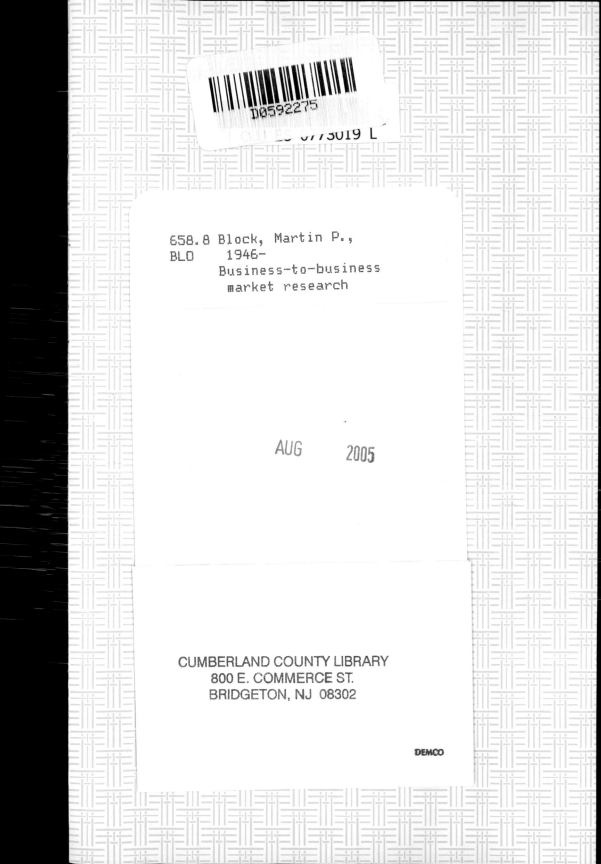

What the Experts Are Already Saying about the new edition of *Business-to-Business Market Research*:

An updated and managerial approach to research in the 21st century marketplace. An integrated B2B approach with techniques and approaches that have been proven in the marketplace. A veritable handbook of research every B2B manager should have.

DON E. SCHULTZ

. . . a comprehensive review of the available research tools, and providing a clear and readable explanatory text.

RUTH P. STEVENS,
President, eMarketing Strategy,
former chair of the DMA B-to-B Council,
and adjunct professor, Columbia Business School

This book is a *must* for managers who have to evaluate and use marketing research as part of the marketing decision-making process. Isn't that just about everybody?

RICK KEAN,
Executive Director,
Business Marketing Association

The definitive work in business-to-business market research . . . a "must have" for anyone researching today's challenging, turbulent, and exciting business markets.

RALPH A. OLIVA
Executive Director,
Institute for the Study of Business Markets
Professor of Marketing,
Smeal College of Business, Penn State

. . . provides such a straightforward, clear explanation of the b-to-b research process and methods that you don't have to be a researcher or statistician to understand it all. It is an excellent primer for those interested in conducting basic secondary research on their own; it also provides very good information that would help a company evaluate the capabilities and proposals of research suppliers. *Business-to-Business Marketing Research* is the new bible for b-to-b market research specialists. It does an a excellent job of explaining how b-to-b and b-to-c research applications differ and provides a crystal clear roadmap for planning and implementing a wide range of b-to-b research projects.

Gary L. Slack
Chairman & Chief Experience Officer
Slack Barshinger

Business-to-Business Market Research

2ND EDITION

Martin P. Block
Tamara S. Block

RACOM
COMMUNICATIONS

AMERICAN MARKETING ASSOCIATION

THOMSON
™

Australia • Canada • Mexico • Singapore • Spain • United Kingdom • United States

THOMSON

Business-to-Business Marketing Research, Second Edition

Martin P. Block, Tamara S. Block

COPYRIGHT © 2005 by Texere, an imprint of Thomson/South-Western, a part of The Thomson Corporation. Thomson and the Star logo are trademarks used herein under license.

Consulting Editor in Marketing: Richard Hagle

Composed by Sans Serif, Inc.

Printed in the United States of America by R. R. Donnelley, Crawfordsville

1 2 3 4 5 08 07 06 05

This book is printed on acid-free paper.

ISBN 0-324-40072-1

For permission to use material from this text or product, submit a request online at http://www.thomsonrights.com.

Library of Congress Cataloging in Publication Number is available. See page 278 for details.

For more information about our projects, contact us at:

Thomson Higher Education
5191 Natorp Boulevard
Mason, Ohio 45040
USA

Asia (including India)
Thomson Learning
5 Shenton Way
#01-01 UIC Building
Singapore 068808

Australia/New Zealand
Thomson Learning
Australia
102 Dodds Street
Southbank, Victoria 3006
Australia

Canada
Thomson Nelson
1120 Birchmount Road
Toronto, Ontario
M1K 5G4
Canada

Latin America
Thomson Learning
Seneca, 53
Colonia Polanco
11560 Mexico
D.F. Mexico

UK/Europe/Middle East/Africa
Thomson Learning
High Holborn House
50/51 Bedford Row
London WC1R 4LR
United Kingdom

Spain (including Portugal)
Thomson Paraninfo
Calle Magallanes, 25
28015 Madrid, Spain

Contents

1 The Business-to-Business Research Landscape

The need for information is the stimulus for all business-to-business market research projects. Market research really is nothing more than the systematic collection, analysis, and presentation of information as data. Market research should, therefore, provide the data user with a better understanding of its business and customers than can be obtained from anecdotal generalizations. Through market research, a company can focus on what its customers really want and need as well as how those customers go about buying. Market research has robust application in market-driven companies because sales are directly linked to the quality and quantity of available information.

A collection of analytical and qualitative methods and techniques used to solve marketing problems, market research methods have been developed from other disciplines, including political science, psychology, and sociology Because many strategic and tactical business problems are similar in both consumer and business-to-business marketing models, these methods can be adapted to solve business-to-business marketing problems. However, there are distinct differences between consumer and business-to-business markets that influence the execution of research Unfortunately, most research texts are written primarily, if not entirely, from a consumer marketing perspective and ignore the unique problems and applications to business-to-business marketing.

Most business-to-business marketers are selling products and services to other businesses rather than to consumers. The business-to-business marketer often knows such things as customer names and addresses, their annual sales revenue, and industrial classification. Even more detailed information, such as the number of employees or

1

business locations and the names of key personnel within a customer's business, is typically available for purchase in database form. A consumer marketing company generally does not have this kind of detailed information on particular customers, despite claims of having a consumer database.

Nature of Business-to-Business Marketing

In the business-to-business marketing world, both products and services are marketed and sold, much the same as in consumer goods marketing. Business products can be either consumable or longer-term capital investments. Consumable products include those that are directly used up in the operations of a business, such as printer ribbons or raw materials needed to manufacture consumer products. Capital investment products typically consist of nonconsumable or durable items, for example, computers or industrial cooking equipment.

Business services can be viewed in a similar way. There are consumable, operations-type services that are needed in the ongoing functioning of a business, such as insurance or janitorial services. Services that constitute one-time investments might include major consulting projects, legal services, or auditing services that affect the operation of the business.

Regardless of the type of product or service being sold to a business, the business-to-business marketer faces different challenges than a consumer marketer due to the unique characteristics of derived demand, the complexity of the buying cycle and buying influences, the opportunity for negotiation, and the greater emphasis on customer service. Each of these challenges, in turn, has implications for research.

Derived Demand

A business-to-business marketer faces a selling scenario where the motivation for purchase and the demand for a product or service are derived from elsewhere. Derived demand implies that the ultimate demand for your business-to-business products and services is related to the marketplace demand by the customer's customers. For example, if you sell condiments to restaurants and street vendors, the amount of mustard or catsup you sell will depend on the number of sandwiches these establishments sell to their customers. When the consumer demand for housing and services increases, the derived demand for building materials from a lumberyard increases. If you sell office equipment to businesses, what and how much you sell depends on the volume of those businesses. The fewer repair and new-build jobs a plumbing contractor does, for instance, the less sophisticated a copier he needs to process the paperwork. The slower retail sales are, the fewer cash drawers or computers a store needs to transact sales. Even when selling to a business-to-business organization, the end-users of that organization's products are eventually always consumers.

Derived demand means that many business products and services are sold based on their potential to help that business customer sell more of their own products or services, earn more money for the business customer, or solve a business problem. Business-to-business marketers are often selling solutions rather than intrinsic product benefits.

How much business demand is derived from the consumers or other companies a business serves varies considerably from one business category to another. Each industry, and sometimes even an individual business within an industry, operates differently.

For the market researcher, understanding the nature of derived demand translates into the importance of understanding a business and/or the industry in which it operates. Often the first barrier raised in selling to a business is the perception that "you don't understand my business." Knowing the regularities, peculiarities, and history of a particular business is critical in being able to market to it. Just as sales personnel must know their business customers' needs, a business-to-business market researcher must also comprehend a business operation in order to conduct research that has high value for the clients of the research.

Buying Cycle and Influences

The business-to-business buying process is often considerably more complex than its consumer counterpart. First of all, a business purchase is rarely an impulse purchase. Most, if not all, business purchases, especially those in larger organizations, involve some kind of review process. Even routine purchases, because of the larger volume, are often subject to justification based on price points across sources. This buying process is deliberate and may involve a number of employees and buying influencers. Therefore, business-to-business marketers often employ a direct sales force, with individual salespeople responsible for managing the time-consuming sales process with a particular company or within a designated territory.

In selling to a business, you must consider the unique buying cycle and buying influencers for that company. Typically, a business must first recognize or identify the need for a product or service in order to initiate the purchase process. While some products or services satisfy obvious and observable business needs, others may solve problems or offer benefits that a company is not even aware of yet. In this situation, need recognition becomes part of the selling task for the business-to-business marketer.

Once initiated, the purchase process involves the research and evaluation of alternative products and/or buying sources, maybe even requiring requests for proposals (RFPs) or presentations from competitive vendors. Many different personnel or personnel levels within an organization could become involved in this evaluation process. Ultimately, the final purchase decision could be made by one or more persons who have been involved in the evaluation process, or by those who are completely external to these previous deliberations.

After a product or service has been selected and purchased by a business customer, servicing or supporting the product and maintaining the customer relationship are important. Service and support usually become influential considerations upon repurchase.

Replacement or repurchase becomes an issue once a product is consumed, depreciates, or becomes obsolete. If a company has been satisfied with the previous product or service, the subsequent buying cycle could be greatly shortened and more routine. The evaluation process may be much more cursory, or eliminated altogether, resulting in an almost automatic purchase cycle. This can be a problem for the business-to-business marketer trying to sell to a company that is a regular user of a competitive vendor. In this case, the salesperson must somehow interrupt the repetitive cycle in order to present new information or a rationale for reevaluation.

Crucial information when selling to a business includes who is involved in the initiation, the evaluation, and the final decision for a purchase; what the requirements or criteria are for purchase evaluation; and who the key competitors are. This kind of information helps market researchers determine which potential business customers should be approached and what messages should be communicated to them in order to effectively sell. Obviously, the decision-making unit (DMU) can vary from company to company and from product category to category. Business-to-business researchers need to understand the process and the complexity of purchasing in order to capture the relevant information from the appropriate personnel.

Negotiation and the Value of Information

Two selling tools that promote negotiation, generally less accessible to consumer goods marketers, are often present in business-to-business purchase situations. The first is that businesses are often very conscious of controlling costs in order to be profitable, making price an extremely important consideration in the purchase decision. The second is that personal selling is often the means by which a sale is made, and when person-to-person communication is involved, the opportunity for interaction and negotiation arises.

Price often becomes a more critical marketing variable because very small discounts, amounts that would have virtually no impact on a consumer, can make a difference in business-to-business sales. Of course, price is not a simple variable, especially when it comes to capital investment items. Determinants of price include the initial price tag, which often can be negotiated; ongoing maintenance cost; and value, which takes both the price tag and the maintenance cost into consideration.

Because of the nature of the business-to-business buying situation, and the emphasis on criteria such as price, it may appear that decisions are simpler to understand because they are guided by a process and rational considerations. However, you must always remember that you are ultimately selling to people, not companies. Therefore, to be successful you must combine knowledge of a company and its competitive environment with an understanding of what appeals to individuals when selling.

A good salesperson is probably very adept at reading people and knowing how to negotiate a sale. Because they feel they are so close to customers and prospects, and because sales force personnel frequently do not have marketing backgrounds, they often fail to see the need for market research and resist it. This has special implications for the business-to-business market researcher because, even though the need for marketing research is high, it often has to be sold to the sales department in a way that they too see the end benefit.

Customer Service

Once a business-to-business sale is complete, there is typically after-sale activity that follows in order to make the sale successful. Because of the value and complexity of many business products, they require support or customer service during the usage period. The level and quality of this after-sale customer service obviously can become part of the competitive vendor mix.

This ongoing contact with customers, however, is what allows the development and refinement of a customer database, containing not only purchase information, but service history as well. This kind of customer information provides better insight into how to continue to sell customers. It also provides input for segmentation analyses that could offer insight into other prospective customers who have similar characteristics. Knowing the nature of the service inquiries and complaints also provides valuable input into product or service refinements that may be needed down the road.

In consumer marketing today, *relationship marketing* is the term applied to developing customer relationships—a difficult task in a mass-marketing, mass-retailing world. Customer service is the key to building customer relationships in the business-to-business world.

Business-to-Business Marketing Problems

Research can help solve a wide variety of business-to-business marketing problems. The first way of approaching the problems is to organize them around common strategic and tactical marketing decisions.

Identifying Market Characteristics

Almost every market planning discussion begins with the phrase "let's define the market." Applying the concepts of target marketing and market segmentation depends on your ability to define your market in objective terms. In some cases, the market may be hypothetical or desired; in other cases, it may be based upon your actual marketplace experience.

Regardless, objective and measurable characteristics are necessary to define any market. Typically, these would include company geographic and demographic characteristics such as region or zip code, industrial classification, company revenue, years in business, and number of employees. Other characteristics such as the kind of technology employed by a company may be important as well. There is a growing emphasis on using behavioral measures, such as purchase volume and/or frequency, to identify target markets. In fact business-to-business marketing has become the leader in the use of behavioral measures.

In almost every case, the only way you can profile market characteristics and determine target segments is through research. Already existing data, such as government-supplied Department of Commerce data, Dun & Bradstreet lists, or in-house purchase histories, usually requires analysis. Surveying the market also may be necessary in order to provide information not otherwise available.

Determining Pricing

In order to utilize economic theory to set prices, you must first know the demand characteristics of your product or service. In other words, you need to understand the precise relationship between price and sales volume. Unfortunately, a seller rarely knows how buyers would respond if the price were raised or lowered by a given percentage. Every product category varies in its sensitivity to the influence of competitive prices, depending on the extent to which products are viewed as commodities by buyers. Some brands are less vulnerable to price competition while others are more so. Setting prices for new products that have no previous purchase history on which to base the decision, add an entirely new wrinkle to the pricing dilemma.

In cases such as these, market research is really the only place the decision-maker can turn for help. You can experiment with trying different price levels in different markets to see what works best. Alternatively, you can implement small sample projects, especially using trade-off or conjoint analysis, to assist in pricing decisions. If you are lucky enough to have purchase data for your products across a range of pricing conditions, you can analytically derive a demand curve and set the optimal price where profits are maximized.

Developing New Products

For manufacturers, product decisions are among the most difficult because of the tremendous cost and risk involved in bringing a new product to market. One type of research, conducted early in the product development process, is the concept test. It usually involves explaining the idea or concept of a product or service to a small sample of prospects. Often qualitative methods, such as in-depth focus group interviews, are used for this purpose. New insights into design modifications or possible ways to market the product often result.

Especially with new products, it is hard to know what you like until you have seen different options.

Large-scale field surveys are also used in product research, although these typically occur once the product is introduced. Say, for example, a new product is introduced initially in a particular region. Survey research then can be used to evaluate that product's performance and customer satisfaction compared to competing products before the product is expanded into other regions. In some industries, such as health care, there may even be panels of prospects, available through a commercial research supplier, that allow you to track usage, satisfaction, and repeat usage.

Developing Promotions

How you promote your products or services to businesses in order to stimulate demand for them is an important consideration if you are a manufacturer or distributor. If you sell products, as opposed to services, you have inventory costs when a product sits in one place very long. The solution to defraying these costs is to shift the inventories (and the costs of storing product) to someone else—a buyer. As a result, who maintains the inventory and pays these storage costs has increasingly become a negotiation tool. Hence, "just-in-time" inventory (where inventory is shipped just in time to meet the demand in order to eliminate inventorying costs) and electronic data interchange (the capability to electronically track inventory movement) have become important in the business-to-business world. These trends have led to an increase in the use of promotion as a short-term stimulator of sales that runs inventory (and thus the cost of inventory) down. Promotion has long been a tool to shift inventory from manufacturers to other marketing channel members and even final customers. Even where inventory costs are not at stake, promotion is a critically important tool in the selling process.

Research can aid in many ways with promotion decisions. Through research, usually available from commercial suppliers, it is possible to track competitive promotional activity in order to know what others are doing. Research can also be used to test the acceptability of promotional ideas and programs. For instance, you might test the impact of a product-sampling program among potential customers for consumable items (or a demonstration for capital items and some services). Or you may want to know which promotional tool is more effective—a cash rebate with purchase or a premium. When motivational promotion programs are implemented with your sales force or other personnel, research can be used to help design the program and select appropriate prizes or awards.

Creating Sales Force Support

Key to the success of any marketing program is the support of the sales force. Certainly research can be used directly to help understand the concerns and motives of the sales force, but this is not nearly as important as research that can provide usable customer information.

Learning more about customers and prospects is a critically important activity for an effective sales force. Research that provides useful customer and prospect information to field sales personnel is the key. A good way to do this is to create a customer and prospect database that can be readily accessed by all field sales and marketing support personnel. This will be discussed in more detail later.

Getting Distribution

Decisions about how to get the product to the customer are common to all marketers. Decisions about whether to sell direct, through brokers and agents, through distributors, or even through retail stores and catalogs are all part of business-to-business marketing. As the competitive environment changes, new channels or routes to the customer may be needed. A decision to move into new market segments, introduce new products, reduce operating costs, or meet other marketplace changes may dictate reconsideration of the current distribution mix and require research. Distribution decisions can be especially risky because of the relationship of the method of distribution to the image and perception of the marketer and its products. For example, a manufacturer that normally sold direct but decided to offer a "special" low-priced product through warehouse clubs might find its direct business adversely impacted.

Market research can play the important role of assessing the expectations and preferences of a customer. Through survey or qualitative research methods, you can learn how best to reach a customer and the potential impact of any changes.

Evaluating Customer Satisfaction

A fast-growing area within market research has been customer satisfaction survey research. Evaluating the level of customer service has become more important in many business-to-business marketing organizations than evaluating marketing communications activity because of the realization that retaining a customer is less expensive than converting a prospect into a new customer. Regularly and systematically tracking customer satisfaction with products and service via telephone surveys has led some organizations to create customer satisfaction "score cards" to record success.

Whether or not a customer repeats a purchase is certainly an indicator of customer satisfaction. The problem with depending entirely on purchase information is that it may be too late to alter a customer's satisfaction once you recognize that the purchasing has dwindled or ceased altogether. If a customer isn't satisfied, the opportunity to correct the situation before they move their business to a competitor will be lost unless there is some method in place to detect the problem.

The Research Process

Every research project, regardless of its purpose or scope, is ushered through a series of decisions and steps that could loosely be called a "process." This process is briefly outlined in Exhibit 1.1. As shown, the research process involves a set of interrelated, but somewhat hierarchical, decisions progressing from deciding what is to be researched, to determining the research design, sampling parameters, and data collection instruments, to fielding the study, preparing and analyzing the data, and reporting the results in a way that addresses the research objectives formulated in the beginning. The length of time this process can take will vary from study to study obviously, and the degree to which each of these steps is observed will also vary depending on the specific nature of the research study.

Most marketing research books will outline a similar research process, although perhaps with a different number or categorization of steps. Still, almost always the process will begin with defining the problem and end with presenting the results. These two steps are, by far, the most difficult in the process, yet most market research books, including this one, spend most of the time describing the steps in between.

Defining Research Problems

Before you can determine what information is required or how to go about gathering the appropriate data, you must first ask yourself what

Exhibit 1.1: The Research Process

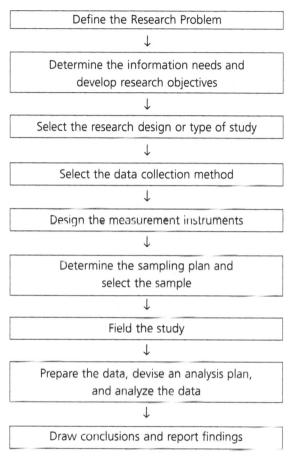

Define the Research Problem

↓

Determine the information needs and develop research objectives

↓

Select the research design or type of study

↓

Select the data collection method

↓

Design the measurement instruments

↓

Determine the sampling plan and select the sample

↓

Field the study

↓

Prepare the data, devise an analysis plan, and analyze the data

↓

Draw conclusions and report findings

the research problem is exactly. This is always the first and most important step in market research. Unfortunately, formulating research problems simply, clearly, and completely is often a tough task that is typically slighted in the research process. Contributing to the difficulty of this task is that the problem stated initially by management is not always the real problem, or it is stated so ambiguously and broadly that it does not provide any real focus or direction for research. Keep in mind that the output of the problem-definition stage is a list of the required information needed to assist in solving the problem.

Nowhere is the lack of a clear problem definition more obvious than to the researcher who must analyze and make sense of the project. Seeing the problem within the context of the management decision process is vital. How will the information be used by management to assist in a decision? What is the situation that has led to the problem emerging or becoming noticed and has motivated the need for research in the first place?

When the problem is stated vaguely, such as in terms of sagging sales or an unmotivated sales force, you need, for instance, to ask yourself if these are not merely symptoms of an underlying problem. Both of these are relatively broad problem areas that could well be the consequence of some other difficulty, such as a product that no longer meets changing customer needs or a fiercely competitive environment. Before investing in research to discover what motivational incentives will appeal to your sales force, learn more about the situation surrounding the suggested problem in order to clarify and better define it.

When multiple parties are funding research (i.e., two different managers within a corporation who work on similar accounts but in different regions, or when corporate headquarters partially funds a regional project), there may very well be different goals and perspectives that complicate this process. Unless everyone involved is clear on what the problem to be investigated is and what the research is meant to accomplish, you can be sure that no one will feel satisfied in the end. Stating the research problem in writing for everyone to approve is a good way to avoid political problems later on. Furthermore, it is not uncommon for managers to change their expectations for the research, and hence the definition of the research problem, midstream as new questions occur to them. Again, time spent early on probing for insight and specifying the problem completely rather than simply jumping into the research fray will hopefully prevent this.

Throughout the problem definition stage, ideas and hunches need to be developed, perhaps even to the formal hypothesis stage. The critical point is that a researcher take time on this first important research phase and continue to question, probe, and speculate even as the research unfolds.

Establishing Research Objectives, Research Hypotheses, and Information Needs

The research problem statement, despite the effort put toward its definition, typically needs to be translated into a more specific form in order to be useful for directing the research design and instrument development. A problem might translate into a series of five research objectives that outline more precisely the exact areas to be investigated that are directly related to the problem. Each of these objectives probably will indicate the need for certain information. This is the nature of the process, where you successively become more exact and focused, flushing out the details as you go along. By doing this, you have an even better understanding of what needs to be gained by the research and, therefore, what research design to use and what specific questions or items need to be included in any research data collection instrument.

In some cases, you may have developed hypotheses as you were clarifying the nature of the research problem. Hypotheses can be incorporated into the development of research objectives as well. Oftentimes, research objectives become formalized as research hypotheses. A hypothesis is a declarative statement that proposes a relationship between two or more variables. Hypotheses are assertions of our assumptions or speculations as to how we think something works. They are stated in such a way that we can test them to see if they are indeed true. In the end, we either accept or reject a hypothesis based on the evidence gathered in the research.

Every time you speculate that this is better than that, or that this is related to that, you are creating potential hypotheses that could be tested. For example, you might hypothesize that smaller companies may be more cost sensitive when buying your products than larger companies. Once you have determined what is meant by "small" and "large" and how to measure price sensitivity, you have a testable hypothesis. If your research objective is to determine what communication methods are more effective when targeting CEOs, and you suspect that visual media are more communicative than the printed word due in part to the extreme time demands, then one hypothesis that you may want to test is: "CEOs prefer watching videotapes rather than reading printed brochures" or "CEOs will comprehend a graphical representation of data faster and easier than data presented in printed tabular form."

Just as a sentence has a noun and a verb, a hypothesis consists of at least one independent variable and one dependent variable. When linking two variables together in an "if x, then y" manner, one variable (x) is presumed to be the cause and the other the effect (y). In the above example, the communication medium (visual or graphical versus printed words and tables) is presumed to influence either preference or comprehension, the dependent variable. This means that hypotheses are predictive in nature. Once you know the relationship between two variables, you can almost predict the value of one variable given some value of the other.

The hypothesis is one of the most powerful tools available for achieving knowledge. Phenomena can be observed; possible causes speculated on, hypothesized, tested, and proven or not proven. Many speculations are incorrect, a mixture of fact and belief and superstition, and sometimes pure myth. A market researcher is obligated to doubt and test explanations or hypotheses. Your understanding of the marketplace should result from the discipline of writing systematic and testable hypotheses.

Presenting the Results

The two critical elements to remember when preparing an analysis and report are the objectives of the study and the audience. If the research is going to be understood and used quite differently by different factions within your audience, then different reports and presentations may be necessary for the same project. The marketing manager, for example, may be more familiar with the technical details of the project and interested in every aspect of the analysis and findings. The field sales force, on the other hand, may be interested only in specific parts of the project without the analytical details. The main point is that reports and presentations need to be tailored to their audiences.

A research report should follow the general sequence of steps outlined earlier in the research process and shown briefly in Exhibit 1.2. A report should begin with a statement of the problem and the research objectives. These should be followed with a description of the methodology used in the study, including how the sample was obtained, any important characteristics of the instrument design, how the data was collected, and so on. This methodological description is critical to the report; without it a reader cannot judge the quality of the information that is presented within. The methodology should be written in terms that can be understood by the appropriate audience. Audiences with less research and technical experience will be less familiar with research lingo and probably require longer, more simply written methodology statements. More analytically sophisticated audiences can understand and get by with relatively short and technically-worded statements. This is especially true with studies

Exhibit 1.2: Major Sections of a Research Report

Executive Summary
I. Introduction of Research Problem and Objectives
II. Methodology
III. Findings
IV. Summary and Conclusions
V. Recommendations
VI. Appendices

that are repetitive, such as the fourth round in a tracking study, since the method has been explained previously many times.

The findings section follows the methodology section and is generally the most substantial part of the report, as it typically consists of all of the appropriate data presentation and associated narrative. The narrative style is typically simple, concise, and direct. It is usually best to organize the findings into sections with their own section headings in a way that is logical and fits with the topics and issues being reported.

Any complex or lengthy numerical data that is important should be presented within simple-to-read tables and graphs, numbered for easy reference within the text, and titled so that they can be identified without the aid of the text. Not only does the use of graphic displays enhance the communication of the information by making it easier for the reader or viewer to understand, it also helps the researcher or report writer. The preparing of a chart or a graph requires planning and thought, forcing the researcher to better understand the information.

Usually, tables and graphs are included in the narrative at the point of discussion rather than appended at the end of the report. Exhibits should only be used when they aid in the reader's understanding; too many may actually distract from the study's purpose.

Ways to Classify Research

There is more than one method to classify and organize research. One way is to consider broadly what the purpose for the research is, dividing projects into one of three types: basic, applied, and methodological research. All three types might be used by the business-to-business researcher.

Basic research is that which is somewhat theoretical in nature and for which the primary purpose is to build your general knowledge in an area. In the business-to-business realm, this kind of project might include one that focused on learning more about risk aversion by corporations as it translates to the purchasing process for capital expenditures, or one which attempted to determine what industry characteristics are related to and predict technology adoption rates across different industry types.

While the information gained from this kind of research is very important and inevitably relevant, it may not be the kind of research project you do to solve the day-to-day problems because it is less immediately applicable. In fact, unless elements of basic research are tied into more specific goals, doing this kind of research is a luxury for which few companies seem to find the time or budget. A larger company may be more inclined to get involved in basic research simply because it has budgets and more products and personnel among which to spread the benefits. If a company is the leader in an industry, it may be more likely to become involved in sponsoring basic research projects in conjunction with university researchers or with industry associations.

Applied research consists of projects that are very focused on an immediate problem or information need. Applied research tends to be very pragmatic. It is designed and conducted for a specific product or client in order to make a very specific decision. Questions such as what promotion should be run during the fourth quarter that would excite the salespeople and clear out specifically targeted seasonal inventories, or what price point should be set for a new service offering, or what retail shelf set is most effective at moving a particular office supply product, define research that is most appropriately classified as applied. The results can be critical to making an informed and profitable business decision, yet they are not generally applicable to other decisions or products. They do not address fundamental, underlying principles and are not linked to any theoretical assumptions in the way that basic research is.

Methodological research is any research that concerns the methods used to conduct research. Methodological research is usually in the domain of research suppliers since they must sell their methods based on objective criteria such as validity and reliability. For business-to-business companies, methodological research might be undertaken when certain research projects are being regularly conducted in-house and procedures are being refined or systematized. If you are implementing ongoing customer attitudinal tracking research at your company, you may investigate alternative ways of administering key attitude scaling questions (different wording, different order or presentation, different scale types, the number of points in the scale, etc.) in order to standardize the process. If your company is developing a customer database, experimenting with alternative sources of prospect information to discover which sources have the cleanest, most accurate data, this, too, represents a methodological approach.

Primary Versus Secondary Research

All research can be broadly classified into one of two basic categories depending on how the information was obtained: primary versus secondary. Primary research is that which is collected by the researcher firsthand for the purpose of a project. This research information, therefore, did not exist prior to its collection as part of the project. Primary research designs would include survey research, in-depth qualitative research, experimental designs, or test marketing, as well as observational studies. In Chapters 5 and 6, you will find a more thorough discussion of survey research methods and qualitative methods. Suffice it to say that most research conducted by business-to-business marketers concerning its products or customers is primary research.

Secondary information is information that has already been previously collected, often by someone else either external to the company or internally, for purposes other than the research project at hand. Secondary information can come from a variety of sources, including, among others, the government, the periodical literature, trade associations, and directories. Chapter 2 discusses secondary sources in more detail.

Custom Versus Syndicated Research

Custom research is designed and tailored specifically to your research goals for your own purposes. The research instruments, all data that is collected, and any of the information gained through the study is confidential and strictly yours to do with what you want. Most applied research projects are probably custom research studies since they are very specific and not easily generalized or useful to anyone else.

Syndicated research is that which a supplier does to satisfy more than just one client. Larger industry studies, or studies on a particular topic that cut across many industries or product types, are often syndicated. The information generated by the research is shared among all those who pay for it. The advantage, of course, is that the costs are shared as well. If multiple clients, sometimes hundreds of companies, buy the syndicated report, then everyone is helping to pay for the project. Often you contract on an annual basis to receive the reports when they are available. In return, you receive more information from a much larger sample than you would probably be able to afford easily on your own budget. Examples of syndicated research are common in the media field: MRI publishes multiple volume sets of audience information by consumer usage on hundreds of product and service categories; Nielsen television ratings are published in syndicated form; BAR tracks advertising for brands and categories throughout the various media for competitive analyses. There is syndicated research for most industries and across most audience types, including business-to-business.

Syndicated research will often go a long way toward giving you valuable information for less cost. However, it will rarely measure everything you would like to know with respect to your market, brand, or situation. Usually, custom research is needed to supplement what is available in syndicate.

Exploratory, Conclusive, and Evaluative Research

Depending on what the goals of a research project are and how the research will be used in connection with decision-making within the company, research could be categorized as exploratory, conclusive, or evaluative. The easiest way to think about these different research types is to consider the decision process most managers go through to solve a business problem.

Initially you recognize a problem, or a symptom of a problem, in some area of your business, for example, sales are sluggish compared to last year. At the early stage of problem detection, you may not really understand why the problem exists or even exactly the extent of the problem. Before you can do anything to solve the problem, you need to understand and define it more clearly. Research can help do this. At this stage, however, research is relatively informal, unstructured, and inexpensive. You may do some research on market trends in the trade and business literature to see if something is happening that could impact your product's sales. You may interview a handful of salespeople or customers to see what insights they can provide. You may go so far as to schedule a discussion with a small group of customers to hear them discuss the product category, the competition, and your brand. All of this is referred to as exploratory research at this point because that is exactly what you are doing—exploring. You are trying to understand the problem better in order to define it.

The next stage for a manager, then, is to document the extent of the problem and determine which course of action is best suited to solving it. Almost always there is more than one solution that could be implemented. Conclusive research is the research that is done to evaluate the situation and the alternatives and provide evidence or data with which to make a decision of what is best to do. Conclusive research can take many forms just as exploratory research can; however, it tends to be quite a bit more formal in nature because of its importance in the decision-making process. If you need to document or describe the problem situation in terms of the market, you probably need to survey the entire market or customers. If you need input on alternative solutions, you also will want to research more than just a handful of customers informally. Larger samples will yield more reliable, conclusive results in which you can have confidence. This is more expensive.

Once you have sufficient data on which to base a decision, you can select the best alternative and implement it. Just because a decision is implemented, however, does not mean that research is no longer needed or useful. In fact, it is in the tracking stage that perhaps more research money is spent than anywhere else. Evaluative research is continuous research that periodically evaluates the situation in order to provide information on an ongoing basis that will alert you to new problems or a reoccurrence of the old problem if and when the time comes. Evaluative research, or tracking studies as they are often called, can take the form of survey research or even periodic analysis of secondary information from syndicated sources or from internal data sources. If another problem is spotted, then exploratory research can once again be conducted to illuminate the problem further and suggest new alternative courses of action.

Decision-making is ongoing. It follows a logical sort of progression from problem recognition through solution implementation. Research is valuable at every step of that process, but the goals of the research are different depending on its purpose with respect to the decision-making. Because of this, the type of research that you do at any point will vary, from being quite loose and unstructured to being very methodical and formal.

Exhibit 1.3:
Business-to-Business Information Checklist

A. Sales History
   1. Defined year by year for a sufficient number of years
      a. In dollar sales
      b. In unit sales
      c. In share of market

B. Price History by Years (Including Promotion)

C. Product History
   1. Quality problems that may have been encountered
   2. Product improvements
   3. Changes in preference between the product and competitive products

D. Competition
   1. Principal competitive brands
   2. Comparison of competitors
      a. In dollar amount
      b. In trend
      c. Competitive advantages and weaknesses

E. Market
   1. Growth trends
   2. User profile
   3. Purchaser profile

F. Distribution
   1. Channels
   2. Market development

G. History of Marketing Communications Expenditures
   1. Media advertising
   2. Collateral materials
   3. Direct mail
   4. Telemarketing
   5. Sales promotion

H. History of Selling Expenditures
   1. In-house sales organization
   2. Agents, brokers, and middlemen

I. Summary of Product Facts

Business-to-Business Information

The volume of information that a business-to-business marketer typically should be able to access in order to make informed and effective decisions is potentially staggering. It is probably safe to bet that it is rare for any one manager to have the most up-to-date information in every area. Nevertheless, Exhibit 1.3 can be used as a guide to organize the various types of information that will be most useful. Sometimes an outline such as this, and there are many different versions similar to the one exhibited, can be very helpful in organizing research materials that have been collected, as well as show what information gaps exist.

The Research Industry

There are a variety of research services and information suppliers that can ably contribute to the research process by substituting for or supplementing internal company resources and capabilities. However, it is helpful to know what the general categories of supplier organizations are and how they are contracted.

One type of research supplier would characterize themselves as full-service suppliers or research organizations, meaning they offer virtually any kind of custom research that you might need. If your project required something they could not provide in-house, such as a particular data collection facility, the full-service supplier would subcontract that service, making it virtually invisible or seamless to you, the client. On the other hand, à la carte suppliers would provide very specific or specialized services. Which approach is best depends on you. If you have the internal resources to handle some part of the research design, fieldwork, or analysis, contracting only what you need from an à la carte service makes some sense because you'll be buying a service with a more intimate understanding of that particular area at a lower cost. Full-service suppliers provide the advantage of their overall research expertise and perhaps better coordination of the whole project, much as a general contractor would in a construction project. Full service is obviously the better approach if you do not have the internal resources.

There are several categories of research suppliers that can provide services for business-to-business market research and each is briefly described next. Most of these suppliers work with consumer research as well. In other words, they do not necessarily specialize in business-to-business research.

Syndicated Research Suppliers

Certainly the best-known market research companies are those that provide syndicated research in the consumer marketplace. Among these are Nielsen Marketing Research, Arbitron, Mediamark (MRI), and Information Resources, Inc. These companies are all considered syndicated suppliers because they sell the same research product to more than one client. This offers you two distinct advantages: lower cost and added credibility. The primary disadvantages of syndicated research are the lack of flexibility and proprietary interest you will have in the research.

One of the best-known syndicated business-to-business firms is Dun & Bradstreet Information Services. Dun & Bradstreet (D&B) offers information on the type of business, number of employees, sales volume, and other characteristics for approximately 10 million business establishments. Often D&B information provides the input data needed to start a business-to-business database or a source of names for business-to-business research samples.

There are other syndicated business-to-business services that specialize in particular markets, such as the health care market. There are several services that specialize in hospital utilization, surgical procedures, and physician locations and specialties. There are also services that specialize in particular classes of retail trade such as restaurants, grocery stores, mass merchandisers, drugstore chains, and convenience stores.

Custom Research Suppliers

Custom research is that which is designed and sold specifically to one client. As the client, you are then able to maintain proprietary interest in the research; the research is known only to the sponsor and competitors have no access to it. You also have complete control over the project as sponsor, so the flexibility problem is eliminated. Custom research, however, is generally much more expensive than syndicated research as noted earlier. You are obligated to pay for all research costs.

There are numerous examples of custom research suppliers, although not very many that claim to do just business-to-business research projects. The larger custom research suppliers, such as Market

Facts, conduct many projects during the year for both consumer and business-to-business clients. Each project would be designed according to the objectives and specifications of the client. Most of the research methods described in later chapters can be employed by custom research suppliers. Certainly some are better suited for particular projects than others.

Field Services

A field service is a supplier that maintains data collection resources. This usually involves a staff of professional interviewers, a telephone facility, and centrally located interviewing rooms. The interviewing rooms have adjacent two-way mirrored observation rooms appropriate for in-depth focus group interviews. This kind of field service facility would be used by a custom research supplier or anyone needing to collect data in a city where they do not have their own resources. Any time you are involved in a project where personal interviewing is needed on a national basis, it is much more cost efficient to hire and train interviewers within several geographically representative locations than to pay to transport interviewers across the country. Field service facilities would also be necessary when conducting qualitative focus group research in, say, six different cities.

The distinction between a field service and a full-service research supplier is not always clear. Many organizations that provide field services also claim to provide all the other research services, including research design and data analysis. An example of an organization that provides field services is Quality Controlled Services. They have facilities within the vicinity of major cities across the country.

Field services, like full-service agencies, almost never specialize in business-to-business research, although some may specialize in specific markets, such as physicians. Generally field services will contract with full-service suppliers, consultants, or the clients directly. The research product or service from a field service is generally of a custom nature and would be proprietary to the client.

Web-Based Suppliers

The Internet has altered the market research landscape. It provides the ability to obtain information about customers, prospects, and competitors directly from the information that they themselves post on web sites as well as information third parties, such as news organizations, write about them. There are numerous Web-based search organizations that will conduct exhaustive searches and prepare summaries and reports.

There are also a growing number of survey suppliers that conduct interviews through the Internet. They maintain large databases of potential respondents and can be a good way to reach a very specialized business-to-business market.

Consultants

A common solution to the problem of not having internal market research expertise is to hire an outside consultant. This may be necessary even if a full-service supplier is used. Consultants can provide specialized research expertise at lower overall cost than a full-time employee. While consultants generally cost more than employees on an hourly basis, they do not work as many hours and don't require long-term financial commitments and benefit liability.

Consultants can be of great help in providing not only expertise but perspective on a problem you may be too close to. However, there are two potential difficulties with using consultants. First, a consultant is not a long-term employee of a client company and, in the end, is usually not responsible for the failure or success of a decision based on his or her research consulting. Second, consultants often work for many clients and the potential for conflicting loyalties among clients is always present. Yet, expertise in a niche specialized area is probably only useful to companies like yours or your competitors. You can insulate yourself from this to some extent by requiring a consultant to sign a confidentiality agreement, much as you would any supplier of custom research.

While the business-to-business market research industry itself is undergoing tremendous change, there are fundamental business-to-business market research concepts that endure. Most important is the absolute requirement to have a rock-solid problem definition. The research plan itself is secondary.

The idea of tried and true market research principles that have evolved over the years and are now being adapted in a rapidly changing technological environment is a primary theme of this book. It will be repeated in virtually all of the more detailed methodological chapters ahead.

2 Managing Business-to-Business Market Research

Any business-to-business marketing research must be designed, executed, and presented within the context of a business's marketing plan. While research can help determine and refine components of the marketing plan, some fundamental decisions regarding marketing objectives and strategy, customer definition, and resource allocation must initially guide and frame the research problem and questions. Ideally, this means there should be cooperation and interaction between the marketing research personnel and the marketing personnel within an organization.

However, traditional line marketing and market research staff has often viewed each other as adversaries rather than partners. Marketing personnel often choose not to get involved in the research projects and the research people prefer not to get bogged down in the marketing details and decisions. The adversarial situation sets the stage, at the very least, for poorly communicated research results, and more importantly, for poorly conceived research in the first place. It's no wonder that getting research used within a marketing organization is an old problem.

Integrating all personnel in a team approach is the ideal situation from which a research project should emerge. This means creating a marketing team that involves all relevant personnel responsible for a product. In fact, the teams might even be called integrated marketing teams. In concept, the notion of an integrated marketing team means that everyone, from marketing, research, and even field sales, is working together. These teams, then, should not only have the responsibility for the development of the marketing strategy, but also for the oversight of the marketing communications tactics and the supporting research. The obvious advantage is that all personnel will become intimately familiar with the research project. Together, they will devise the objectives for the research, be involved in its design, and understand its limitations. They'll better understand the findings and how they relate to the marketing problems and strategy.

Admittedly, this concept is in strong contrast to the more traditional approach that places personnel in separate functional categories. Yet, the idea of integrated marketing teams and communications has considerable merit for business-to-business market research. If you use this integrated team approach, it is almost impossible to conduct a research project that turns out to be not relevant or used.

Value-Based Marketing Perspectives

Organizations have always been judged by their investors and owners using financial measures, such as Return on Equity (ROE), Return on Assets (ROA), Return on Investment (ROI), and Earnings Per Share (EPS).

Increasingly, organizations are moving toward a "value-based" marketing perspective, where quantitative and financial measures are being used to identify and determine their success. Firms have adopted score keeping tools such as Six Sigma[1] and the Balanced Scorecard[2] in order to measure and, indeed, improve their performance. Accordingly, there has been increasing pressure on marketing communications managers by senior management to provide the same type of quantitative financial measures for the impact and effectiveness of the marketing communications efforts to match those already in place for operations, logistics, manufacturing, procurement, and similar departments.

The requirement today is an understanding of dollars out and the measurement of dollars back into the organization as a result of investments in marketing tactics and marketing communications programs.[3] This requirement is the challenge for marketing communications managers today and will become increasingly more important in the future. Because confidential internal financial data is required to determine value, a methodology is needed that can be instituted by the marketing communications group within the organization that does not rely on externally developed measurement systems.

These measures can be easily turned into the needed financial measures over time. Scenarios and relationships are now possible that permit the organization to say: "We invested $X in marketing communications activities A and we received a $Z increase in incremental sales." This philosophy will dominate the approach to business-to-business market research described here.

Increasing Business

Marketing objectives typically revolve around growth or increased business. To this point, there are really only three ways to increase sales: acquisition, retention, or upselling. Acquisition is a strategy to attract new customers or convert prospects into customers. Conventional marketing wisdom says that this is the most difficult and expensive way to increase business. You must first find these prospects which, for any number of reasons, are not buying your product or service and then persuade them to try or buy it, or switch from a competitor's. If they are currently not users of the product category or service at all, this means educating them on the need for it or the benefits of trying it for the first time. If they are currently using a competitive option, it may be an even more difficult sell to convince them to try your product if they are satisfied, or at least not dissatisfied, with what they are already using.

Because acquiring new customers is so difficult, retaining current customers becomes an important strategy. Especially in a competitive marketplace where businesses are continually being targeted by competitors with advertising, promotions, and sales calls, simply maintaining current sales levels is not necessarily automatic. Keeping current customers satisfied is essential and this may mean more or better servicing of the account.

The third marketing strategy is upselling, or attaining add-on sales from your current customer base. This involves getting customers to either trade-up by buying more expensive lines or models or to purchase larger quantities of the current product. If promoting new uses, ways, or situations in which to use the product is not an option, well-planned promotional tactics might help to load customer inventories in the hopes that overall usage will increase and sales will remain at the higher level over time. If a current customer opens new stores or has multiple locations, there may be the opportunity to sell-in more of the product, or a newer version of the product.

Defining Customers and Prospects

Another important element in any business-to-business integrated marketing plan is to understand who the customers of your business are today and exactly who your marketing strategy is targeting. The more information a business has about its customers and/or prospects, the better it can target them with marketing communications or personal selling that speaks to their needs, strengths or weaknesses, increasing sales. Given that a customer is an organization that has made a purchase in the past, it is likely that you may already have a great deal of information that can be used to guide future marketing efforts. Some customers are worth more than others because they have purchased more in the past and can be expected to purchase more in the future. Categorizing customers on the basis of past behavior is beneficial because it can help to prioritize your marketing and selling efforts. Such categorization, or segmentation, is typically the task of the market researcher.

Prospects are those organizations that have not made any purchases in the past and which, without evidence to the contrary, are potential customers. Often these companies have been doing business with a competitor or have not purchased in the category. Distinguishing between legitimate prospects and those organizations that will never make a purchase is another important research task.

Building and Maintaining the Marketing Database

Regardless of the marketing strategy pursued, understanding your customer base requires the maintenance of a marketing database. If this database doesn't already exist, building one should become a priority. It is probably the most important marketing tool a business-to-business marketer can have. It should be noted that the marketing database needs to be separate from whatever database is in place to prepare your organization's financial reports because the *marketing* database should be organized and maintained in such a way that customers can be identified and categorized (segmented). Over time, it also should be supplemented to include data on prospects as well as current customers.

It is critical that the business-to-business market researcher have access to a marketing database to develop both strategic analyses as well as supplemental projects. All other research should be done in conjunction with the database and the consequent understanding of the customer's real behavior.

Historically, for most organizations, marketing and marketing communications measurement has been an external activity based on external measures and conducted through external measurement systems. The marketing organization has attempted to understand the success of its marketing programs and activities among its various groups of external customers and prospects using external organizations to collect and analyze the necessary data that then provides the firm with various measures of success. A vast array of external organizations including vendors, research companies, syndicators, consultants, and the like have emerged to service the marketer's needs by measuring the impact and effectiveness of various types of marketing communications activities.

This external approach probably worked well in the past. Today it is often too slow and cumbersome to be effective. Further, such an approach often ends up measuring the wrong variables and providing the organization with too little information and direction to enable marketing managers to cope with the increasingly sophisticated and dynamic marketplace. Arguably the measurement of marketing and marketing communications results, particularly those relating to the impact, effectiveness, and return on investment of marketing communications investments, should be moved back inside the marketing organization.

Because building an internal marketing database is such an important tool for marketing strategy and research, an overview is given here of the steps involved in creating a database. Later chapters, Chapter 4 specifically, spend more time discussing the issues and fundamentals of the marketing database.

Building the Marketing Research Database

The process of building a marketing database for use in research consists of four distinct steps: assembling the appropriate data, preparing the data so that it can be analyzed, selecting the appropriate statistical modeling tools, and then subsequently applying the analysis to the research problem or hypotheses at hand.

It is important to note that what is proposed is a process, not a model. While the approach will rely on models of external results, it is based on a series of models used in a particular way and developed for the individual organization. It is based, designed, and developed specifically for the individual marketing communications organization, its communication tools, its markets, its distribution system, and the needs of its management.

The major advantage to this approach is that consulting or service models tend to be static while processes are fluid. Thus, the marketing research manager should start to think about how to create processes that can be used and adapted, rather than static models that specify relationships that may change over time.

Assembling the Data

The internal data necessary for a marketing database may already exist, but typically has been prepared and stored for purposes other than managing the marketing process or measuring marketing or marketing communications effects. It often exists in different formats, for different time periods, and in varying levels of detail within different functional departments within an organization. Therefore, at the outset, the biggest challenge when assembling the data is maintaining consistency—consistency in the way the data is coded and categorized and consistency in the time periods over which data is aggregated.

Sales data is usually a good place to start because this information is typically in the best condition for analysis. Sales data will have dependable price, quantity, and date information connected with it. However, sales data often comes with arbitrary product and customer identification codes, which require "dictionaries" in order to convert the data to meaningful market and marketing information. Preparation of these dictionaries can be onerous and is usually the most difficult task in the assembly process. There can be hundreds of thousands of product codes to sort through and differentiate from one another.

Sales history refers to the length of time (years) that sales data is available. The more history you have, the more you can do with the database analytically, and the better the results. In fact, the amount of historical sales data is normally the limiting factor in the sophistication of the analytical work that can be performed. However, changes in the way data is recorded over time, or even what data is recorded, has the potential of introducing new issues and problems for the market researcher. Such variables as new accounting systems, new product introductions, or even new packaging, all contribute to inconsistencies in the data that need to be sorted out in order to make sense of it.

Marketing expenditure data presents another analytical challenge. Marketing expenses are often defined in terms of budgetary categories and may or may not reflect the actual activity itself. For example, trade show expense may be shown as advertising because there is available budget in that accounting category. How expenses are categorized also tend to depend on the personalities and styles of the managers involved and sometimes change from budget period to budget period. For instance, what is a trade show in one period may be referred to as an "event" in another time period or by a different manager. It is also common to find that expense payments are not carefully related to their relevant time periods. The date shown in the marketing communications expenditure data may reflect when an item was paid, rather than when the activity occurred. A change in accounting practice, moving from a 30-day payment schedule to a 90-day payment schedule, for example, could have profound impact on how the value of a marketing communications program might be determined. As a side benefit, the work of assembling the marketing database will spur the need for better activity description, more detail, better consistency, and generally more discipline by all managers.

Time aggregation is always an issue when assembling data into a consistent datafile. Generally our experience shows that sales or expenditures compiled week by week work best analytically, but data is commonly only available by month or on a quarterly basis. As time periods become more aggregate, changes tend to average away, making it more difficult to show the direct impact of marketing activities. It is typically the marketing expenditure data that dictates the need for longer time periods of analysis.

This first step in assembling the data and creating the data dictionary is the most time-consuming and difficult of the four steps. Yet, understanding and interacting with the data is critical to the success of this process. Clearly the necessary intimate connection with the data can only be accomplished within the organization as most firms simply could not or would not allow external organizations to access such seemingly competitive-sensitive information.

Preparing the Data

Once the data is assembled, it must be prepared for analysis. Statistical packages generally require data to be assembled into a single matrix of variables by time periods. This requires that all the data from all the various sources must be assembled into a single analysis file. If the data during its assembly has been recoded for consistency, then appending one file to another is not a difficult task. But often before analysis can occur, the data must be scrutinized for anything that might interfere with the analysis or the interpretation of the analysis results.

One such concern is the presence of "outliers" in the sales data. Almost always, historical sales data will contain some unusual one-time sales blips that usually have nothing to do with the marketing activity of the organization. This may mean sales to a particular customer, of a particular item, or of a particular date or time period may need to be deleted from the analysis file. If these data anomalies are not removed, they may end up distorting the modeling or analysis later on. Obviously, data should not be deleted without strong evidence that it represents a true outlier and not simply a relatively infrequent purchasing occurrence.

Sometimes data will need to be recoded further to enable computer analysis. Dummy coding is a process whereby categorical variables (such as gender, the presence or absence of a particular promotional activity, or the distribution channel by which an item is sold) can be converted to binary numerical data that the computer can understand and manipulate. Variables that are highly inter-related or correlated might need to be aggregated or combined, since statistically they will serve to cancel each other out in any statistical analysis.

Another issue of concern is whether the data contains seasonality effects. Sales data almost always show seasonal characteristics since most products sell more at some times of the year and less at others. Seasonal fluctuations in sales are natural and somewhat predictable over time. Finding the pattern typically requires multiple years of data but identifying it is important so it can be statistically controlled in the analysis. Otherwise, there is potential to mistake a seasonal sales fluctuation for sales resulting from some marketing or marketing communications activity. Often a sales increase that appears to be associated with a marketing expenditure is really just a seasonal increase, or a true increase is hidden by a normal seasonal sales decline.

Selecting the Statistical Model

Once the analytical data file has been prepared, a statistical model can be chosen. It is here that most marketing managers run for cover and gladly hand off the analytical task to external suppliers. It is where the term *black box* applies and where the marketing manager is most likely to be misled in the process. The problem, of course, is that this step is not independent of the data assembly and preparation steps.

Certainly the most common model for analyzing marketing databases is regression. Regression modeling (discussed in greater detail in Chapter 5) is an analytical procedure that uncovers statistical relationships among a set of variables. It results in a statistical equation or model that can be used to predict sales (or another criterion variable) from a set of predictor or independent variables such as customer demographics, marketing communications expenditures, or price. The more history a manager has, the better the model that emerges from the process.

Interpreting a regression model takes an understanding of the marketing and communications variables involved, not just knowledge of the statistical procedure itself. This is why it is so important for the entire integrated marketing team to work together. Any modeling must take into account such things as lead-lag or carryover effects (for instance when advertising in one week impacts sales the next week and the following week) or interactions among variables (for instance advertising and promotion working together to create a synergistic effect). Identifying these relationships and building them into the model is vital if the model output is to be meaningful.

There are times when a logarithmic regression model would work better than a simple linear regression model. When price is one of the predictor variables and the criterion sales variable appears to vary widely, then a log model (which converts data to its logarithm or exponent) can smooth out the data for better results. For those uncomfortable with traditional linear statistical models, such as regression, there is the supervised artificial neural network. A good back propagation model, found in most data mining packages, can quickly sort out the relationships among predictor variables and the criterion sales variable.

It is important to understand that there is no one model that can be used to measure the impact and value of all marketing programs. There are multiple models that require different assumptions about the nature of the patterns and relationships among the variables such as sales, media investments, promotional allowances, and the like. It is clear from our experience that many models should be run and compared. The models should be only partially judged on their ability to explain the criterion variable or sales. They should also be judged on how well they fit the development of the marketing strategy. This strengthens the case for making measurement and database creation an internal process. These issues will all be discussed in greater detail in later chapters.

Applying the Analysis to the Problem

Whatever problem the marketing manager is facing, this internal analytical process should provide guidance. The best models can be used to answer the fanciful "what if" questions so popular today or to evaluate hypothetical scenarios. The model, however, should not be used independently of the manager's intuition and instinct. It should be used as a supplementary tool. If advertising is not showing much sales response or lead generation, it might be that the message is not on target and a different creative approach should be tried.

Static models that focus on single point-in-time results are interesting but generally less than relevant to the marketing manager charged with generating financial returns from investments in marketing. The market is simply too dynamic for a static model to work over the long term. Therefore, any model needs to be applied and then updated or revised. At each application, the model should continually improve and become a more useful tool; yet it will never be perfect and it will always need long-term revisions.

The real value to the marketing manager of the approach outlined is using the model as a tool and learning from its continuing and ongoing revision process. Even when the model doesn't successfully predict sales or adequately explain past results, there is learning that will help refine the model. The value of internal marketing measurement is in the journey, not just reaching the destination

In summary, it is our strong belief that the dynamic marketplace requires a re-thinking of how the impact and effects of marketing can be measured and evaluated. The need for different forms of analysis has made this measurement process increasingly dependent on internal data and a more focused marketing analytical approach. Indeed, marketing and marketing research managers must become the master of their own fate. This means the development of the measurement skills and abilities within the organization, not simply the tendency to source external supplies and resources for the task.

The Research Budget

The costs associated with a research project typically can be divided into those pertaining to research and instrument design, data collection (or fieldwork), data preparation and analysis, and final report and presentation.

Research and Instrument Design

The costs associated with research design include mostly someone's time to define the purpose of the research, outline the fundamental research method to be used, establish contractual relationships with the necessary sub-contracting suppliers, and determine an appropriate time schedule for the research. Often there are research materials that need to be designed, such as questionnaires, data collection forms, or protocol sheets, and this is categorized here as well. If the research involves an experiment where test materials or procedures need to be put in place, these costs would also fall in the design stage.

The costs associated with the design and launch of a project are the easiest to underestimate or overlook. Since most of the cost is someone's professional time, it is often work assigned to a consultant or a full-service research supplier. Research suppliers that understand the true cost associated with this phase of the research process may appear expensive when compared to a supplier that is only providing data collection and simple analysis.

How much you budget for this research expense depends primarily on the complexity of the research project. The best cost criterion is the number of hours or days of professional time that you estimate would be required to accomplish the tasks involved. There might also be some support overhead for professional staff and additional expenses, such as travel that might be necessary to get a project underway.

Data Collection

A second budgetary consideration for a research project is what it will cost to collect the data. This is generally the first cost that may come to mind when you first start budgeting for research. Depending on the project, data collection might simply be the subscription fee to a syndicated supplier, which supplies you with the secondary data you need. It might also be what you pay to a field service or full-service supplier to conduct the primary fieldwork.

If the project involves survey research, the costs associated with the fieldwork may become the largest cost component. There is almost no economy of scale in fieldwork. The cost of a telephone or a personal interview is the same whether ten interviews or a thousand are completed. Typically, fieldwork is estimated on a per-completion basis. Therefore, the more completions you need, the more costly the fieldwork component. The cost per completion will mainly depend on how difficult it is to reach your desired study subjects and how long the interview takes because both of these factors influence the hourly completion rate. Business-to-business fieldwork, especially when it concerns elite, difficult-to-reach individuals such as company CEOs and presidents, can be quite expensive on an individual completion basis. Even with a very short, five-minute phone interview, several interviewers, and a clean list of qualified phone numbers with respondent names, only two to three completions per hour are probably possible. To obtain cooperation, an incentive might also be required, which can dramatically increase the fieldwork costs.

Obviously, the cost of fieldwork varies considerably and depends entirely on what is involved. For focus group research, the fieldwork might consist of recruiting costs plus incentives paid to participants, the facility cost, moderating cost, and audio- and videotaping. The fieldwork costs associated with an in-store observation study would consist only of hours spent observing plus travel expense for interviewers.

There may be some cost efficiencies in data collection if the same data can be shared or used for more than one project. This is the same principal by which syndicated suppliers operate. For instance, if you can piggyback your information needs with someone else's in the company, and meet the objectives of two studies in one, the data collection cost can be spread across two budgets. Sometimes the re-use of syndicated data may be so common within a company, that there are no project costs associated with it at all. Dun & Bradstreet data, for example, may get purchased once and re-used so many times by different personnel that its cost becomes part of the general overhead.

Data Preparation and Analysis

The third cost component to a research project is the analysis of the data and any related data preparation costs. The preparation cost involves transforming any data into computerized form so that the data can be computer analyzed. The analysis cost is determined by the analyst's professional time. Assuming that the necessary hardware and software computational tools are in place, the cost criterion is again the number of hours or days it takes someone to do the required analysis. Be careful of making the same mistake that too many have made, which is to simply allow someone to generate all conceivable tabulations, without any thought given to what is really useful and needed. The result will be a very impressive stack of computer printouts or a very thick report that will almost never get used, simply because it is so voluminous and mindless in form. It is well worth the

Exhibit 2.1:
Telephone Tracking Survey Budget Breakdown

300 completions among company purchasing agents
   —Sample list purchased from D&B
   —Five minute interview, approximately 20 items

Project Cost Estimate

D & B sample of 1000 names	$1,000
Fieldwork (300 completions @ $50 ea)	15,000
Printing of materials	500
Data entry & editing	1,000

Professional Time

Preparation of questionnaire	2,500
Analysis and top line report	9,000

TOTAL $29,000

cost to explain to an analyst what it is you need from the data and let them perform the appropriate analyses in a logical fashion.

The type of analysis that is performed will partially determine the cost. Specialized or more sophisticated analytical techniques may require extra knowledge or skills and be more costly on an hourly basis.

Final Report and Presentation

The last budget component for research is for the preparation of the final report and/or a final presentation of the findings. A good final report relates the findings of the research project to its objectives. It should be written so that the appropriate decision-makers understand it and will spend the necessary time with it. The traditional belief is that a busy executive won't read more than a page or so. This should be amended to say that they won't read more than a page of poorly written, irrelevant material. However, if a report is lengthy and complex, it is often customary to have an executive summary that highlights the key points.

The cost of a good final report and presentation again is a matter of the professional time it takes to prepare them. Depending on the audience for the presentation, some production costs might be involved as well.

Exhibit 2.1 shows a hypothetical budget breakdown for a telephone tracking survey with the specified parameters.

It is easy to overlook some of the costs involved in conducting market research, especially the cost of necessary professional time. High-quality market research can be relatively expensive. However, the cost of not doing research can be considerably higher to an organization if a competitive advantage is lost because the information was not available. The cost of poorly conducted research, or research that is not well-communicated within the organization, should also not be forgotten.

Notes

1. Pande, Peter S., Robert Neuman, Roland Cavanagh, et al. *The Six Sigma Way: How GE, Motorola and Other Top Companies Are Honing Their Performance* (Chicago: McGraw-Hill Trade, 2000).
2. Kaplan, Robert S., and David P. Norton. *The Balanced Scorecard* (Cambridge, MA: Harvard Business School Press, 1996).
3. Schultz, Don E., and Jeffrey S. Walters. *Measuring Brand Communication ROI* (New York: Association of National Advertisers, 1997). Chapters 1 and 2.

3 Secondary Sources of Information

When you have a research question, it is often a good bet that there exists some information on the topic already. Before investing the time and money into primary data collection, or making a decision based on no information at all, consider what secondary sources of information might be available to you.

Secondary information can meet a variety of tasks and objectives. By doing a careful search of existing sources, you can sometimes very quickly compile sufficient information to address your questions. Time is an important advantage. Since the data already exists, you don't need to wait for primary data to be collected—which can take weeks or months. With secondary information, it is simply a matter of the time it takes to find and access the data. With on-line or library computerized search capabilities, a review of all that the periodical literature can provide can take place in a matter of minutes. With today's overnight delivery services, faxing technology, and computer modems, the information is on your office desk almost immediately.

Secondary information also has the advantage of costing very little—especially compared to the cost of primary data collection. Some information, such as information from internal company records or articles in trade publications, is free. Other secondary information is available for a fee. For instance, associations often engage in projects to benefit their membership, offering reports for sale at a minimum cost. Syndicated industry reports are often available at a price that would be far less than the cost of doing the research firsthand.

Another advantage is that much secondary information is acquired through sources such as the government or commercial syndicates.

When this is the case, the information available can be of a larger scope generated from larger samples (perhaps a census) employing higher standards of data collection and verification than would be possible through singular primary research efforts.

There are obvious disadvantages to using secondary information as well. First, since the information was originally obtained for a purpose other than your specific research problem, it may not answer your immediate question. This problem of "fit," or relevance, is the classic drawback to using secondary information. Fit often has to do with how the questions are asked or how the data is aggregated. For instance, you may need the characteristics of potential customers within a company "trading area," but the information that is available is reported only by county or census tract and does not align with your designated geography.

You may need weekly sales data for individual stores within a chain over the last year, yet sales are only documented at the chain level in bi-monthly increments. When data is not defined precisely the way you would want it, or it is aggregated to a level that is inappropriate, it becomes difficult to use without some guesswork and finessing. This drawback has helped precipitate the need for computerizing information in order to facilitate "re-analysis" to fit the parameters and questions at hand. Today, many syndicated sources offer on-line computer access to data in order to provide more flexibility in the way the data can be tabulated and presented.

The problem of fit is more serious when the information available is not as complete as you would like or sufficient for what you need. For instance, you might want to know the spending statistics of three companies in your market and the secondary source only reports data for X and Y and not Z. You may know *what* activities a company participates in but not *how often*; you may have media *exposure* information but have no idea of its *impact*. In such situations, you may need to turn to primary research efforts in order to supplement the available secondary information.

A second drawback to secondary information is that it may not be as up-to-date and accurate as you would like. Typically, time has passed since when the data was collected and when you access the information. This timing issue is especially a problem in industries where there have been dramatic changes in the business or competitive environment. Advances in technology and technology adoption, a new product introduction, or new governmental regulations can quickly change the nature and structure of the competitive framework or customer expectations and behaviors. Data collected even one or two years prior may be too outdated to be of use.

A third disadvantage that can plague secondary research is when different sources provide contradictory information. Published information, especially numerical information, gains an almost mystical credibility. When those published reports conflict, which do you believe? For instance, published market share, sales, or media expenditure figures by company within an industry can often vary substantially from one secondary source to the next. Often the reason for the differences lies in the methodology used by the original source to collect the information. Methodological differences might include such things as how the questions were asked, exactly who was included in the sample and how the sample was generated, or the time period over which the data was collected. Furthermore, the sponsor of the research must always be considered and evaluated for credibility and potential bias since the original context and purpose of the report could influence the way the information was reported.

In other words, two published reports could conflict, and both be absolutely correct—simply because they were reporting essentially different things. Market share or sales information might vary because sources have based the numbers or trends on different assumptions of how the market is defined and who (what companies or geographies, for example) are included in the base. Associations frequently report such information based on their membership only, which may or may not be representative of the entire industry. For this reason, there are some corporations that do not rely on syndicated market share data at all to gauge their relative position within the marketplace or to benchmark themselves.

This problem is aggravated by poor or ambiguous reporting of the methodology by the secondary source. Information can be published or quoted in the media without reference to any methodological specification. This methodological detail is generally perceived as boring and, therefore, excluded, but it has obvious implications for data validity and generalizability.

Despite the data drawbacks, doing your homework with secondary research can reduce the risk of a market venture or decision by giving you some background information and insights from others who have had experiences of a similar nature. This applies to developing marketing strategies, as well as to designing primary research projects. The historical record of business ventures is typically contained in secondary information, and marketers can almost ensure failure by ignoring it. By routinely examining what has been done in the past by others in the industry or by others in your own company for that matter, you equip yourself with additional tools for analysis and evaluation.

Secondary information also offers a range of perspectives on the immediate problem. It is generally very useful to see the research problem from outside your immediate corporate culture. It helps to see where the biases are and where errors in interpretation are likely to be made.

Furthermore, in many instances, secondary information is the only information available in the time frame available to you. This last point is very important. Examination of secondary research is much better than the examination of no information at all.

Commercial Databases

To say that secondary information is rapidly becoming dominated by the computerized database is a dramatic understatement. Most libraries have replaced their manual card cataloguing systems with computerized systems, microfiche, and digital compact disks. Most published information today is already in digital form before it is printed, making it easy to store and maintain in digital form. Selling access to computerized databases has become a commercial enterprise.

Conducting on-line computerized data searches greatly reduces the time it takes to find relevant material and offers the added convenience of conducting the search in-house rather than traveling to the nearest library. Of course, there are costs associated with searching this way. There is the telephone line charge for the time spent searching on-line and usually a connect charge in order to access the database. If abstracts or articles are printed, there is also the cost of printing.

The computerized database industry is one of the most dynamic and the fastest growing. It is becoming increasingly important for the market researcher to keep abreast of the latest developments and available services in order to have access to such useful and important information. There are four broad categories of commercial databases: bibliographic, numeric, directory, and encyclopedic.

Bibliographic Databases

A computerized bibliographic database contains references to existing periodical literature or other published documents. It lists the coordinates of articles, such as the name and author, journal title, and publication date. Typically, key words that describe the content of the article, or abstracts, are also listed; sometimes the entire document might be available. Relevant articles can be accessed through key-word searches. By entering a single word, such as "carbide," a database can provide all of the documents (or references to them) that have that word in them. Multiple words can also be used, such as the words "carbide and drill." Such a query would automatically provide all of the documents containing both words. Most databases even allow for complex logical statements, which can narrow the focus of the search and keep the number of documents to a manageable number.

A market researcher would access a bibliographic database to short-cut and expand old-fashioned library searches on newspaper and magazine articles, reports, press releases, and so on, in order to quickly learn more about an industry—information on market competitors, marketplace trends, business issues or concerns, financial/managerial issues, and personnel changes—anything that might be written in the trade or business press. When selling to publishers, for instance, knowing what the hot buttons are within that industry should be of value.

When considering a new marketing venture, it would be possible perhaps to find out what obstacles others in similar situations have encountered. Analyzing the content and tone of articles written by the press about your company would give you insight into how it is communicating to the public through its press releases and what image is being portrayed to the public about your company. This last example explains why this kind of bibliographic service has become a critical tool for the public relations industry.

The number and names of the available bibliographic databases are too numerous to list here and will certainly change over time, but some of the better-known services are worth mentioning. LEXUS is probably the best-known legal bibliographic database, originally designed for the legal community to simplify searching case law. It has since expanded to include a news-based service, NEXUS. LEXUS/ NEXUS, then, is a commercial database containing most news-oriented periodical literature, along with case law. Other bibliographic databases offer access to different sources. For instance, Dow Jones, the parent company of the *Wall Street Journal*, would be a good source for business and financial information published in the *Journal*. There are a number of commercial research syndicates that catalog market studies based on either primary data or reanalyses of census data. Many provide Internet access, but often require a subscription fee.

Numeric Databases

Numeric databases can be financial or statistical. Financial databases, such as Chase Econometrics, generally are used by economists to support their analyses and forecasts. Statistical databases consist primarily of numerical information that has been collected by either the government or a syndicated data supplier. Much of the federal government information, such as that from the Bureau of the Census and the Department of Commerce, is available in computerized form, either on computer tapes or diskettes or through an on-line service called CENDATA. Other examples of computerized statistical databases include Donnelly Marketing Information, which maintains consumer household and health care information; Simmons Media/ Marketing Services, which reports media audience exposure for both print and broadcast, cross-referenced by product usage information; the Nielsen Television Index with its television program ratings; the Nielsen Retail Index reporting store audit information on retail prices, promotional activity, and product sales; and Nielsen's SCANT-RACK service, based on in-store scanner data of product sales.

The advantage of accessing numeric databases is probably somewhat obvious. You can extract just the information you need, in more or less detail, and manipulate it or reanalyze it in the way most useful for your own specific purpose. U.S. population or retail trade statistics from the Census Bureau could, for example, be analyzed by state or any given major metropolitan area, or by a particular class of retail trade, to suit a marketer's needs. In many instances, numeric databases contain data that is not published elsewhere in print. An example, of course, is again the Census Bureau which, although it publishes many print reports based on census data, offers much more statistical and geographical data, in greater detail, in computerized form than would be economically possible to offer in print.

Directory Databases

Many commercial enterprises or associations compile membership directories for the purpose of doing business or for the convenience of their memberships. These directories might include such information as names, titles, addresses, telephone numbers, and other relevant member statistics. They are often computerized and made available, usually for a fee, to anyone wanting access to the information. Directory databases are different from bibliographic databases in that they are created by an organization from that organization's own internal or primary information. By contrast, a bibliographic database is essentially created by sources outside of the information provider; that is, the information to be accessed originates from the periodical literature or the media, not the database provider. The telephone company, for instance, has computerized all of the nation's residential and business telephone listings into a directory database available to interested parties and used by suppliers of business and consumer survey samples.

Dun&Bradstreet (D&B) is a good example of a directory database that is useful to business-to-business market researchers. For companies nationwide, it contains name, address, and SIC information, as well as statistics such as revenue and number of employees. It is, therefore, a good source of information to assist in identifying both customers and prospects. Companies can pay to have on-line access of the most current company data. This would be especially handy if you needed, for instance, a count (and specific names and addresses) of the manufacturers of industrial equipment or fabricated metal products as designated by SIC, within a particular geographical area that earn revenues of $200 million or more.

Encyclopedic Databases

Encyclopedic databases store large volumes of textual or pictorial data. Encyclopedia Britannica, for instance, can offer its entire encyclopedic knowledge on CD-ROM for easy search and retrieval. However, this type of database is not restricted to encyclopedias. It refers to any encyclopedic, or comprehensive, collection of original information rather than mere references to them.

The clear advantage to using an encyclopedic database is the cost factor. Volume sets as large as these in print are costly to buy and update. Buying the set on CD-ROM or accessing it via on-line services is cheaper. Furthermore, updating can occur electronically and, therefore, more quickly and cost efficiently, resulting in a more accurate information reference. The problem holding this area back currently is the lack of standardized disk formats and often the need for custom software to access or interface with these complex databases. Currently, searches can only be conducted on the text; searching pictorially is still not available.

Encyclopedic databases have not been specifically developed yet for business marketing applications, but almost certainly will be available in the future.

Internal Information

A very large source of secondary information is internal information—data from within your own company that is often routinely collected for various departmental purposes.Customer purchases, inquiries, lead qualification programs, customer service and service requests, accounting and sales reports, sales personnel reports, and previous market research that has been done for the company are common sources of such information. Most of this information exists in various departmental files, some of it is probably in computerized form, and some is probably buried in storage facilities. The researcher's hope is that it has not been thrown away. One of the biggest mistakes a company can make is to not retain this type of information. Unfortunately, new personnel often like to clean house and throw out the old files. While you can argue that the data takes up too much space or is costly to retain and maintain, not having the information when it is needed can cost far more than the cost of storage.

By accessing sales and inquiry information from previous time periods, you can see the seasonality patterns or buying cycles for a product, become aware of downward sales trends that might indicate a problem, compare sales from this year to last or one department to another, or evaluate the effectiveness of a marketing strategy. By looking at the absenteeism or productivity level for company personnel, you can begin to benchmark and see what kinds of employee motivational programs work best. The decision of what kind of communications program to run could be affected by inspecting the results of previous promotional efforts and analyzing their relative impact. What a shame it is that many companies receive warranty cards from customers for products sold and never bother to read them. Analysis of this purchase information, along with customer comments, could supply a researcher with much valuable information, including product problems, geographical sales information, and knowledge of a customer's potential repurchase cycle or related product needs and services. This information could certainly provide input for a company's customer database.

Because much internal information is routinely collected, it already exists and should be readily available to you just by inquiring, at no cost. Of course, since data collected internally is usually collected for some other purpose unrelated to marketing, it may not answer the specific questions at hand or may not have been collected in the most convenient form to analyze. It is possible, too, that some of the data may be biased, particularly if it is provided by sales personnel—a sales report may have been written with different goals in mind than selling the product.

Internal Financial Information

In most business organizations, the functional area with the longest database history is typically the accounting department. Often the accounting department was the first to get involved in computing and may still have control of the information technology function. Accounting departments are often quite technologically advanced.

Accounting information is usually financial in nature—sales revenues, expenses, overhead costs, and profits. Accounting reports are generally prepared to satisfy either tax reporting requirements or other managerial purposes. These documents probably report sales and invoice data that have been aggregated across product lines or geographical markets, rendering them almost useless for marketing comparisons. Therefore, when approaching the accounting department, your main difficulty will probably be getting information reformatted or re-arranged to suit your particular purpose and interests.

Sales Information

Every time a sale is made, an invoice full of important marketing information is created. Invoices often include customer identification, product(s) purchased and number of units sold, price paid, discounts used, salesperson identification, store location, and shipping information. These invoices usually are processed by the accounting department into aggregate sales revenues and then tracked by the receivables department to ensure payment. Traditionally, this important sales transaction is lost once the payment has been received and processed.

As marketers, you should see to it that this sales information becomes the heart of the customer database. All of the individual purchase information should be retained and organized so that the current purchases can be related to all prior purchases this customer has made.

Registration and warranty cards that customers complete and mail in are another source of sales information. These cards also contain additional information depending on what is requested, such as customer feedback on the sale itself and the product, more refined address information, product use information on the purchased item plus product ownership and usage in other related categories, and customer or company demographics.

The field sales personnel doing the selling are certainly important internal sources of information as well. They generally are required to file "contact" reports or similar documentation that describes their interaction with both customers and prospects. In an automated system, this information is directly entered into a computer database by the sales personnel. This secondary information, the "paperwork" of sales personnel, then can be systematically analyzed to understand sales trends, individual customer purchasing patterns, or even employee productivity.

Talking directly to the sales personnel will also provide you with meaningful insights into the market or customers, although this is not technically secondary research since you are the one gathering these insights firsthand. However, on this point, you should remember that information from field sales personnel, especially those on a commission-based compensation system, may be somewhat biased. What is profitable for the salesperson may not always be in the best long-term interest of the company. A sales rep is typically focused on selling an individual account rather than promoting a company-wide marketing strategy. He or she may also be focused more on the immediate micro issues—making an immediate sale or making this month's goal—that he or she is facing at the time rather than on a broader macro view of the marketplace. Still, a good market researcher should frequently consult with field sales personnel both directly and indirectly to keep abreast of trends and potential problems.

Customer Information

As the importance of customer service seems to increase, the need to collect more information on customers also increases. Every time a customer makes a service request, the information should be transferred to the customer portion of the marketing database. Certainly service requests provide information about potential product problems. The request also presents, however, an opportunity to interact with and ask the customer additional questions that may lend even more insight into their needs and purchasing behavior. Company demographics such as revenues, number of employees, and SIC classification can all be useful data for selling to them again down the line, as is information on who the end user of the product or service is and how and when the product is used, what the budget and purchasing cycles are, and who is involved in the decision of what to buy. Many companies rely on this kind of customer information to better segment and more effectively target customers in the future.

Personnel Records

Company employees are important information sources: They sell the product, fulfill the services, and interface with customers on a day-to-day basis. Corporations are increasingly recognizing the value of loyal, long-term employees and are involved in motivational programs to increase productivity, as well as educational and training programs to develop employee skills and professionalism. Keeping the sales force motivated and the customer service personnel friendly and knowledgeable is obviously related to sales and profits. Therefore, information on employees that can be used to track productivity and satisfaction are also invaluable sources of information to the marketing researcher. While employee satisfaction surveys can be employed, there is probably much internal secondary information that could substitute for or supplement these surveys, including individual employee sales levels and quotas, sales and loss ratios, absenteeism, telephone records, and so on.

Governmental Information

The most important source of external secondary information for the business-to-business market researcher is the U.S. government. The federal government is a rich source of statistical information on a variety of topics. In fact, there is so much information available that there are commercial suppliers that do little else than re-analyze and repackage government-supplied information to sell to market researchers.

A variety of federal agencies collect and supply information. Much of the information is collected in the normal course of their operations, such as during the collection of taxes. Certainly, the Department of Commerce is by far the most prolific supplier of information, but there are other, equally important agencies that prepare information as well: the Internal Revenue Service, the Federal Reserve System Board of Governors, the Department of Labor, the Council of Economic Advisers, the Office of Management and Budget, and the Congressional Information Service, to name a few. Most government publications are published through the U.S. Government Printing Office and can be obtained through the National Technical Information

Service (NTIS), 5285 Port Royal Road, Springfield, Virginia 22161, which provides a catalog of available publications upon request. Much of this information is also available in computerized form or on CD-ROM, depending on what it is. Again, NTIS is the source of this kind of information.

Department of Commerce

The Department of Commerce is the most important source of business-to-business information because it houses the Bureau of the Census. Census data, which is collected for both consumers and businesses, is generally comprehensive and of very high quality since consumers and businesses alike are required by law to participate. The data is available in tabulated and printed form, as well as in computer-analyzable form on tape or diskette. Computerized census data is available for a nominal fee and allows for tabulating or analyzing data to meet any specific need. Analysis of this data has provided a lucrative opportunity for commercial data suppliers.

Of special interest to business-to-business marketers are a variety of publications and computerized data coming from the Bureau of the Census: the *Census of Agriculture*, *Census of Construction Industries*, *Census of Government*, *Census of Manufacturers*, *Census of Mineral Industries*, *Census of Retail Trade*, *Census of Service Industries*, *Census of Transportation*, and the *Census of Wholesale Trade*. All of these publications provide the fundamental descriptive statistics for these business markets. A business might use these statistics to identify promising new company retail locations or sales opportunities based on the demographic characteristics of the prospective customers, population numbers and projected growth, and retail volume for similar businesses.

Not all census data is collected at the same time because of the scope of such a task. The business census that supports most of the publications mentioned previously is taken every five years—in the years ending in "2" and "7." In several of the categories, more frequent bulletins and publications are issued as well. There is, for example, the *Annual Census of Manufacturers* that covers the years in between censuses. In some categories there are even monthly publications, such as *Monthly Retail Trade* and *Monthly Selected Services Receipts*.

Of course, the Bureau of the Census also publishes information about consumers. This consumer information appears in a long list of publications beginning with the *Census of Population*. Population and housing information is collected every decade in the years ending in "0," as you probably are aware. Other consumer-oriented publications might also be useful for business-to-business purposes, such as the *Census of Housing*, *County Business Patterns*, and *County and City Databook*.

Census Bureau products are available in a variety of places. Libraries usually will have a section designated for government publications in print and on microfiche. Almost all states have data centers through private and public organizations registered with the Bureau's National Clearinghouse, and the Bureau has regional offices throughout the country that can provide information as well. A list of these and other sources can be obtained through NTIS or through the Data User Services Division, Bureau of the Census, Washington, D.C. 20233.

The Department of Commerce itself publishes a variety of materials that can be very helpful to the market research process. *Business Statistics*, for example, is published every two years and provides a historical record of the data published in the monthly *Survey of Current Business*. *U.S. Industrial Outlook* is published annually and includes five-year projections, as well as a summary of past activity. Needless to say, the Department of Commerce is an extremely rich source of secondary information.

State and Local Agencies

State and local governmental interests are found where there are licensing requirements or taxing authority. Lists and other information are often maintained that are public records and can be useful in defining markets.

There are also state and local agencies that are created for the purpose of promoting business activity in a particular geographic area or market category. Examples are convention bureaus, tourism boards, Chambers of Commerce, and agricultural extension services. State and local agencies typically do not have the information-gathering and publication sophistication of the Department of Commerce, but they still can be important sources of information.

Standard Industrial Classifications

A very important categorizing scheme for the business-to-business marketer is the Standard Industrial Classification (SIC) on the newer

North American Industry Classification System (NAICS) issued by the Office of Management and Budget of the Executive Office of the President. This coding system was devised as a way to classify business establishments by industry type or the type of economic activity in which they engage. For the government as well as for the business-to-business marketer, the code establishes a much-needed standard of uniformity and comparability when presenting statistical data on these various companies. The codes themselves have been developed, and recently revised in 1987, by a multi-agency federal committee, with obvious primary input from the Bureau of the Census. The SIC is used by all federal agencies as well as state, county, and local governments. It is also widely used in business-to-business marketing as a way of classifying and identifying businesses by industry types.

The SIC is important for the business-to-business marketer in that business prospects and customers will be other businesses. Therefore, having a common language to classify these customers and their characteristics is essential when accessing government and other statistical databases in order to build a customer or prospect database. As a manufacturer of dairy food products, you are most likely selling to food stores or eating and drinking establishments, defined by two specific SIC codes within a much wider range of retail trade establishments. D&B, as well as the Department of Commerce, will use these identifiers to access specific retail names and addresses or demographical data on these retailers, as should you. When developing databases or mailing lists for advertising to, communicating with, or researching prospects, the SIC system is invaluable.

Establishments

SIC coding is based on establishments. An *establishment* is defined as an economic unit, generally at a single physical location where business is conducted or where services or industrial operations are performed. For instance, a factory, store, hotel, movie theater, farm, bank, railroad depot, airline terminal, sales office, warehouse, or central administrative office would each be considered an establishment and given a code. Where distinct economic activities are performed at a single physical location, such as when a lumberyard also operates a construction business, or a manufacturer also has separate retail operations, each activity is treated as a separate establishment and given a distinct SIC. In other words, if there is no SIC designation that combines these activities into one code and there are distinctly separate operations (i.e., separate employees and wages) that can be associated with each activity, a business enterprise could be interpreted as consisting of multiple establishments, with multiple SIC classifications.

Each operating establishment is assigned an industry code depending upon its principal activity. Where there are multiple activities, the establishment is coded according to the one that has the most economic importance.

Code Structure

The SIC codes themselves are divided into industry groups in a hierarchical manner. There are two-digit, three-digit, and four-digit industry groups, each with successively more industrial detail. The codes are categorized into eleven major divisions designated as A through K: Agriculture, Forestry and Fishing; Mining; Construction; Manufacturing; Transportation and Public Utilities; Wholesale Trade; Retail Trade; Finance, Insurance and Real Estate; Services; Public Administration; and Nonclassifiable Establishments. The major divisions and the two-digit and three-digit codes associated with each are shown in the chapter appendix.

To illustrate how the SIC codes work, consider the commercial marketing research industry. As shown in Exhibit 3.1, marketing research establishments are found in Division I, Services. This division is defined as establishments providing a wide variety of services for individuals as well as business and government establishments. This major division includes the two-digit codes ranging from 70 to 89. Marketing research establishments would fall in the two-digit Major Group 87: Engineering, Accounting, Research, Management, and Related Services. The appropriate three-digit code that is more specific is 873, for Research, Development, and Testing Services. The four-digit code, fine-tuning the classification even more, would be 8732, or Commercial Economic, Sociological, and Educational Research. This is defined as those establishments primarily engaged in performing commercial business, marketing, opinion, and other economic, sociological, and educational research on a contract or fee basis. This category is distinguished from 8733, which consists of noncommercial research organizations.

Depending on the level of specificity or aggregation you desire in classifying businesses, you may decide that the two- or three-digit code is sufficient. However, four-digit SIC codes are considered standard.

Exhibit 3.1: Breakdown of Standard Industrial Classification Codes for the Marketing Research Industry

A: Agriculture, forestry, and fishing (01–09)

B: Mining (10–14)

C: Construction (15–17)

D: Manufacturing (20–39)

E: Transportation, communications, electric, gas, and sanitary services (40–49)

F: Wholesales trade (50–51)

G: Retail trade (52–59)

H: Finance, insurance, and real estate (60–67)

I: Services (70–89)
    70 Hotels, rooming houses, camps, & lodging places
    72 Personal services
    73 Business services
    75 Automotive repair, services, & parking
    76 Miscellaneous repair services
    78 Motion pictures
    79 Amusement and recreation services
    80 Health services
    81 Legal services
    82 Educational services
    83 Social services
    84 Museums, art galleries, and botanical & zoological gardens
    86 Membership organizations
    87 Engineering, accounting, research, management, & related services
        871 Engineering, architectural, and surveying services
        872 Accounting, auditing, and bookkeeping services
        873 Research, development, and testing services
            8731 Commercial physical and biological research
            8732 Commercial economic, sociological, & educational research
            8733 Noncommercial research organizations
            8734 Testing laboratories
        874 Management and public relations services
    88 Private households
    89 Miscellaneous services

J: Public administration (91–97)

K: Nonclassified establishments (99)

D&B offers a commercial service, known as Dun's Market Identifiers. This is a list of most business establishments in the United States with their SIC identification. An additional enhancement of the code that gives a more precise breakdown is also offered. D&B also has names and titles of key personnel in many cases. The list is well maintained and contains the most current available information. The D&B list is an excellent way to start a prospect database.

One point to keep in mind is that D&B will accept more than one SIC code for any company listed in its database. When doing searches on a particular SIC four-digit code, unless you specify otherwise, all codes listed by a company will be included, even cases where the SIC may not be the primary or first designated business activity. Therefore, you may end up with some companies that are technically classified as retailers because they are involved in some retailing activity, but consider themselves manufacturers rather than retailers for all other purposes.

Some industries are more prone to have businesses with multiple SIC classifications, such as the advertising or publishing industry. Here an advertising agency could also be classified as a direct marketer or a research operation *and* have a production division that does typesetting and commercial printing. Or a book publisher could be cross-listed as a magazine or newspaper publisher or even a commercial printing operation.

Other Secondary Information

Beyond government sources and commercial supplier enhancements, there are a wide variety of available secondary information sources. These include both commercial and noncommercial suppliers.

Directories

Directories provide listings of organizations and individuals. Certainly the most familiar directories are the telephone white pages and yellow pages that are in every home and office. There are several other commercially prepared directories that are useful to the business-to-business marketer and can be quickly found and consulted in the reference section of any major public library.

The National Register Publishing Company publishes, among others, the *Directory of Corporate Affiliations* and the *International Directory of Corporate Affiliations*, both of which list corporations and their subsidiary holdings. National Register Publishing Company also publishes the *Standard Directory of Advertisers* and the *Standard Directory of Advertising Agencies*, which lists key personnel, locations, and descriptive statistics for those companies or agencies listed within.

The *Fortune Directory*, published by *Fortune* magazine, lists information on the top 500 largest corporations, including names of key employees. The *Thomas Register of American Manufacturers* is a multivolume directory that lists individual product information, addresses, offices, and subsidiaries of manufacturing companies. D & B publishes the *Million Dollar Directory*, which lists the offices, products, sales, and number of employees for companies with assets of $500,000 or more. Standard & Poor's *Register of Corporations, Directors, and Executives* provides listings of officers, products, sales, addresses, and phone numbers for most U.S. (and Canadian) corporations.

Predicast's F & S Index provides information on companies, products, and industries from a variety of sources, including current periodicals and news literature, as well as special industry reports. This index is published weekly and includes information on new products, technological developments, mergers and acquisitions, and so on.

There are also a variety of very specialized directories. One of the best known is Standard Rate and Data Service (SRDS), which publishes listings of media advertising rates. *Business Publications* is one of the SRDS directories that contains listings for most of the business periodicals. Gale Research also publishes specialized directories. *Consultants and Consulting Organizations Directory*, *Encyclopedia of Information Systems and Services*, and *Encyclopedia of Associations* are a few examples of their publications.

Syndicated Information

Beyond directories, there are a number of suppliers that compile business-related information. Among them are two quarterly Predicasts publications, *Predicasts Forecasts* and *Worldcasts*, which forecast industries and products. *Moody's Manuals*, including *Banks and Finance, Industrials, Municipals and Governments, Public Utilities*, and *Transportation* are published by Moody's Investors Services and contain balance sheets and income statements for most companies and governmental units. Standard & Poor's publishes *Corporate Records*, which contains financial statistics and recent news items; *Industry Surveys*, which includes analyses of most industries; and *Statistical Service*, which provides monthly statistical data. Another service,

FINDEX, The Directory of Market Research Reports, Studies and Surveys, lists thousands of research reports produced by research suppliers.

Periodical Literature

All of the business, trade, and professional publications are full of articles and information about a range of topics potentially useful to marketers. The difficulty is in finding the issue with the article that is needed. Once the article is located it becomes a low-cost source of information.

To cut down on the labor involved in article research, you might well consult a number of indexing services that help locate relevant articles. The *Business Periodicals Index*, published by the H. W. Wilson Company, indexes articles published in about 350 business periodicals by subject matter. *Dissertation Abstracts International*, published by University Microfilms, contains most of the doctoral dissertations done around the world for a more in-depth review of a particular study on a research topic. The *Wall Street Journal Index*, published by Dow Jones, catalogs everything appearing in the *Journal*, dividing stories into general news and corporate news.

Most public and university libraries have these and other services, which can make finding good articles fast and easy. Additionally, much that is relatively recently published is accessible through computerized on-line services. A library or an on-line service is an important tool for a business-to-business market researcher.

Associations

Industry and professional associations are another rich source of information. Associations almost always maintain directories of their members and also collect and compile information about their industry or profession. Generally, information is not available about individual association members beyond simple name and address identification. Information is generally aggregated to represent the entire industry. There are anti-trust considerations in some industries, and personal privacy issues in some professions.

There are enough associations to warrant their own directory, as described earlier. One association's directory you'll likely refer to from time to time is the American Marketing Association's *International Membership Directory and Marketing Services Guide*. This contains a listing of many potential business-to-business research suppliers.

APPENDIX

Historical Standard Industrial Classifications (1987 Sectors and Subsectors)

A: Agriculture, forestry and fishing

    01 Agricultural production—crops

    02 Agricultural production livestock and animal specialties

    07 Agricultural services

    08 Forestry

    09 Fishing, hunting, and trapping

B: Mining

    10 Metal mining

    12 Coal mining

    13 Oil and gas extraction

    14 Mining and quarrying of nonmetallic minerals, except fuels

C: Construction

    15 Building construction—general contractors and operative builders

    16 Heavy construction other than building construction—contractors

    17 Construction special—trade contractors

D: Manufacturing

    20 Food and kindred products

    21 Tobacco products

    22 Textile mill products

    23 Apparel and other finished products made from fabrics and similar materials

    24 Lumber and wood products, except furniture

    25 Furniture and fixtures

    26 Paper and allied products

    27 Printing, publishing, and allied industries

    28 Chemicals and allied products

    29 Petroleum refining and related industries

    30 Rubber and miscellaneous plastics products

    31 Leather and leather products

    32 Stone, clay, glass and concrete products

    33 Primary metal industries

    34 Fabricated metal products, except machinery and transportation equipment

    35 Industrial and commercial machinery and computer equipment

    36 Electronic and other electrical equipment and components, except computer equipment

    37 Transportation equipment

38 Measuring, analyzing, and controlling instruments, photographic, medical and optical goods, watches and clocks
39 Miscellaneous manufcaturing industries
E: Transportation, communications, electric, gas, and sanitary services
   40 Railroad transportation
   41 Local and suburban transit and interurban highway passenger transportation
   42 Motor freight tansportation and warehousing
   43 United States Postal Service
   44 Water Transporatation
   45 Transporatation by air
   46 Pipelines, except for natural gas
   47 Transporation services
   48 Communications
   49 Electric, gas, and sanitary services
F: Wholesales Trade
   50 Wholesale trade—durable goods
   51 Wholesale trade—nondurable goods
G: Retail Trade
   52 Building materials, hardware, garden supply, and mobile home dealers
   53 General merchandise stores
   54 Food stores
   55 Automotive dealers and gasoline service stations
   56 Apparel and accessory stores
   57 Home furniture, furnishings, and equipment stores
   58 Eating and drinking places
   59 Miscellaneous retail
H: Finance, insurance, and real estate
   60 Depository institutions
   61 Nondepository credit institutions
   62 Security and commodity brokers, dealers, exchanges, and services
   63 Insurance carriers
   64 Insurance agents, brokers, and service
   65 Real estate
   67 Holding and other investment offices
I: Services
   70 Hotels, Rooming Houses, Camps & Lodging Places
   72 Personal services
   73 Business services
   75 Automotive repair, services, & parking
   76 Miscellaneous repair services

78 Motion pictures

79 Amusement and recreation services

80 Health services

81 Legal services

82 Educational services

83 Social services

84 Museums, art galleries, botanical & zoological gardens

86 Membership organizations

87 Engineering, accounting, research, management, & related services

88 Private households

89 Miscellaneous services

J: Public administration

91 Executive, legislative, and general government, except finance

92 Justice, public order, and safety

93 Public finance, taxation, and monetary policy

94 Administration of human resource programs

95 Administration of environmental quality and housing programs

96 Administration of economic programs

97 National security and international affairs

K: Nonclassified establishments

99 Nonclassificable establishments

North American Industry Classification System (1997 subsectors matched to historical 1987 SIC sectors)

Agriculture, Forestry, Fishing and Hunting

111 Crop Production

112 Animal Production

113 Forestry and Logging

114 Fishing, Hunting and Trapping

115 Support Activities for Agriculture and Forestry

Mining

211 Oil and Gas Extraction

212 Mining (except Oil and Gas)

213 Support Activities for Mining

Utilities

221 Utilities

Construction

233 Building, Developing, and General Contracting

234 Heavy Construction

235 Special Trade Contractors

Manufacturing
   311 Food Manufacturing
   312 Beverage and Tobacco Product Manufacturing
   313 Textile Mills
   314 Textile Product Mills
   315 Apparel Manufacturing
   316 Leather and Allied Product Manufacturing
   321 Wood Product Manufacturing
   322 Paper Manufacturing
   323 Printing and Related Support Activities
   324 Petroleum and Coal Products Manufacturing
   325 Chemical Manufacturing
   326 Plastics and Rubber Products Manufacturing
   327 Nonmetallic Mineral Product Manufacturing
   331 Primary Metal Manufacturing
   332 Fabricated Metal Product Manufacturing
   333 Machinery Manufacturing
   334 Computer and Electronic Product Manufacturing
   335 Electrical Equipment, Appliance, and Component Manufacturing
   336 Transportation Equipment Manufacturing
   337 Furniture and Related Product Manufacturing
   339 Miscellaneous Manufacturing
Wholesale Trade
   421 Wholesale Trade, Durable Goods
   422 Wholesale Trade, Nondurable Goods
Retail Trade
   441 Motor Vehicle and Parts Dealers
   442 Furniture and Home Furnishings Stores
   443 Electronics and Appliance Stores
   444 Building Material and Garden Equipment and Supplies Dealers
   445 Food and Beverage Stores
   446 Health and Personal Care Stores
   447 Gasoline Stations
   448 Clothing and Clothing Accessories Stores
   451 Sporting Goods, Hobby, Book, and Music Stores
   452 General Merchandise Stores
   453 Miscellaneous Store Retailers
   454 Nonstore Retailers
Transportation and Warehousing
   481 Air Transportation
   482 Rail Transportation

483 Water Transportation

484 Truck Transportation

485 Transit and Ground Passenger Transportation

486 Pipeline Transportation

487 Scenic and Sightseeing Transportation

488 Support Activities for Transportation

491 Postal Service

492 Couriers and Messengers

493 Warehousing and Storage

Information

511 Publishing Industries

512 Motion Picture and Sound Recording Industries

513 Broadcasting and Telecommunications

514 Information Services and Data Processing Services

Finance and Insurance

521 Monetary Authorities - Central Bank

522 Credit Intermediation and Related Activities

523 Securities, Commodity Contracts, and Other Financial Investments

524 Insurance Carriers and Related Activities

525 Funds, Trusts, and Other Financial Vehicles

Real Estate and Rental and Leasing

531 Real Estate

532 Rental and Leasing Services

533 Lessors of Nonfinancial Intangible Assets (except Copyright)

Professional, Scientific, and Technical Services

541 Professional, Scientific, and Technical Services

Management of Companies and Enterprises

551 Management of Companies and Enterprises

Administrative and Support and Waste Management and Remediation Services

561 Administrative and Support Services

562 Waste Management and Remediation Services

Educational Services

611 Educational Services

Health Care and Social Assistance

621 Ambulatory Health Care Services

622 Hospitals

623 Nursing and Residential Care Facilities

624 Social Assistance

Arts, Entertainment, and Recreation

711 Performing Arts, Spectator Sports, and Related Industries

712 Museums, Historical Sites, and Similar Institutions

713 Amusement, Gambling, and Recreation Industries
Accommodation and Food Services
    721 Accommodation
    722 Food Services and Drinking Places
Other Services (except Public Administration)
    811 Repair and Maintenance
    812 Personal and Laundry Services
    813 Religious, Grantmaking, Civic, Professional, and Similar
    814 Private Households
Public Administration
    921 Executive, Legislative, and Other General Government Support
    922 Justice, Public Order, and Safety Activities
    923 Administration of Human Resource Programs
    924 Administration of Environmental Quality Programs
    925 Administration of Housing Programs and Urban Planning
    926 Administration of Economic Programs
    927 Space Research and Technology
    928 National Security and International Affairs

4 Marketing Databases

The use of both internally generated data and syndicated data sources in developing marketing databases, along with the analysis and segmentation of those databases, is an important business-to-business marketing research activity. The marketing database not only provides ongoing definition of customers and prospects for the marketer, but also provides a mechanism for the development and evaluation of marketing strategies and marketing communication programs. Marketing databases, however, are expensive and time-consuming to create and maintain, requiring great care in both their initial design and continuing operation.

One mistake business-to-business marketers sometimes make is to hastily assemble something called a database that is never analyzed and, therefore, never used to support market research activity. When marketing and sales personnel have very limited access to the database, and very little information ever seems to come from analyzing the database, then this is evidence that the database is not being used the way it should be.

From a business-to-business point of view, having a marketing database is absolutely crucial in successfully selling to customers, converting prospects into customers, and understanding the market. However, advance planning and attention to detail are required to make the database one that is capable of being meaningfully analyzed to provide this valuable information.

Database Fundamentals

A marketing database is a dynamic collection of facts about customers and prospects stored in computerized form. The information contained in a database minimally includes individual customer and/or prospect name and address identification. The database should also contain detailed purchase information for each customer as well as a record of inbound and outbound communication for each customer and prospect. All of these activities should have time references. Time, and all time-related activities, are some of the most important pieces of information in the database. A good database chronicles all the contact points made between marketer and customer or prospect through time.

It is the interactive, dynamic nature of a marketing database that characterizes it and distinguishes it from a simple list or file of information. For it to be dynamic, the database must be continually updated and supplemented with new information, as that information becomes known. For the database to be interactive, it must also be understood by and accessible to all the relevant decision makers or ideally all members of the integrated marketing team. They must actively take part in keeping the information current and feel comfortable enough to go to it any time they have a need for information. A database that no one uses or understands is wasted and valueless to a company.

Customer Data Sources

Most marketing databases begin with your company's internal customer sales records. These records consist of all the traditional paperwork processed during a sales activity up to receipt of payment—company names and addresses, personnel names and titles, all purchases made itemized by type and by amount, methods of payment, any service requested and provided, and the corresponding dates for each activity. Most likely this is already in computerized form as part of the accounting system, and, depending upon the nature of your business, it may also be part of your inventory or manufacturing system. Converting the information for use in a marketing database is usually not difficult, but it is not a trivial matter, either.

Usually, it is the accounting department staff that makes the necessary file conversions to transfer purchase information from the accounting system into a marketing database. Unfortunately, the data that is computerized for accounting purposes may not be in the form that is best for research analysis. Often, time and date information are not immediately accessible in computer form and need to be added. Sometimes the purchase information has been purged or aggregated over time so that the detail of a customer's purchasing history is lost, making analysis less sensitive. For instance, a customer's purchasing amounts may have been totaled over a particular time period and only these totals kept in the computer file, or purchases might be aggregated across an entire store or region in the same way. Also, because of the amount of information that can accumulate, sometimes the purchase history is truncated and only the previous two years' worth of data is maintained on the system. If possible, as much of this detail that can be, should be reinstated into the database. This, of course, requires time and money.

In addition, information on marketing communication efforts, and other types of customer or prospect contact, does not come through the accounting department and usually does not already exist in computer usable form. This means that it is necessary to enter this information into the database. Furthermore, to keep this information up-to-date, this process must be an ongoing one. Many companies are not staffed to handle this extra burden.

In order to have data that can be analyzed for marketing purposes, a record needs to be put in the database whenever communication materials are sent out. If the outgoing communication is a mailing, then the name and address list can easily be matched against the database and a code created and automatically entered by the computer for those customers. However, other communications without a computerized record still would require manual entry. To keep this task manageable, field sales personnel, for example, should be entering into the database daily the contacts they have made, either directly or through data entry personnel. As with purchase information, customer or prospect communications must be associated with a date and time reference. This cannot be stressed enough. Time is just as important for communications analysis as it is for purchase analysis.

External Data Sources

By acquiring external data on companies, you can expand a customer or prospect marketing database. Dun & Bradstreet (D & B), for example, maintains information on virtually all businesses in the United States. Included in their information are such things as industrial classification, number of locations, number of employees, sales revenue, and the company's credit rating. A good marketing database should be designed to readily accommodate outside or external data sources, such as D & B. These external sources may supply critical supplementary information on current customers and become the basis for the development of the prospect portion of a database.

In fact, external sources are the only way of developing a prospect database. A general business information compiler will provide an excellent starting point. Other, more specialized information sources may be better suited to provide industry- specific information, such as in the health care field. The prospect portion of a marketing database will almost certainly require more communication tracking and data entry than will the customer portion.

File Structures and Languages

Organizing the technical part of a marketing database takes some consideration. There are many computer hardware and software alternatives available, although there is probably no one perfect alternative. For many small business-to-business marketers, a good marketing database can run on a stand-alone personal computer. Very large businesses may need mainframe computer capability to accommodate the larger customer files and complex user networks. Most companies, however, probably should have a computer network to handle the database.

Most marketing databases, in computer terminology, would be configured as a relational database requiring some "structured query language," or SQL. In other words, every piece of information on a customer or prospect—such as the company name—would be related to other elements—such as the number of employees—through a system of pointers that only a special computer language—an SQL package—can sort. In the microcomputer market, there are many well-known packages, such as dBase and Paradox. There are also packages for mid-level or mini-computers and, of course, for mainframes. Important things to consider in selecting an SQL are the software's ease of use and its ability to accommodate files in a variety of formats, including those from other relational database packages.

If hardware is not already available to support the database, then it too must be acquired. Since a database should be accessible to more than one employee, there is merit in acquiring a computer network. Depending on its size, a network can be expensive to install and maintain and can add considerably to the cost of a database. Providing network access, however, can also add substantially to the value of a database; the more people who can easily access the information, the more this important marketing tool can contribute to the sales and marketing efforts of your company.

Defining Variables

Most variables, or items in a marketing database, are entered as text, such as the names of the companies. There are also many coded identification numbers, such as a product or part number. These variables, or fields to use the database terminology, are in categorical or nominal format. This makes them especially difficult to statistically analyze.

Categorical variables will need to be numerically coded or recoded in order to be analyzed, a process that will be discussed in more detail later in this chapter. What is important at the database design stage is to keep a record of the different values or codes that are entered into the system to facilitate the coding process. This means making sure that text is always entered in a consistent manner. For instance, using the official two-letter postal code for states is far better and more useable than entering a haphazard collection of state abbreviations. All variables should be unambiguously defined in this way. Analysis later on will be much easier if this kind of thought goes into the coding at this early variable definition stage.

Data quality will probably always be a problem, and human error will always be a factor in data coding. External suppliers may not be as careful with their data as you would hope, and there may even be data elements that are correct but that appear wrong because of some unusual, undocumented circumstance. In these cases, there is really nothing that you can do except make the best of the situation and stay on top of the problem. Focus on quality and make documentation a good habit. Keep meticulous written records describing all of the definitions, processes, and special exceptions that can be referenced later when needed. The database and future marketing efforts will reflect the strength of your efforts.

Access

Limiting internal access to a database is one of the biggest mistakes any marketer can make. Certainly anything of proprietary interest should be carefully guarded, but those within the organization who have both strategic and tactical marketing responsibility should have access to the database. In fact, they should be encouraged to use it. They should also be required to record their activity, especially contact or communication with customers or prospects, on a regular basis. Field sales personnel should also have access to the database from remote locations via portable computers.

To preserve order and confidentiality where necessary, a hierarchical access scheme can be designed and implemented. This means that different employees would have differing levels of access to information and differing capabilities with respect to entering, changing, or deleting information from the database. For instance, only certain employees might be able to delete an entire company from the system. Others might be able to alter only certain designated fields, or to add fields. Restricting access in this way helps prevent major errors.

The database is a critical marketing tool. Everyone on the marketing team should participate in its creation and utilize it regularly. This means that a database should be networked and provide easy access. The stand-alone PC-based database is appropriate for only a very small organization if access is considered.

Maintenance

Companies and personnel change. A marketing database must stay current with the marketplace it represents. One of the quickest ways a marketing staff will lose confidence in a database is to find too many instances where the information contained within it is out-of-date. Perhaps the most expensive, but essential, element of database management is keeping it maintained or as current as possible. The database is not something to be built once and then used indefinitely. It must be viewed as a dynamic process to manage. Typically, this means hiring staff to do nothing but enter changes and updates to customer and prospect information.

The Principle of Segmentation

Market segmentation is based upon the belief that individuals and businesses will respond differentially to marketing programs. At the extremes, some individuals may be much more likely to respond, while others may never respond at all. And, of course, the gradations in between can be almost endless. The individual's particular circumstance, needs, experience, perceptions, beliefs, abilities, or whatever else might be relevant to the message may influence the likelihood of his or her response. Marketing and communication textbooks are filled with examples and explanations of how individuals are different and are more or less likely to respond.

Defining and targeting market *segments* is a way to leverage knowledge about individuals' or companies' differential responses. Aiming a particular marketing communications program at a segment of your market that is more likely to respond for a particular reason will invariably produce better results than aiming a similar effort to everyone en mass or targeting those segments that have been shown to be less likely to respond.

Market segmentation has been heralded as one of the most fundamental principles of marketing. However, in the past it has been largely a guiding conceptual principle for developing marketing plans and strategies, rather than a call for empirical data analysis. And even conceptually, the principle of segmentation will carry you further than ignoring the notion altogether. For instance, if your business sells bar code readers, then obviously you know your market must be companies that process and need to keep track of lots of small items. This assumption then leads to the identification of certain distribution and manufacturing categories, described by SIC code undoubtedly, where this would be true. By aiming your selling efforts at these prime prospect candidates, you have essentially segmented your market and narrowed your focus in order to achieve better response.

It is, of course, possible for you to just know which individuals are the likely responders, just as a good automobile salesperson might feel confident in his or her ability to size up prospects when they walk into the showroom or a bar code salesman knows that certain types of distributors are key candidates. Today, however, some form of quantitative measurement is typically required for the task of segmenting your customers, if for no other reason than the sheer size of most potential market segments. Rather than deriving segments solely on subjective judgments, they can be statistically derived from an empirical analysis of what is known about the market and actual response evidence. Quantitative analyses always dramatically outperform subjective analyses, thereby providing companies that use them a definite competitive edge.

Quantitative audience and market segmentation analysis represents one of the most important tools for the marketing strategist. Perhaps more important than the specific competitive advantage that segmentation provides is the more general revolution in the approach to the development of marketing communications strategy. Before audiences could begin to be segmented on the basis of their purchase behavior, media time and space were bought and sold on the basis of which had the most efficient delivery of the largest audience at the lowest cost per thousand. Now that markets can be segmented by their response to communications, the result is declining advertising revenue for many mass media.

Accepting the idea that individuals respond differentially is easy enough. It is in applying the concept that the difficulty begins. Two general problems quickly emerge. The first problem is in the selection of characteristics or variables to use in defining the segments. Knowing that segments will respond differentially is one thing; knowing what variables can be used to define them is quite another. The second problem becomes readily apparent once more than one characteristic or variable is specified: How do you fit the variables together in a meaningful way to create a sound segmentation scheme? Both of these questions are answerable using statistical analysis procedures.

It is obvious that these kinds of statistical problems would be extremely tedious and difficult to solve without the aid of computers. When the numbers of customers and prospects become very large, segmenting an audience quickly becomes a statistical task. However, the availability of increasingly lower-cost computing power has made market segmentation much more than just a conceptual principle.

Data-Driven Marketing

At the risk of oversimplification, direct marketers can be distinguished from other general marketers because of their knowledge of customer names and addresses. It is because business-to-business marketers also have this kind of information that direct marketing principles could be and have been applied relatively easily. Other general marketers, such as consumer package goods, durables, and services, are just now starting to apply direct marketing segmentation principles because these marketers have generally had much less information about who their customers are and their customers' purchase histories.

Consumer package goods marketers are beginning to record the names and addresses from redeemed coupons and sweepstakes entries in an attempt to create the beginnings of a customer database; airline continuity or frequent flier programs are now able to identify business travelers; radio stations use card promotions; and most durable goods manufacturers generate names and information through their warranty registration cards. Even credit reporting agencies can offer customer information in some major product categories or where a credit card is likely to be used. And all of these sources of consumer information depend on the computer for the collection and storage of the data.

The most important application of data collection for retailers has been the checkout scanner, which is currently installed at most super-markets and is moving into other classes of retail trade such as office supply stores, as well. With the addition of a check-guarantee card or other customer identification at checkout time, retailers have the same information as does the catalog marketer. The nature of the re-search supplier, the advertising agency, and the media have all changed because of the scanning technology. The common reference to scanners and scanner data is, however, something of a misnomer. The scanner is nothing more than an input device, transforming bar code to numbers for a computer. Computerized data collection and analysis are what make the concept of market and audience segmen-tation possible and practical.

The implication for the business-to-business market is obvious. With a customer database, and the collective learning from direct marketers and consumer goods marketers, business-to-business mar-keters are in a very good position to improve the way they sell.

Segmentation Variables

Historically, market or audience segmentation are discussed in terms of three general classes of variables: demographics, psychographics, and purchase behavior. Each class of variables has its own traditions and utility.

Certainly the best-known class of variables is demographics. Demo-graphics in consumer marketing refer to those characteristics of a person likely to be of interest to the Bureau of the Census. They in-clude age and gender, income, education, marital status and occupa-tion. Demographic variables are commonplace in survey research and are generally used to describe survey participants in lieu of names and addresses. Since broadcast and print media use survey research to describe and document their audiences, they also tend to describe their audiences in demographic terms.

It is important for business-to-business marketers to keep in mind that they, too, are selling to people, not companies; hence, the demo-graphics of purchasing agents and company CEOs, for instance, are always relevant. Furthermore, businesses themselves can also be de-scribed in demographic terms. SIC codes, company revenue, and length of time in business are used in the same way as occupation, income, and age or education might be for consumers.

Geodemographics are those variables that apply to where people or companies reside in geographic terms. Because census data is in computerized form, the data can be readily sorted and arranged by geographic units such as zip code areas or census tracts. Such geodemographic segmentation is less useful for businesses, unless they are relatively small, local businesses that specially cater to the residents in their area. For instance, knowing where a General Foods or Caterpillar is located really does not help to identify who their customers are. Nor does it help a business-to-business organization to segment these companies in a meaningful way. Consider segmenting Procter & Gamble, General Foods, General Mills, Quaker Oats, and Kimberly Clark, for instance, by geography. What does it really tell you?

On the other hand, perhaps for some categories—retail food, restaurants, or physicians—geodemographics may be useful. There are enough of these businesses in any given area that they will most likely be differentiated by the clientele they serve. You have some idea of how these businesses may be different from one another and how you might sell to them differently.

The problem with both demographic and geodemographic variables is that they are relatively weak predictors of purchasing and/or response. If the idea underlying segmentation is that some groups are more productive in terms of response than others, then demographics are not very good at separating and describing those groups. Despite this shortcoming, demographic variables are easily and widely collected and employed in segmentation because they are so standardized and universally known.

Psychographics are those variables that measure the psychological aspects of human behavior—developed in part to overcome the poor predicting power of demographics. Believing that an individual's state of mind is linked to response, many attempts have been made to measure these psychological states, including such things as perceptions, opinions, attitudes, and beliefs. The problem with psychographic variables is that they are difficult to measure and almost everyone that measures psychographics does it differently, making it difficult to compare measures across different databases and analyze for segmentation purposes. In addition, these measures are rarely available in business-to-business situations without extensive and expensive survey research effort.

To measure psychographics, you must ask personal and subjective questions of those whom you are studying. This makes psychographics impractical variables to collect for anything but a relatively small sample. It would be very expensive to obtain psychographic measures on customer groups that are larger than a few hundred individuals, for example. Furthermore, psychographic variables, despite their apparent promise, have been shown to predict response poorly as well.

Lifestyle variables, including variables that represent how individuals use their time and the activities they engage in, are probably the most useful of the psychographic variables. But even these variables still suffer from the data collection problem. As a result, psychographics are not often found as segmentation variables even though they might first appear as likely candidates.

The most powerful segmentation variables are those related to actual purchase behavior in both consumer and business-to-business marketing situations. Prior purchase behavior is, by a wide margin, the most powerful predictor of response or current purchase behavior. In fact, with knowledge of an individual's or company's purchase history, demographic and psychographic variables are generally rendered impotent.

In the past, purchasing information was difficult and expensive to collect because it, too, required asking questions of buyers. Now that scanning and bar code technology is becoming readily available across more product categories, this is less true. In fact, many marketers have the opposite data problem; they find themselves drowning in so much scanner data that that information accumulates at a much more rapid rate than it can be absorbed and analyzed. No doubt, in the near future, collecting purchase data through survey research will be a thing of the past.

Direct Marketing Purchase Variables

Direct marketers have had the luxury of having individual purchase behavior data for a relatively long period of time. As mentioned, it was the direct marketer who first saw the statistical relationship between prior purchase behavior and current purchasing and thus understood the value in maintaining purchase history data. Direct marketers think of segmentation in terms of the acronym "RFM," which stands for Recency, Frequency, and Monetary value. Each of these variables represents a different aspect of a buyer's purchase history, and they work together to predict future purchase.

Recency is the purchase variable that refers to the amount of time that has passed since the most recent purchase was made. The empirical evidence from catalog selling is that the longer the time since the last purchase, the less likely the individual is to make another purchase.

Frequency indicates how often a buyer has purchased over some uniform time interval. Many catalog marketers set a standard time interval, such as the previous two years, for analyzing frequency. For instance, the number of actual purchases would be tracked across the two-year time span and designated as the frequency for that individual. Buyers who purchase more frequently during the time interval tend to be the ones who are more likely to repurchase or respond in the future.

Monetary value, obviously, is a measure of the total dollars spent over the same time interval. Again, the direct marketing evidence shows that buyers who spend more, are more likely to spend again.

Direct marketers are also currently struggling with another variable—type of merchandise—that has shown promise in developing assortments of merchandise for particular market segments. Together, these four variables are so powerful as segmentation variables that direct marketers pay little attention to any of the other potential segmentation variables.

Purchase Variables

Business-to-business marketers are replete with purchase variables. The problem is knowing what to do with them. Since the advent of scanning, consumer marketers have had the advantage of considerable purchase data as well. This is an area, therefore, where it is worthwhile to consider what approaches consumer marketers have taken in their analyses of buying behavior.

It is worth noting that package goods experience is distinct from direct marketing because of the differences in the buying situation. Most package goods products are frequently purchased, have relatively low prices, and commonly have brand-name reputations that have been built over many years with media advertising. This is a somewhat different situation than what the typical catalog marketer faces since catalogers deal with relatively infrequently purchased, high-priced, higher mark-up, durable and soft goods that generally do not have strong customer brand loyalties. Therefore, it should not come as a surprise that package goods marketers have discovered three critical purchase-related variables that direct marketers do not use: product usage, brand loyalty, and deal proneness.

Product usage is clearly related to the direct marketing concepts of recency and frequency. A package goods marketer, however, will designate someone as a user or a nonuser based on whether he or she has purchased the product in some reasonable time period. Obviously, individuals who have never purchased the product in this length of time are classified as nonusers. Users are generally divided into categories according to the amount of the product purchased. Heavy users buy the most—for example, a heavy beer purchaser buys at least one six-pack per day—and light users purchase considerably less. A distinction is generally made between light users and one-time buyers. A one-time buyer has purchased only once in the category compared to the light user who has purchased in the category more than once, but buys the category much less often than the heavy user.

Not only do the heavier users tend to continue the prior established purchasing pattern, buying more than the lighter, one-time, and nonusers in the future, heavy users respond very differently to advertising, price promotions, and in-store promotions such as displays than these other usage segments. Again at the risk of oversimplification, heavy users probably respond the best to price promotions, light users best to in-store displays, and the one-time buyer or nonuser to advertising. Knowing this, a marketer can tailor the promotion and advertising mix to leverage whichever of these product usage segments is most desirable. This empirical link between purchase and promotional response illustrates the utility of the segmentation concept.

Brand loyalty is perhaps the most controversial of the potential segmentation variables. Essentially, there are two groups among product category users: brand loyals who always purchase the same brand and brand switchers who purchase multiple brands within the category. Some argue that brand loyalty is really a state of mind and that various psychographic variables are needed to fully understand and measure loyalty. But loyalty can be based on behavioral purchasing patterns. The concept of brand equity, or the value of a brand name, is a similar and related variable. Brand equity is considered the premium price that the buyer is willing to pay over another brand and it can be measured or calculated without the use of psychographic measures as well.

When a buyer has purchased only a single brand within a product category, then there is little disagreement that the individual is brand loyal. When a buyer is not exclusively brand loyal, purchasing other brands a small percentage of the time, there needs to be a rule by which to designate that buyer as either brand loyal or not. Usually the rule of thumb that is applied is that when 80 percent or more of a buyer's category purchases are of a single brand, they are brand loyal. Buyers who have not purchased any one brand at least 80 percent of the time are classified as brand switchers. Prior brand loyalty has generally been one of the most important factors in predicting future brand purchases.

Deal proneness is based upon the proportion of prior purchases, across some time frame, made in association with some form of special price incentive. In supermarket package goods, there is a considerable range of deal proneness and responsiveness to price promotion across households, with a given household buying anywhere from 5 percent of their goods on deal to more than 70 percent. What is most interesting is that deal proneness—that is, making a high proportion of purchases on deal—is unrelated to other variables such as age, income, or education. Yet, prior deal proneness is a strong predictor of acceptance of future deals and, consequently, a critical segmentation variable.

Usage and deal proneness are two purchase variables that could apply to the segmentation of a business-to-business marketing database; both can be estimated from the customer portion of the database. Loyalty is much more difficult to estimate and apply without some sort of competitive information in the database as well.

In summary, purchase behavior variables are the best candidates for any audience or market segmentation scheme, as both direct marketers and package goods marketers have independently realized. There is little doubt that the distinctions between direct and package goods marketing will blur over time and that the variables and strategies used by each in segmenting their customer databases will blend as well. However, the increasing availability of purchase history data makes the consideration of these variables practical for the first time.

Defining Segmentation Variables for Analysis

The first step in segmenting a marketing database lies in defining the variables that should be included in the segmentation analysis—in other words, which variables potentially differentiate the companies in the database from one another. Initially, demographic, geographic, and purchase behavior variables, as well as any psychographics that may be available, should all be considered as potentially useful. Then these variables need to be defined in such a way that they can be analyzed using a statistical model. This presents new considerations.

Levels of Measurement

When you study a phenomenon and attempt to measure it, strictly speaking you are really measuring the attributes or characteristics of the phenomenon rather than the object itself. When you measure the object, you are usually quantifying those attributes so that you know how much of a particular characteristic is present. Quantification allows you to compare attributes across people, objects, or situations in an unambiguous and unbiased way so that you can analyze the various levels and differences mathematically. It is much more precise and useful than simply using judgment to assess a situation. A measurement system, then, is really nothing more than a set of standardized rules to quantify or assign numbers to represent the quantities of these attributes.

During the process of operationalizing concepts and variables, you often have the liberty of assigning different rules, or different *levels* of measurement, to whatever you are trying to measure. In other words, you can quantify at differing levels of mathematical sophistication. In market research terms, this means either classifying an attribute as belonging to one of multiple categories, or assigning a scale value or number to represent an amount or intensity of some attribute. The former is normally associated with counting, whereas the latter is associated with measuring.

There are four levels of measurement, usually described in a hierarchical manner, each level becoming increasingly precise and mathematical in its application. They are: nominal, ordinal, interval, and ratio measurements. Each is described briefly in the following sections.

NOMINAL MEASURES. Classification of attributes into mutually exclusive categories that have no quantitative relationship among them is commonly referred to as nominal measurement. In other words, the variable feature being measured can be divided into varying groups, where the name of the group is its identity. Because these groups have no mathematical relationship among them and have no quantifiable meaning, this level of measurement is considered the lowest in analytical sophistication. That is not to say, however, that it is any less important in market research than any other level of measurement.

There are many examples of nominal measurement when you consider demographic or geographic variables. For instance, gender is a well-known nominal variable. Gender can be divided into two attribute categories: male and female. These categories have no quantitative relationship between them. One is not bigger, greater, more than, or less than the other. The categories are mutually exclusive since, for all practical purposes, someone is either a male or a female, and not both. To determine how much of each attribute level there is, you simply count the number of males and the number of females, and percentage these counts. However, mathematically, that is all that really can be done to quantify gender.

A respondent's martial status, occupation, company title, and position are all nominal variables. A company's SIC code and geographical location in terms of state or zip code are nominal measures. Establishing if someone or some company is a product owner or not, a user or nonuser, the particular distribution channel used, and what specific brand was purchased—all of these are nominally measured variables.

In many instances, variables only make sense being measured at the nominal level. Even if you could scale gender, from completely male to completely female, with a continuum of more or less of each gender type in between, this data would not be very useful for most marketing research purposes. It is sufficient to know the percentage of males and females in a sample.

It is when a variable can meaningfully be measured with more precision that using a nominal measurement device makes less sense. For instance, consider the concept of product usage. Knowing whether or not a business has purchased a product in the last year or not can be very useful information. Knowing, however, how *much* of the product the customer has used in that same time period tells you far more about the product usage for this business. You still know if a company is a user or not, but you can begin to compare the amount of usage across customers as well.

One characteristic of nominal questions that is hard to deny is that they are usually quite easy for interviewers to administer and for respondents to complete. When time is of the essence, having someone simply indicate if they do or do not own a product is much quicker than asking someone to indicate exactly how many of each of the products they own.

RATIO MEASURES. At the other end of the measurement spectrum is the ratio level of measurement. Ratio measures quantify attributes by scaling them along a continuum. Ratio scales are easy to understand because they are familiar in everyday life. When you talk about measuring distances, weight, height, age, or time, you automatically think of measuring in miles, pounds, inches, years, or minutes, respectively. As demonstrated in these examples, there is always some kind of standard scale used that consists of equal units of measurement to determine how far, how heavy, how tall, how old, or how long. It is critical to the scale utility that whatever the measurement units are, they always be equal regardless of where they appear in the process. In other words, the first pound should weigh the same as the last pound. It is also usually true that there is an absolute zero point, where *zero units* literally means "no units," or "none at all." If you are zero years old, technically you have not been born yet.

In business research, you have many ratio-level scales that potentially could be applied: company revenue in dollars, number of employees, number of branch locations, number of customers, years in business, cubic feet of warehouse space, number of trucks in a shipping fleet, units of product sold, market share, percent of budget spent on advertising, and so on.

Ratio-level scales are generally analyzed by computing averages, for instance, the average distance people drive to work or the average daily temperature for Chicago in August. Because scale units are equal, they can be added, multiplied, subtracted, or divided. Any mathematical computation is possible, making ratio-level scales much more flexible and useful analytically than any other measurement type.

You will notice, however, that averages do not always compute to whole numbers. The average age of a sample might be 57.3 years and the average number of locations a sample of companies may have might be 2.7. This is due to the fact that you are taking advantage of using an equal-unit continuum where technically you can calculate to the nth decimal, the portion of a unit.

With ratio scales, you know more; yet you have the flexibility to present that information with whatever level of precision you decide. To use the product usage example from earlier, a ratio scale will tell you more than if a business has used or not used a product—you know precisely how much. From this, then, you can always easily determine how many businesses are users or nonusers. You can also divide usage up into several categories of your own choosing; for example, you might classify customers as heavy, moderate, and light users. You also can talk about the average amount used by the group overall.

With this flexibility, however, comes a warning. You must realize that if you purposely and permanently reduce the level of measurement from a ratio level to a categorical level, you lose the precision and flexibility. If you have ratio-level age data for a group of customers (i.e., how many years old each person is), by collapsing the age scale into several age categories, say under 18, 18–24, 25–34, 35–54, and 55 and older, you lose the knowledge of how old each individual is since he or she is placed in a broad category that is less precise. You also lose the ability to do many mathematical maneuvers such as adding and subtracting years, or calculating the average age. In a database, it would be safer to retain variables at the ratio level so that you always have the option of what level of precision to use for any given analytical procedure or purpose.

As you might expect, most market researchers have a bias towards higher level, more sophisticated measurement such as is possible with ratio scales. It is much easier to find relationships among scaled variables than among categorical variables. Certainly the statistical tools that can be applied to scales are considerably more powerful.

INTERVAL AND ORDINAL MEASURES. The interval scale is sometimes thought of as a variant of the ratio scale because it is also an equal-interval scale. However, the assumption of a standard, real zero point, or a zero that means the absence of the characteristic, no longer holds true. Interval scales have arbitrary zero points that are not "real" in the sense that they do not mean "the absence of."

There are few really good examples of interval scales. In science, temperature is the textbook example. On a Fahrenheit temperature scale, zero degrees represents the point at which a saturated saline solution freezes, which is an arbitrary meaning. On a Kelvin temperature scale, zero degrees truly means the absence of heat, and this is considered a true ratio scale.

An index provides a similar example of the concept of an arbitrary zero point, although the base is usually set at 100 rather than 0. With an index, one value is set equal to 100 and every other value is compared to that base value. Those above the base have indexes above 100 and those below the base have indexes of less than 100. All the indices on the scale are relative to the base and cannot be interpreted concretely without that knowledge. An index of 150 means that there is 50 percent more of the attribute compared to the base level. You must know what the base is in order to know how to interpret the 150. This is the same as having an arbitrary zero point; you cannot interpret the rest of the scale without understanding what that zero means.

An ordinal scale is categorical in nature. What distinguishes the ordinal scale from a nominal scale is that the categories are logically rank ordered in a meaningful way. There is an indication of relative standing or rank order among the categories. In other words, some categories are greater than or less than others, or higher/lower, shorter/taller, younger/older. The most straightforward ordinal scale is one that simply rank orders: "Please rank these five brands from most to least preferred." In this case, there are first, second, third, fourth, and fifth place brands. However, you have no idea how much more or less one brand is preferred over another. There is no unit of measurement as with an interval or ratio scale that calibrates preference.

Any measure that has multiple categories that are in logical rank order but not equal sized is considered ordinal level. Consider this education question:

> Please indicate the highest level of education that you have completed.
>
> ❑ Less than high school
> ❑ High school graduate
> ❑ Some college/technical degree
> ❑ College graduate
> ❑ Some postgraduate work
> ❑ Graduate degree

Each category represents successively more education. Yet there is no presumption that the categories are equal. A college degree may take four years to complete; but a graduate degree can be obtained in less than two years, and a high school diploma takes twelve years. This is ordinally scaled.

In many instances, a potentially ratio-level scale is condensed into fewer, broader categories, becoming an ordinal scale for all practical purposes. Consider these two questions:

How long has your company been in business?

Ratio:	Ordinal:
❑ years	❑ Less than 5 years
	❑ 5–14 years
	❑ 15–24 years
	❑ 25–49 years
	❑ 50 years or longer

The answer format to the right is an ordinal scale, whereas the one to the left is a ratio level. By asking respondents to place themselves into one of the ordinal categories rather than to write the exact number of years, will produce less precise and less useful information in the long run. However, this is often done in survey research on the presumption that it is easier for respondents to place themselves in a category than to estimate an exact number. Sometimes there is the fear that respondents *won't* give an exact number because of confidentiality, such as with questions involving income and revenue.

With an ordinal-level scale, you can count the number of responses within each category and percentage, just as you can with nominal measures. You can also show the midpoint as a way of showing the "average" on the distribution, since the categories can be ranked in a high/low manner. You cannot, however, calculate a real average unless you estimate one by using the midpoint of each category to represent the entire category.

Scales and Level of Measurement

Scales present an interesting measurement dilemma. Technically, most scales are probably, at best, interval-level measurement because the end point that anchors the continuum is somewhat arbitrary and is not necessarily standardized across every individual. If you have a 0–5 attitude scale, where the 0 means you are extremely dissatisfied and a 5 means you are extremely satisfied, the 0 may not mean the same level of dissatisfaction to everyone using the scale. When the zero does not have the same meaning for everyone, the mathematics of comparison become unclear. It is as though there is no standard zero point—a necessary characteristic for the scale to be considered ratio level.

There is also a problem with scales when the intervals cannot be assumed to be equal. To make a comparison to ratio-level scales, this would mean that the length of an inch might vary according to where its position on the scale. Some argue that rating scales suffer from this problem. To put it simply, the distance between "strongly agree" and "agree" on an agreement scale may not be perceived as the same distance as between "agree" and "neutral." Sometimes, people view the middle categories as broader than the end categories, for instance, the "excellent" interval may be perceived as somewhat narrower than the "good" interval on a quality scale. If this is the case, then a scale without equal intervals becomes an ordinal, rank-order scale.

You can think of the intervals as being stretched to all different widths using an elastic ruler of sorts. In this light, ordinal scales might be considered as simply unreliable interval scales. The problem with them is that the statistical and analytical tools that can be used are not nearly as powerful. If you can't assume equal intervals, then you cannot use the more powerful mathematics; you merely can count and percentage as though it were a nominal measure.

The controversy for attitude scaling, then, is whether to refer to them as ordinal-, interval-, or ratio-level scales. If you can assume that differences in the way people standardize their perceptions and the widths of the intervals will average themselves away—in other words, those that are more stringent balance out those who are less stringent—then you can treat these scales as though they were ratio scales and calculate averages, using the more powerful analytical procedures. The risk would be that the data might be misleading if the underlying assumptions are being violated. If you take a more purist approach and treat scales as ordinal or interval level, then you sacrifice this analytical flexibility and power.

For most marketing and business-to-business market research purposes, attitude scales are used as though they are ratio and equal interval scales.

Criteria for Measurement Quality

Since there are so many ways to operationalize a variable or concept, how do you know when it is a quality measurement? There are three criteria to consider in this regard: validity, reliability, and measurement precision. The ideal measurement instrument or question will be all three—valid, reliable, and precise. However, there are usually compromises you need to make along the way, and there is always error in any research you do. So, it is rare to find a perfect measurement system. This is especially true in the marketing area where so much of what is studied is subjective in nature.

Validity

Validity represents the degree to which a measurement reflects the "true" meaning, or true score, of the variable or concept under consideration. In other words, did you actually measure what you *intended* to measure? You can talk about the validity of an entire study or the validity of one item or question in a survey. Validity is not an all-or-nothing concept, for rarely would you develop a question or conduct a study that was completely missing its goals; and, likewise, rarely will you write a question or conduct a study that is completely 100 percent valid in every respect. Therefore, the goal is to strive for as much validity as possible.

Validity is compromised when there is some source of error or systematic bias in the way the study was conducted or the way a question was asked. Systematic bias means that the distortion of the truth happens in a uniform, almost predictable, way rather than in a random, haphazard fashion. This kind of bias can enter into a research project at many points.

Here are just a few examples of where validity might suffer as a result of the way the research was conducted. If an interviewer raises his or her eyebrows consistently when respondents answer questions a particular way, then this might "teach" or encourage respondents to distort their answers to coincide with the way they think they should respond. If the respondent learns or is told who the sponsor of a competitive brand study is, there is the potential for a bias to result in his or her evaluations for that sponsoring company. If a question is written in a way that leads respondents to answer one way more than another, then there is a constant source of bias that will decrease the validity of that question. If the first brand presented to respondents in a preference question is consistently ranked most preferred, there may be an order bias that is affecting the validity of that data. If you conduct your research in the evening and there is reason to believe that respondents are more fatigued and less responsive at this time of day, then the research findings are probably less valid.

The issue with validity is to be constantly alert to the potential of bias entering into the research process so that you are able to avert or eliminate as much of the obvious systematic bias as possible.

You will hear two kinds of validity discussed in research: internal and external validity. Internal validity has to do with the procedures and instruments of the research itself and whether they are themselves free of systematic bias that could affect the outcome of the research and distort the truth. The examples given above all refer to bias that can *internally* affect the results. External validity, on the other hand, has more to do with how realistic the findings are, or how well the research results can be generalized back to the "real world." Even the most internally valid piece of research can suffer from external validity problems if the way the research was conducted didn't truly reflect the manner in which people *normally* go about their business outside the research environment. When you bring customers into a research setting and ask them to view advertising or ask them to estimate their likelihood of buying a product, their reactions may not always reflect what they do once they leave. External validity has always been a problem for "laboratory" type research experiments and tests. That is why most marketers will spend a great deal of money to field-test a new product or marketing strategy in a real-world test market situation.

It is unfortunately true that you rarely can have research results that are both internally and externally valid at the same time. If you field-test a new product, for example, people will discover, buy, use, and either repurchase or shun the product in a realistic way. However, the researcher has absolutely no control over the environmental variables that could unduly affect this process. The reasons a potential customer might not discover, buy, or rebuy the product may have little to do with the product itself, but rather other influences such as the fact that the competition had put their product on sale just before the test research began and many customers who would normally have been interested had already stocked up on the sale-priced product. Therefore, the study results may not truly reflect the potential success of your product and are invalid.

Reliability

Reliability is another important reflection of how good a measurement is. It is the extent to which your measurements are consistent and dependable, usually over time. You, of course, would like any measurement you implement to yield the same results when measuring the exact same phenomenon. If you ask the same person the same question twice, assuming that their disposition has not changed, you should get the same answer both times. That is reliability.

Again, reliability is not an all-or-nothing characteristic. Your goal is to have an instrument that consistently measures something in the same way each time so that you can depend on the stability of the results. An unreliable research instrument or procedure is one that is inconsistent, unpredictable, and variable in its ability to measure. In other words, sometimes it works better than other times.

Reliability is usually a function of random errors that can creep into the research process. A reliable athlete is one who again and again leads his team to victory. And even the most reliable of athletes can have an off day. But if that athlete is "on" one day and "off" the next in an unpredictable fashion, then it is very hard to rely on his ability. If a question is worded in an ambiguous way, it may be interpreted differently each time it is answered and it is, therefore, unreliable. If you use a different team or person (whose styles and criteria may be different) every time you administer a product quality inspection, you will be lucky to get consistent results.

There are ways in which to test for reliability. One way is to look for stability over time as in a "test-retest" situation. Simply administer the test twice on identical or comparable respondents and compare the results. If you are worried about respondent consistency in a survey, ask the same question twice, once in the beginning and again toward the end and look to see if the person is inconsistent in the way he or she answered the question.

Reliability is not directly related to validity. You can, for instance, have an instrument that consistently produces invalid results or a relatively valid instrument that is, unfortunately, unreliable. Ideally, you want research that is both valid and reliable.

Measurement Precision

Precision has to do with the exactness of a measurement or how finely the distinctions among the attribute levels are. For instance, a stopwatch that measures time in terms of microseconds is much more precise in its timing than one that only keeps track of seconds or minutes. Knowing that a company has been in business for four years is much more accurate than only knowing that it has been in business less than ten years. Recording purchase history on a weekly basis is more useful than aggregating purchases to a monthly level. A 10-point satisfaction scale is more precise in its estimate of satisfaction than the same scale with only five intervals. In other words, the more gradations a measurement scale has, the closer it can come to reflecting the true, exact level of the attribute. Generally, this is the goal.

However, precision is related inversely to reliability. The more precise you try to get in measuring something, the harder it becomes to get the same results, even from the same individual, again and again. If you scale attitudes on a 3-point Like/Dislike scale, it is very probable that you will find that someone who is favorable toward the product will mark the Like position without fail every time you administer the question. If, on the other hand, you measure attitudes using a 100-point scale, even someone who is favorable and remains favorable may one time mark a 5 and another time mark a 10. If the respondent doesn't perceive very much difference between the 5 and the 10, then this degree of precision may be producing unreliable results.

Therefore, while precision is a worthy goal and reliability is also an important criterion of quality, you may need to sacrifice a bit of one in order to get more of the other. Some researchers would argue that while a 100-point scale may not be as reliable as a 10-point scale, if you have gained ten times the precision with some of the respondents, this far outweighs the small differences in the other scores. Others will argue that if a 100-point scale is potentially unreliable, then why not use a 10-point scale, which is a bit less precise but still much more precise than a 3- or 4-point scale.

Perhaps there is no one best answer. As with all else, it is a matter of degree.

Outliers

A variety of situations can cause outliers (responses at either extreme end of the answer spectrum). Some are software related, when infrequently occurring conditions generate extreme data or programming errors generate spurious results. Some outliers result from redefinitions of a product code. Such redefinitions can cause abrupt changes in transaction counts, dollars per item, or average items per transaction. Many conditions can cause extremely high values that may not correctly reflect the true activity.

The outlier, however, may reflect truth, in that the purchases actually occurred, but they reflect situations so unlikely that one may not wish to include them in the analysis of data. In this case, the observed values of purchase volume are reduced to more reasonable values.

As an example, a small business, such as a restaurant, may make an unusually large purchase following a flood that wiped-out previous inventories.

Missing Data

Data that is generated continually over time, such as sales or tracking measures, often contain data points with no value. Marketing databases are notorious for such missing data. During this process data may be lost due to system failures or software problems. If there is a fixed summarization cycle, data from some outlets may be received too late for inclusion in the summarization.

In some instances, only part of the data may be collected. Syndicated data suppliers have extensive quality control routines to identify periods of missing data and to correct for such occurrences. Correction methods include adjustment of projection weights and imputation of missing data based on past sales history and current promotional data. For panel data, missing data represent a much more serious problem, as imputation is not robust at the customer level over short periods of time. In this case, either the customers with missing data must be dropped from the analysis or the analysis period must be shortened to exclude the times of missing data.

5

Analytical Tools

Statistical analysis is necessary to make sense of the quantitative data that has been assembled. Traditional statistical analysis is divided into two parts, description and inference. Description analysis involves the summary of data, and inference analysis involves generalizing from samples.

Descriptive Analysis

Most research findings are in the form of quantitative information, which requires the use of statistics. The first stage of any analysis is to summarize the responses for each question. This is typically accomplished using descriptive statistics, or summary statistics, such as averages and percentages. Obviously, the level of measurement used to collect question responses will affect what kind of descriptive statistics you can apply.

As mentioned previously, categorical responses (nominal and ordinal) are described using percentages. Percentages are easy to calculate and easy to understand. However, percentages can be misleading if sample sizes become very small. A percent calculates a ratio on a per hundred basis and, therefore, assumes large samples of more than 100 respondents. When the numbers are smaller than this threshold, a percentage becomes less meaningful and less stable.

In some cases, even when the overall sample is very large, the number of respondents who actually answer a question can be very small. In fact, rarely will every respondent answer every question on a questionnaire; the sample sizes (n's) will vary from question to question. If a particular question is difficult to answer or does not apply to everyone, you will have large numbers of missing responses, effectively lowering the sample n on which the percentages are based. Because of this, sample *n*'s probably should be reported to place these figures in perspective and avoid misleading anyone.

Percentages are typically not as precise a measurement as ratio level scales. However, it is easy to create the illusion of precision by reporting percentages to the *n*th decimal place. For example, if 9 respondents out of 21 claim to have purchased a particular brand, this could be reported as .4285714, or 42.85714 percent. This gives the appearance of being very scientific and accurate, when in truth the numbers are quite small and not very reliable. Usually, carrying decimals out more than one or two places at the very most is all that the data will realistically support.

Categorical data can also be described in terms of the most frequent response, or the modal category. The assumption here is that the most frequent response is the most representative response. But, depending on the number of categories and what the percentage distribution actually looks like, this may not be entirely true.

If the categories can be arranged in a rank-order progression, such as with an ordinal scale, then you can describe the distribution in terms of the median or the midpoint—the category that divides the sample in half. In other words, half the sample is above and half is below this category. This is perhaps more representative than the modal category since it takes the entire distribution into consideration.

Continuous metric measures are more precise than any categorical measure, even with smaller sample sizes. Much more can be done statistically to summarize this information as well. Not only can percentages, a mode, and a median be reported, but a mean or an average can be calculated as well. Means are calculated simply by adding up all the responses and dividing by the sample size. In this way, a mean accounts for all the variations in response across the entire distribution. Rating scales that have respondents indicate the degree of agreement or an excellence rating across an array of items can easily be compared by ranking the means. You must be sure to note, however, which end on the rating scale is positive and which is negative. If the lower number indicates a positive evaluation, for instance, then lower means indicate more positive overall ratings. To compare by ranking the means also assumes that all items being compared have similar scales and that the positive end is the same for all.

Averages suffer sometimes from the fact that they are based on *all* responses. If one respondent writes in a scale value that is considerably higher than all others, the mean will skew high when that large number is added into the total. In other words, that one company's radically high response will distort the mean in a way that makes it less descriptive or representative. If you aren't careful of this, you could be badly misled by the descriptive statistics you see in a report. For instance, consider the following summary information on a sample of manufacturers:

Number of locations		Number of employees	
Range	1–25	Range	1–850
Median	2.5	Median	50
Mean	5.0	Mean	165

As shown, the median in both cases is much more representative as a whole than the mean, which is being skewed by the very few companies in the upper range. While a mean is more precise than a median, it is not always the most representative. Good analysis requires knowing when to use the most appropriate statistic regardless of the measurement used.

A summary of research findings will usually start with a presentation of the descriptive statistics for the study questions. However, invariably questions of how this variable relates to that variable or how one segment of the population differs from another will arise. A statistical relationship or difference is found by doing a statistical test of significance.

Statistical Significance

When comparing two or more samples or subsegments within a sample, you are looking for meaningful differences in the ways those samples or subsegments are composed or how the individuals within those subsegments responded to a question. Yet, how do you determine what is meaningful? A statistical test of significance can be useful in this regard. In fact, it is probably important to conduct a significance test before you automatically assume that *any* difference that is found is real. Because all survey data is taken from samples, which may or may not represent the population as a whole, the differences found across samples could be due to sampling error or chance fluctuations of the data, rather than real, meaningful differences.

Sampling standard error can be estimated for any random probability sample. Error estimates are based on the sample size and the extent of the variation among the sample respondents. The larger the sample, the less error typically. The less variation found in responses, the more stable those responses are and, therefore, the less error there is. Standard error can be calculated for any statistic in your data.

When you compare responses across segments, you will almost always find differences in the percentages or the means. The problem is in knowing how much of those differences are due to the error present in the sample and how much can be credited to truly different attitudes in the groups being compared. True differences are always of interest because these differences could be the basis of a segmentation scheme or they could be the justification for targeting different segments with separate marketing or communications strategies that take advantage of this knowledge.

A significance test compares the actual differences found in the question responses for the groups to an estimate of the amount of error present in the data in order to statistically determine how significant or meaningful the differences really are. You must realize, of course, that you never really know since the error is estimated based on probabilities. But you are essentially given the odds of the findings being significant or real. If the significance of a data difference is shown to be .30, this means that there is a 30 percent probability that the differences found are simply due to error and chance—not very promising. Usually to be of consequence, you want your data differences to be significant at the .05 level or less. This would mean that the probability of finding such a difference by chance is only 5 percent or less, making the odds of it being a real difference 95 percent. These are much better odds. The lower the significance figure, the less the probability of the difference across the groups being only due to error.

The point of conducting statistical tests of significance is to find relationships among the variables in your study that are meaningful. It cannot be emphasized enough that you should be careful of overinterpreting very small, insignificant differences across segments. The difference between 69 percent and 75 percent may be due entirely to error in the data. If you begin to treat these differences as more important than they really are, then you may mislead yourself into believing that one segment of the population is considerably more interested (or more favorable or more whatever the measure represents) than another segment when this is simply not true.

Graphical Analysis

Graphics help in summarizing and presenting data in the same way that descriptive statistics can—maybe even better. More than this, a good graph can help the researcher understand the relationships in the data as well. While this is not meant to be a comprehensive guide to graphing techniques, the importance of graphical analysis is discussed.

The physical sciences and engineering have long understood the power of graphical methods in analyzing complex relationships among variables. Business and marketing have lagged in this recognition, in part because the analysis of complex multivariate data has not been an everyday necessity until relatively recently with the advent of scanner data and other database information. It is especially difficult to understand how variables, especially when there are more than two that are being analyzed at one time, relate to one another. Trying to understand the numerical evidence can be overwhelming and confusing. In many cases, the adage that a picture is worth a thousand words is very true. Graphing can give a much better understanding of the patterns and relationships that may exist among data.

The choice of the type of graphical presentation depends on the nature of the data and the relevant comparisons being made. Graphs that are prepared to support an analysis should match the original goals for that analysis. You need to pay special attention to make certain that a graphical display does not contain superfluous clutter and does not draw attention to nonessential points. Graphs should demonstrate the purpose of the analysis as clearly as possible.

Several basic styles of graphs are available as a feature of spreadsheet or presentation software. Again, the level of data measurement plays a role in the selection of the graph type that is best.

A pie chart shows the relative size or contribution of each variable category relative to the whole. The data being graphed must be categorical, and the categories must be mutually exclusive, adding to 100 percent. A pie chart can present only one variable at one point in time, which makes it probably the most limiting of all graph types. An example is if you were graphing your market share along with your main competitor's. Together all market shares add to 100 percent and could be graphed in one pie chart, with the largest slice going to the brand with the largest share of market. However, if you wanted to compare market share trends across time, for example, across the past five years, or across geography, for example, for five different regional territories, one pie chart alone could not show this, and several pie charts would be ridiculously difficult to compare. For this analysis, you need a graphing technique that takes advantage of two-dimensional space.

Bar charts and line graphs can graph more than variable—one representing the x-axis, or horizontal dimension, and the other variable representing the y-axis, or vertical dimension.

A bar graph has vertical or horizontal bars that represent the various categories of a categorical scale. The length or height of the bars indicates the differences in the percentages or frequency for each category. You can add more than one variable, but a bar graph can quickly become very difficult to understand if there are very many comparative bars. If the bars represent nominal items, which have no temporal or logical relationship to each other, they should be arranged in descending or ascending order to demonstrate which categories are biggest or smallest comparatively. The only time this would not be the case is if the bars represent ordinal categories for which you want to show how the percentages vary as you progress up or down a scale.

For instance, consider graphing the volume shipped each day of the week. Even if Monday has the least volume and Wednesday the highest, you should retain the MTWTF sequence in order to show the pattern through the course of a week. Graphing revenue or educational categories is similar: You should maintain the hierarchical relationship among the categories regardless of the differences in the values for each.

Exhibits 5.1a and 5.1b show compact disk purchases plotted across the regional sales territories. By way of comparison, the line straight across shows the national sales average. This draws the eye immediately to the territories that are above and below the average and gives a standard for comparing the numbers or bars. The graph to the right is identical except that the sales territories are ordered in terms of their sales. In this graph it is visually easier to see what the graph is obviously meant to show, which territories are the biggest sales generators and which are the weakest.

A line graph is similar to a bar chart except that a continuous line, instead of discrete bars, shows value differences by its height. While a line is often shown graphically representing categorical data, because of its continuous nature and the way it draws the eye, it is best used for plotting a continuous variable. Line graphs are usually used to show patterns and trends over time. Sometimes a line is plotted over a bar chart to draw a distinction between the two variables being plotted, as in the previously described plot.

Bars and lines can be combined for interesting and useful effects if you know what you are trying to demonstrate. The graph in Exhibit 5.2 shows the volume and price points for XYZ product across time. The bars along the bottom represents weekly volume across one year scaled

Exhibit 5.1: Examples of a Graph and a Bar Chart

5.1a XYZ Industry Compact Disk Purchases

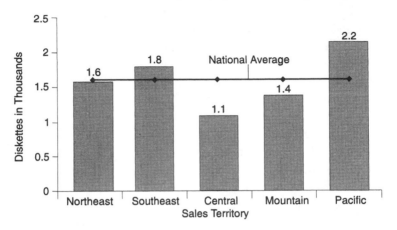

5.1b XYZ Industry Compact Disk Purchases

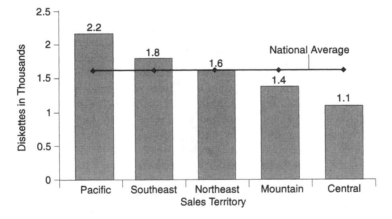

on the left in terms of units. The dotted line at the top shows variations in price across the same time intervals, scaled in dollars and cents to the right. This kind of graph is very clear in its purpose and takes advantage of both lines and bars to overlay a considerable amount of data into one picture that shows patterns, trends, and relationships.

A scatterplot, or X-Y graph, uses both axes of the graph page to plot two variables at a time in relationship to one another. If you wanted to look at the relationship between price and volume, you'd plot price on one axis and volume on the other and end up with a se-

Exhibit 5.2:
XYZ Product—Graph of Volume and Price Over Time

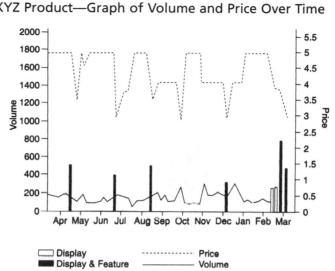

ries of points in two-dimensional space. Inspecting the pattern of these points could tell you about the price elasticity for the brand, or how volume levels change as price increases or decreases. If you plotted volume and price separately as two lines or two series of bars, you would never see the relationship between the two.

The graph in Exhibit 5.3 shows a scatterplot that relates customers'

Exhibit 5.3:
Scatterplot Relating Budget Size to Likelihood of Purchase

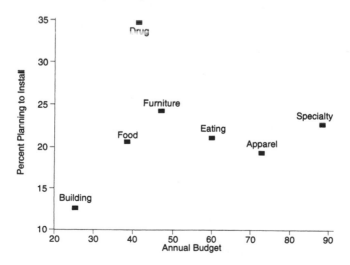

Exhibit 5.4: Bubble Graph Relating Budget,
Likelihood of Purchase, and Industry Size

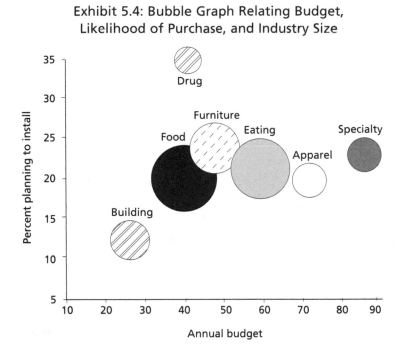

budgets to their intent to purchase or install a product in the near future. The points show a slight trend toward companies with larger budgets having more intent to install than those with smaller budgets. The graph in Exhibit 5.4 shows the same plot with two more pieces of information overlaid—industry type and number of companies within each industry. The points become bubbles and the size of the bubble represents the size of the industry. Now you can see where your best sales opportunity lies and can strategize where to aim your selling efforts.

As these few graphs have shown, there is much more to graphical analysis than making a bar, line, or pie chart to describe each variable in your study. In fact, except for presentational purposes in a meeting, such simple graphs are probably not necessary in a report; the data can be just as easily and more efficiently presented in a table. But graphing can help show patterns, trends, and relationships among variables in ways that numerical tables never could. However, you need to think about what it is you are trying to say, look at the kind of data you have, and determine how you can use the various graphing capabilities to display and prove your point.

For both line and bar graphs, you can change the scale with which the data is plotted by widening or narrowing the incremental units along the axis on which the data is plotted. If you wanted to dramatize differences, you could do so easily by increasing the widths of the intervals. Even a minute change could be made to look like a giant leap. Changes in scaling in this way can mislead and misrepresent and should be avoided.

Traditional measurement theory divides quantifiable variables into four types: nominal, ordinal, interval, and ratio. As mentioned previously, these can, for all practical purposes, be categorized as two broader types: metric, or continuous, and nonmetric, or categorical. Metric measures have an equal interval scale, such as distance, weight, and dollar amount. Nonmetric measures are characterized as having mutually exclusive categories that cannot easily be scaled, such as the months of the year, presence or absence of a special mailing, and readership of a professional magazine.

Before any analysis can be performed, all available variables in the database must be defined as either metric or nonmetric. Nonmetric variables must be specially coded, a process called *dummy coding*. In this case, a nonmetric variable, such as the presence or absence of a characteristic, is reduced to a scheme of 1s and 0s—a 1 to represent presence or a 0 to represent absence of the characteristic. If this coding is done, the nonmetric variable can be analytically treated much the same as a metric variable, allowing more sophisticated analysis to be applied.

Once the variables have been characterized, then you need to determine whether or not one of them can be designated as a dependent variable. A *dependent variable* is one whose value is dependent on the input or influence of other variables. It is also a variable of some importance in that it is usually a criterion of business success or a measurement associated with some desired impact or response to a marketing effort. For instance, product sales is a pretty good indicator of business success and the size of a company's technology budget is a pretty good indicator of how much they plan to spend on technology-related items. These are appropriate dependent variables since learning what is related to sales or budget, and therefore how to predict them, would be very worthwhile. The remaining variables are then designated as potential *independent*, or *predictor*, *variables*—variables whose influence may help to predict the level of the criterion variable. If no criterion variable can be designated, then all of the variables are considered as predictor variables and the analysis proceeds somewhat differently.

Another consideration when defining variables for analysis is how the variables relate to each other. If the variables can be assumed to be independent of one another, then their relationship can be characterized as additive. If the relationship between two or more variables is such that they work together interactively, then it should be considered as nonadditive and the statistical problem of interaction must be dealt with.

An example that demonstrates interaction among variables is that of relating a shelf price reduction and a special display to sales of a brand in the store. If a given price reduction generates one level of sales response, and a display in the store boosts sales to another level, then if the price and display were additive, you could simply add together the estimated sales response for each by themselves and predict the sales for when a sale product is displayed. If the sales—when both a price reduction and the display are present—is actually *greater* than the predicted sales, the best model to describe this relationship would be nonadditive. In this example of price and display, the evidence points to the fact that these are indeed nonadditive, or that they have a synergistic, interactive effect when in the presence of one another.

Interactions considerably complicate both the analysis and your ability to understand the relationship between variables. In real life, interactions are everywhere. Recognizing this, rather than ignoring it, means that analyzing data for interactions can help to identify key variables and relationships important for segmentation.

Criterion-Based Statistical Models

Selecting the appropriate statistical model or technique to use is based upon the above considerations. If you determine that there is a dependent criterion variable, then several dependence methods including multiple regression, logit analysis, discriminant analysis, and chi-square automatic interaction detection, or CHAID, can be used to derive segments. If no criterion variable can be designated, and you simply have one big set of independent variables, then cluster analysis, an interdependent technique, is the appropriate choice.

Multiple Regression

Multiple regression is one of the most familiar statistical tools. It is a technique that statistically relates a series of predictor variables to the criterion variable in an additive equation-like manner. Regression coefficients are derived that express the strength of the relationship for each variable to the criterion, or the "elasticity" of that variable. The multiple correlation coefficient can be used to describe the strength of the relationship between the entire set of predictor variables and the criterion variable. This technique will automatically select those predictor variables that significantly impact the dependent variable, hence determining which variables to use in the segmentation scheme.

Exhibit 5.5 shows a hypothetical regression equation to predict product sales. The two variables in the equation are family ownership (a categorical dummy-coded variable) and number of years in business. Without going into a great amount of statistical detail, the regression coefficients are the weights for each variable in the equation. Where these coefficients are negative, this means that the variable is inversely related to sales. For instance, family-owned companies in this example produce less sales than nonfamily-owned companies. Where the coefficients are positive, the variable is positively related to sales: the longer a company has been in business, the higher the level of sales. The correlation coefficient shows how well the equation predicts sales. In this case, a value of .44 indicates a moderate relationship between family ownership, revenue, and product sales. Knowing this information on companies would explain just about 20 percent of the variation you see in sales among them, or in other words, you could correctly predict sales with only this information about 20 percent of the time.

Direct marketers commonly use regression to develop scoring models that then predict a criterion value (i.e., sales) for each individual member of a database based on the important variables. Individuals with higher scores are thought to represent greater potential sales and individuals with lower scores lesser potential. The implication, of course, is that individuals with higher potential can be solicited differently than those with lower potential. Most direct marketers will establish a cutoff score, below which no solicitation should occur. Scoring models, usually developed on RFM principles, are used by virtually all catalog marketers. A similar concept is applied by credit-granting institutions as well to determine who are worthy prospects and who are not.

Regression lends itself very well to large data files. It does not

Exhibit 5.5: Hypothetical Regression Model to Predict Sales

Sales = -7.19 + 19.28 Family owned + .31 Years in Business
Correlation Coefficient (R2) = .34

require manipulation of large matrices that limit its applicability to large numbers of cases as do some of the other techniques. Regression is a common feature of many software packages, is familiar to most traditional researchers, and, thus, is widely used. It is, despite discussion to the contrary, the most widely used segmentation tool by a wide margin.

Logit Analysis

Logit analysis is often suggested as an improvement on regression in segmentation applications. Logit analysis involves changing the criterion variable into odds, or the probability of purchase, instead of a continuous metric variable such as amount of purchase, as would be the case in regression. The rest of the analysis is very similar to regression, however.

Discriminant Analysis

Discriminant analysis is also similar to regression analysis in that it is based on an additive model that predicts a criterion from a set of predictor variables in an equation-like format. The difference is that one uses discriminant analysis when the criterion is not continuous but rather is categorized. For instance, rather than predicting an exact level of sales, the goal would be to predict whether or not an individual will fall into a low-spending category or a high-spending group.

In applying any of these statistical techniques to segmentation, you run into problems with defining the variables and handling the very large data files. Variables often must be dummy coded or mathematically transformed to better fit the assumption of linearity and additivity (or the independence of all variables) that all of these are based on. While today's unprecedented computing capabilities can handle the large marketing database files, it is still a good idea to work with smaller subsets of the data, or sample files, that might be drawn using a systematic sampling procedure from the larger database. This allows analysis to be accomplished more quickly and on a microcomputer rather than on a mainframe computer.

CHAID

The dependence techniques described previously assume linearity and are based on additive statistical models. They assume all variables are independent of one another or additive, or at least ignore the possible interactions between variables. CHAID (Chi-Square Automatic Interaction Detection), on the other hand, depends upon them. This analysis assumes that interactions are present and proceeds to find the ones that explain the greatest differences between groups.

With CHAID, variables are nonmetric, or categorical, rather than continuous. (A similar process, AID, works with metric variables, or those that are defined as continuous.) The CHAID process begins by identifying the potential categorical predictor variables and selecting the binary split among all the variables and categories that explain the greatest difference in the criterion or dependent variables. The data is then divided into two groups. Each group is then further divided among the remaining variables. After the second division (two splits and two predictor variables), first order interactions are identified. Second-order interactions appear with the third split, and so on. The analysis proceeds, creating a tree-like analysis, until either the groups become too small to further divide, or no remaining predictor variable will generate a significant split.

What results can be a moderately complicated hierarchical segmentation structure that defines each group in terms of a sequence of values of predictor variables. In practice, with very large data files, many splits occur, making the task of identifying segments somewhat cumbersome. Most of the time the resulting model predicts better than the simpler regression model, although not always better enough to justify the additional complexity.

Exhibit 5.6 depicts a typical CHAID tree diagram that shows the variables that interact and explain or best predict the response achieved from a particular direct mail program. As shown, the tree begins with the number of companies mailed, or 85,800. The overall response rate for this mailing was 17.8 percent. To better predict response, however, the CHAID tree shows that companies with revenue over $20 million were much more likely to respond, a 28.3 percent response rate. The other 63,400 companies had revenue less than $20 million and an overall response rate of only 14 percent. Both of these groups then were split again. The larger revenue group split just once based on family ownership. Family-owned businesses tended to respond more. For the smaller revenue companies, family-owned companies also responded better, and of those, younger companies (less than ten years in business) responded the best. In the end, this analysis derives five different segments:

Exhibit 5.6:
CHAID Tree Program Response

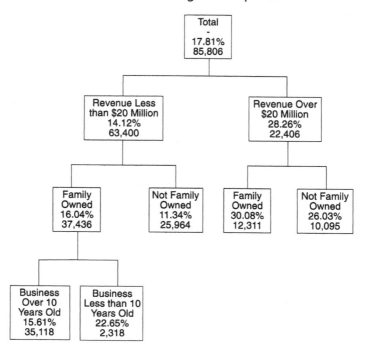

Segment	Response Rate
I. Revenue over $20M, Family owned	30%
II. Revenue over $20M, Not family owned	28%
III. Revenue under $20M, Family owned, Less than 10 years in business	23%
IV. Revenue under $20M, Family owned, More than 10 years in business	16%
V. Revenue under $20M, Not family owned	11%

Cluster Analysis

When there is no criterion variable, then the remaining statistical tool is cluster analysis. The idea of cluster analysis is to identify groups of individuals who are similar or homogeneous on some set of characteristics, yet different from other groups. The diagram in Exhibit 5.7 gives a visual idea of what three clusters might look like in just two dimensions, or from classification on only two variables. The vari-

Exhibit 5.7:
Depletion of Three Clusters in two Dimensions

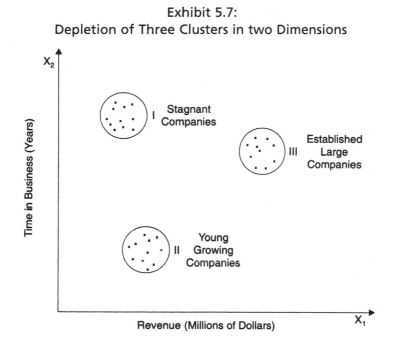

ables used to create the clusters are selected based on hypotheses of what should be important or on other analyses, such as regression or discriminant, which identify these variables as important. In the exhibit, for example, the horizontal dimension might be defined as revenue and the vertical dimension might be years in business, thereby creating three clusters: (I) Stagnant Companies, oldest yet least in revenue, (II) Established Large Companies, highest in revenue and in business for some time, and (III) Young Growing Companies, companies with low revenue that haven't been in business very long.

Cluster analysis has gained some notoriety with commercial geodemographic clustering schemes. These geographical clusters are based on the demographics and presumed lifestyle differences among different zip code areas. In practice, these geodemographic clusters are more useful than demographics by themselves, but they pale in comparison to purchase behavior data. Almost every time purchase histories are available, this kind of geodemographic segmentation adds nothing to the ability to predict.

Cluster analysis requires the calculation of some kind of "distance" measure between individuals in order to be applied. Direct distance measures are rare and usually need to be derived from other variables.

A correlation ratio is often used to represent similarity or distance since it represents the strength of the relationship among variables. Variables that are more similar or more related would have higher correlations than variables that are not. Preparing variables for a cluster analysis is perhaps more of a problem than for a regression analysis.

There are two basic types of cluster analyses: hierarchical and divisive. Hierarchical cluster analysis begins without any assumptions about the number of clusters and attempts to show the possible linkages between individuals, ranging from as many clusters as there are individuals, in other words, each individual as its own cluster, to one large, single cluster. Divisive cluster analysis begins with a fixed number of groups or clusters and fits individuals to them to maximize the differences among them on the selected variables.

Hierarchical cluster analysis requires considerable computer resources and, therefore, is usually limited in its use to situations where there are a small number of individual cases. Few hierarchical procedures work for databases of more than a few hundred individuals. This makes hierarchical clustering impractical for most segmentation applications. While hierarchical cluster analysis is not used very often as a segmentation tool, it might be used with a very small subsample in order to help determine the number of groups for a divisive cluster analysis.

All cluster analyses, however, have limited value because they are not guided by a direct relationship of the predictor variables to a criterion variable. Generally, the technique doesn't perform as well as the criterion-based methods.

Database Applications

Once the database is developed, your focus should shift to its analysis and research applications. The application of a database for market segmentation has already been discussed, and many of the same principles and requirements for segmentation apply to other research applications, such as generating leads, answering marketing queries, developing marketing strategies, and evaluating marketing tactics. These are briefly discussed.

Lead Generation

An important application of the marketing database is in generating leads for the field sales force. This application may not be the most important from a direct research perspective, but it is the kind of application that will demonstrate the usefulness and value of a database to an important employee constituent—the sales force. If the sales force is ever going to be actively involved in supplementing and updating the information on customers and prospects, they need to derive some very tangible benefit from it. Segmentation of the prospect portion of the database could very well result in the identification of profitable leads that will win over the sales force since they profit from those leads. Lead generation is also important from a research perspective since it is a lead generation program that is most likely to expand the marketing database.

If analysis of current customers shows particular variables to be somehow related to spending/sales/response, then segmenting prospects on these same variables is a way to qualify and select the best prospects to call on or send marketing communications. Developing a "scoring model" such as that used by direct marketers is one way of determining who those best prospects are.

Of course, the challenge for business-to-business marketers is to learn what criteria are most important in qualifying a good customer or prospect. These qualification criteria are found through research using one of the segmentation analytical techniques described previously. For instance, to establish those criteria that predict purchase, you might use regression analysis to examine the purchasing patterns of customers who already have purchased and to find the variables that seem to be statistically associated with purchasing. Once these criteria are known, a scoring model can be created. This model is similar to an equation into which you input the various characteristics of a company, and from which a company's likelihood of purchase can be scored and predicted. Good salespeople always size up their prospects and try to meet them in the best way to sell them. A lead generation scoring model should be seen as an extension of this.

Examples of simple questions that could help determine the likelihood of future purchases include: "When do you anticipate purchasing?" "What brand of XYZ do you currently purchase/have installed?" Or, you might ask prospects to apply rankings: "Please rate each of the following reasons for purchasing XYZ." "Please rank the following applications in terms of how critical each is in the operations of your business." You may even find that some SIC industries or particular company demographics are associated with higher or lower responses and much of this information you would probably already know from any general compiled database.

The biggest problem with most lead generation programs from the point of view of field sales personnel is that the leads are out of date or cold by the time they are received. This is the same kind of problem found with all marketing database work and underscores your need to work as expeditiously as possible to keep your database current.

TELEPHONE METHODS. There are several ways that a lead generation program can be operated. A good way to collect the necessary information is through the use of the telephone, or as it has become known, telemarketing. This involves both making calls (outbound telemarketing) and receiving calls (inbound telemarketing).

Outbound telemarketing requires a list of numbers or prospects to call. Lists can come from data compilers and other sources. The problem for many complied lists is that the number of prospects is relatively small, and they are often called by competitors and other telemarketers, making them difficult to reach. In general, however, most telemarketing suppliers claim greater success with business markets than with consumer markets.

Inbound telemarketing means usually that a company or potential customer is responding to your 800 number. The challenge is to somehow get the 800 number to the potential caller in the first place. Print advertising and direct mail are especially popular ways of targeting the appropriate prospects or customers and providing them with information on how and why they should call or inquire. Leads generated via inbound telemarketing are especially good because the callers have already expressed enough interest in the product to pick up the telephone and call. However, this kind of lead generation does not separate out those calls that are from prospects who are likely to buy from those calls that are from curiosity seekers (or those who are out to collect information rather than buy, such as college students writing term papers). If you are establishing an 800 number for lead generation, you probably will need to maintain a telephone facility or contract with a telemarketing supplier in order to answer and follow up on the incoming calls.

An example of a telephone-based lead generation program for an equipment manufacturer is shown in Exhibit 5.8. The program depends on inbound responses from an 800 number that appears in business magazines. When people phone in, they are asked a series of simple questions such as dollar amount purchased in the category in the last twelve months or last twenty-four months. Therefore, both the monetary value and some measure of the recency of purchase are then known. From this, based on a scoring model developed through regression analysis from prior data, which showed which prospects were the best, these incoming leads are qualified and rated as A, B, C, D, or E based on an assumption of their purchase likelihood. Only the upper three categories—hot (A), very good (B), and good leads (C)—are immediately passed on to the field sales force. Those that do not qualify are suspended. Unless an incoming call is determined to be of no value and completely disqualified, however, all calls and information are included in the marketing database.

MAIL METHODS. Generating leads through the mail requires the prospect to complete a simple self-administered questionnaire for the purpose of providing the appropriate information. The prospect can obtain the questionnaire through any number of means: at a trade show booth, via direct mail, or as part of a print advertisement. Response cards that are sewn into the binding of a magazine are one form of this type of lead generation. The questionnaire is usually returned by the prospect through the mail.

One shortcoming of the mail lead generation method is that the questionnaires do not have the benefit of a live "interviewer" and may be completed with varying degrees of care. Reading handwriting also can be a problem if names and addresses are necessary to follow up on the lead. Not every question may be understood or properly answered. Timing is also problem: the time between when the prospect first responded to the time they are identified and contacted could be too long and their interest may have waned or they may already have taken action with another supplier.

Marketing Queries

Unanticipated questions always seem to arise in the normal course of business. A new competitive threat, a proposed governmental regulation, or litigation can generate new questions. For example, it might be necessary to know how many customers have purchased a particular product. Or how many of your customers who have purchased a particular product are located in a particular state. Other similar questions can be answered from information contained in the marketing database.

Special requests for information such as these usually require an analyst to access, sort, or aggregate companies within the database in different ways in order to answer the question at hand. Developing a database with this in mind means having as much data as possible coded into the database and utilizing an SQL (structured query

Exhibit 5.8: Telephone-Based Lead Generation Model

Lead Rating	Qualification
A	More than $5,000 sales last 12 mo
B	More than $2,500 sales last 12 mo
C	Less than $2,500 sales last 12 mo
D	Less than $2,500 sales last 24 mo
E	None within last 24 mo

Qualified Leads

A	Hot Lead
B	Very Good Lead
C	Good Lead

Suspended Leads

Consultant
Duplicate
Follow up not justified
Customer info important—review
Inaccurate customer information
Literature collector
Bought competitor's product
No contract after four attempts
Seeing sales rep
Not telemarketed
Wrong product application

language like Microsoft Access) that allows this kind of ad-hoc analysis to be easily and quickly accomplished at someone's beck and call. Answering questions, after all, is one of the most common, and perhaps most important, uses of the database. The marketing database truly works in this scenario as a tool to aid in the decisions made in the course of doing business.

Marketing Strategy Development

Developing marketing strategy requires knowledge and understanding of your market and your customers. Usually if you have applied any kind of market segmentation analysis to your database, you already have some understanding of the differences across businesses in your market that should aid you in developing tailored marketing strategies. Applying this knowledge through the development of marketing strategies that meet customers' needs and fit with your company's competence, can give you a distinct competitive edge.

If, for example, you know that one segment is more prone to solicit the guidance of external consultants or industry experts than another, or that they use your product in association with another product frequently, you may develop strategic relationships with other vendors or industry associations to make it easier for prospects to learn about and buy your product. If you learn that the most critical element for one company segment's operations is delivery time, you may come up with a new distribution strategy to move your product more speedily to their front door. If there is a segment in the market that is crying out for a service that you can easily add to your current service and that capitalizes on your strengths, the database analysis may have led you to a new opportunity. Product purchases can be compared to buyer characteristics to evaluate product positioning. Buyer profiles can be compared to prospect profiles, and so on. The point is, without analyzing the information in the database, you may never have realized these needs and segments existed.

Marketing Tactic Evaluation

The marketing database can also be used to test marketing tactics. If your creative agency has developed several different direct mail offers or different print executions for trade publications, randomly drawn subsegments of your database can be used as test groups for each tactic. The different tactical executions can be sent to the various groups using an appropriate controlled, experimental design so that you know who received what tactic. Then as response information is recorded into the database, you can monitor the response from each group to determine which offer or advertisement seemed to pull the best leads or inquiries. Using the database this way is similar to a direct marketer's use of lists to evaluate different executions. This is the reason why it is so important that you include and continually update the communication information in your marketing database.

Time and Activity Measures

While the individual identification information and the purchase information are critical components of the marketing database, time measures are the key analytical components. Time variables make possible the calculation of recency and frequency variables that are commonly used by catalog direct marketers. Certainly, the same variables can be used by the business marketer.

Time has been generally overlooked as a critical variable within marketing. This is partially because it is very difficult to obtain good temporal measures. It is also due to a lack of analytical or theoretical tradition. The only place where time has become a critical variable is in management science with time and motion studies.

Time has several important elements and makes the most sense when associated with some activity, such as making a purchase or receiving a mailing. Time-based activity analysis is divided into two types of variables: frequency and duration. *Frequency* refers to how often an activity occurs over some time period. *Duration* refers to how long an activity takes, or how much time is in the interval between activity events. The latter is the more likely measure to come from a business marketing database. How often a marketer sends and receives communications from a prospect becomes a critical variable. How much time elapses between communications or purchases becomes another. Tracking time in this way may reveal problems that need to be corrected or may explain why leads and/or customers are lost over time.

Always remember that time is very important in applying your database.

6 Designing Survey Research

When there is a need to come to a conclusion on a research topic, talking to only a few individuals is often not representative enough to enable generalization back of your larger customer base. In addition, the unstructured, exploratory manner in which most small-sample, qualitative research is conducted, will not be sufficient to give you the hard evidence you need to make a business decision. Yet, when you talk to large numbers of individuals, the methods and guidelines that work for small-sample qualitative research no longer apply. Research instruments and protocols must be much more structured and quantitative in their very nature, or else any information collected will be difficult to analyze and use. This chapter will discuss some of the sampling, data collection, questionnaire design, and analysis issues that apply to survey research.

Surveys have traditionally been the most-used research method in business. Survey research, in fact, probably constitutes the backbone of most company research departments since any in-house research talent most likely spends the majority of their time designing, conducting, analyzing, and presenting survey research. Every company has periodically conducted a survey among their customers or among their potential market(s) in order to assess satisfaction, understand wants and needs, evaluate marketing strategies, and so on. In addition, most marketing-oriented companies conduct more than the occasional survey research project to keep in touch with their customers or track their progress in a market.

Part of the reason for the popularity and use of survey research is that surveys are generally quite cost-efficient for the volume of information gained. Regardless of whether you implement a survey through the mail or over the phone, you can collect an amazing amount of data in a very short time period. Therefore, you can execute and finish a survey project in a relatively speedy manner. And even though you are typically contacting large numbers of respondents, you can maintain tight quality control over the process and the data.

Describing your audience or customers' key characteristics, buying behavior, or decision making processes, usually involves using percentages, i.e. the percentage of companies falling into this revenue category or that, the percentage of companies with this or that equipment installed or who buy this or that brand of product, the percentage who are satisfied or dissatisfied, and so on. Percentages require larger sample sizes in order to have stability and meaning. That is why you'll hear researchers state that samples should be 100 large at a minimum—just so they can use percentages reliably to report findings. When segmenting and comparing subgroups of respondents, it is nice to have at least 100 in each subgroup, hence the need for larger samples.

Someone working in consumer marketing research is normally dealing with markets consisting of millions of individuals. In the business-to-business realm, the size of the market is considerably smaller—with companies numbering in the thousands perhaps. In some specialized categories, the business-to-business market may be as small as only a few hundred companies, or even less. In this context, large-sample surveys may seem out of place since the market itself is quite small. You might logically conclude, then, that large-sample survey research is not necessary or that smaller samples are acceptable. This is misleading since, again, for analytical purposes, larger numbers are still desirable.

Generally speaking, the size of the required sample is independent of the size of the market. Regardless of how large the market is, you would still want to have a minimum sample size of 100 (more if any segmentation analysis is needed). As a practical matter, when the number of companies in a particular market is close to the minimum sample size, you are probably better off surveying the entire census. On the opposite side of the size issue, if a market numbers in the thousands, you rarely need a sample larger than 10 percent of the population, and samples of more than 1,000 to 2,000 become difficult to manage and do not increase the reliability of your data.

It is in the area of large-sample surveys that business-to-business market research overlaps the most with consumer research. The methods that a market researcher employs to survey a consumer market are virtually identical to those employed by a business-to-business market researcher. In some business categories that have a significant work-at-home segment, the distinction between consumer and business-to-business research might be further blurred. However, because you are dealing with smaller numbers in some cases and working exclusively with individuals within a work environment, there are certain constraints and issues that arise that are not issues with consumer survey research. These distinctions are mentioned wherever possible to tailor this material to your needs.

When Survey Research Is Appropriate

There are a number of instances in which survey research is important in business-to-business research. Some of the general applications are described in the following sections.

Evaluating and Tracking Communications Programs

Most business-to-business marketers, similar to those working in consumer marketing, develop and use a wide array of communications to help sell their products or services. At some point, however, two questions are always asked: "Have our communication efforts improved our ability to sell?" and "Has it been worth the money?"

These questions have traditionally been answered by conducting survey research among the intended audience of the communication. Based on some performance criteria, the success or failure of the communication is documented quantitatively and tracked over time. Surveys for this purpose are generally conducted by telephone so that the top-of-mind awareness and reaction from the respondent can be obtained efficiently and expediently with maximum geographic coverage of the market.

These tracking studies are done in almost the same way for consumers as for businesses, the major difference being that consumer interviewing is usually conducted during evening hours while business interviewing takes place during business hours. Depending on the objectives of the communications campaign, the survey may target chief executives, senior managers, purchasing agents, and/or various product users. Any tracking research would need to be conducted among the appropriate target groups. Great care is required in a business tracking study to be sure that the correct individual is contacted and interviewed.

The criteria used to track performance have conventionally been communication measures falling into one of three categories: awareness, preference, or intention to consider or purchase. Typically, communication performance is not directly tied to sales because of the many other variables, such as price, that can affect whether or not an actual sale took place. Awareness measures usually take the following form—"When thinking of long-distance carriers, what company comes to mind first?" Top-of-mind awareness questions like this can really only be asked over the telephone or in a face-to-face interview if you want to get an immediate response. If you were to ask this question in a mail survey, respondents would have the time and opportunity to ponder the question or even investigate alternative brands/companies, hence their response would no longer be considered top-of-mind. Preference is usually measured by asking the respondent to rate or rank the brand or company alternatives in a particular market category. For instance, you might ask, "How would you rate MCI in terms of its (quality/value/service)? Would you say it is excellent, above average, about average, below average, or poor compared to other long-distance telephone carriers?" Intention measures generally begin by asking "If you were going to buy today, how likely is it that you would consider/buy (BRAND)?"

Standard questions like these are then administered more than once to independent samples of businesses over a specified time interval in order to track performance. If a new campaign is about to be launched or targeted to a new customer group, an initial baseline survey is typically conducted before the campaign starts. This, then, provides a basis for comparison once the communication has been sent or run in the media. The time interval for conducting successive follow-up surveys might be as short as weekly or monthly. However, in most business-to-business applications, the time intervals tend to be longer, i.e., follow-up surveys are done on a quarterly or annual basis. This style of tracking is most associated with companies that have larger media advertising budgets and run television and radio advertising as part of a campaign.

Recall Versus Recognition

There are two variants of the awareness measure that deserve special mention: recall and recognition. Recall scores tend to be used more to measure the impact of television commercials and large-circulation magazines advertising and, therefore, are a suitable research method for consumer advertisers targeting mass audiences. Since recognition tests require actually showing a respondent the advertising, practically speaking, they are predominantly associated with magazine advertising rather than television or radio. Both recall and recognition are used by and have application for business-to-business advertising.

A recognition score is computed by calculating the percentage of respondents who say they have previously seen an advertisement when they are shown the same advertisement during an interview. Of course, the first problem for a recognition interview is to establish that the respondent has previously looked at the test magazine. This is usually done through a series of questions that require the respondent to provide information about the main editorial content of that magazine as evidence that they have indeed had the opportunity to read the magazine earlier. Generally respondents are shown many advertisements during the interview, perhaps as many as 100, which diverts attention from any single advertisement.

It is obvious from this discussion that measuring recognition is best accomplished in a face-to-face interview with the interviewer paging through the test magazine. This method, however, may prove to be impractical for business to business audiences because of their wide geographic dispersion and the relatively specialized nature of many trade magazines. Measuring recognition via a mail study is possible since the ads can be viewed in this way, and some services today syndicate mail business-to-business advertising recognition scores, but the control of the interviewing situation is lost.

A criticism of recognition measures is that you can receive false positive responses; in other words, it is relatively easy for a respondent to indicate that they have seen an advertisement before when in reality they have not, especially when the time they have to view the ad is increased as it is in mail surveys. Because of this, recognition scores are suspect in the eyes of some, but for specialized markets and magazines, they are sometimes the only measure of advertising performance available. While you would want to be careful of comparing recognition scores with other advertising measures, such as recall, comparing the recognition of one ad or audience to that of another, has some merit in terms of measuring the attention-getting power of an ad. Nonetheless, recognition scores should be used with full knowledge of how they were obtained.

Recall scores were developed to improve upon recognition

measures. In this scenario, a respondent, without seeing the advertisement, must first say that he or she remembers seeing it and then report something about it that indicates they are in fact remembering that particular advertisement. The amount of lead in or the type of cue given to a respondent to solicit recall can vary. Unaided recall questions cue the respondent only as to the product category: "Do you remember seeing any advertising for long-distance telephone carriers?" Aided recall questions typically aid the respondent more by naming the actual brand or company ("Do you remember seeing any advertising for MCI last night while watching television?") or even relating some part of the message or visual/action within the advertising to help the respondent remember. The percentage of those respondents that simply say they have read or seen the advertising is referred to as *claimed recall*. The percentage that, from memory, can prove they saw the advertising by also reporting something about the advertisement—a visual or audio element or something specific about the message—is referred to as *related recall*. The related recall score is the most commonly used measurement of advertising performance.

Recall scores have their problems as well. Some respondents who claim to have seen the advertising may actually be remembering advertising that ran in another media vehicle; others may have seen the advertising but may not have a good memory for details. Furthermore, because recall tests are a common way to measure the effectiveness of advertising, the talent involved in creating the advertising often create it in such a way as to induce recall for the sake of higher recall scores—rather than to sell. It is easy, but dangerous, to be trapped into playing the numbers, if the goal of the advertising is forgotten and ignored in the testing of it.

On a cost-per-advertisement basis, recall scores are quite expensive. Far fewer advertisements can be tested in the same amount of interview time using the recall method than can be tested using the recognition method. The recognition method employs a relatively simple check-off question for each advertisement a respondent claims to have seen or read. This makes recognition methods more cost-effective than recall tests in the business-to-business setting.

Segmenting Markets

One of the greatest frustrations of the business-to-business marketer is working with existing business databases that have limited information. Trying to segment the market based only on company SIC codes and employee numbers is tough since obviously so much information about a company is just not captured in these variables and more information is necessary to identify those businesses that are the best prospects. The just as obvious solution to this lack-of-information problem is to conduct survey research.

A market segmentation study can provide information on variables that are critical to the description of both customers and prospects and their arrangement into key groups or market segments. A market segmentation scheme allows the marketer to more efficiently direct a business's marketing effort and, therefore, should be part of most marketing plans. Segmentation defining market segments within a customer database was discussed previously in more detail in Chapter 4.

Before you undertake a large-sample segmentation survey, you first must ask yourself a number of basic questions. To begin, do you fully understand the facts about your product or service? Is it purchased as a normal replenishment or restock, or is it a capital good? You must define what it is physically; what it's designed to do; how it works; how it compares with the competition; how it is priced; and what the trends and developments are in the marketplace, both for your product or service and for the competition's product or service. You should approach a segmentation survey, then, as a way to understand the market, for you need to know and understand the people and compa nies to whom you are selling. This approach should be the frame of mind that guides the selection of variables and issues to be included in the survey.

Exhibit 6.1 outlines just some of the variables that might be impor tant in segmenting a business-to-business market. Obvious variables that should be added to your customer database are the physical or demographic characteristics of the organization that might not already be known: sales revenue, company organization and ownership, length of time in business, number of locations, geographic coverage, and so on. Even knowing what business the organization considers itself to be in can be very revealing. Standard industrial classifications alone can be quite misleading, especially in the case where an organization has more than one SIC (or NAICS [North American Industry Classification System])code. You may miss critical processes or technologies that a business organization may strongly identify with if you do not have a complete picture of all industries within which a company operates.

The current ownership or usage status with respect to your market is important information. Is a company a current customer and, if so,

Exhibit 6.1:
Key Segmentation Variables

Relating to the Company

Number of employees
Number of branches/plants/warehouses
Ownership
Revenue
Market share
Type of business(es) (SIC or NAICS)
Business (SIC or NAICS) ranked by importance
Time in business
Geographic coverage
Distribution channels
Management style
Corporate structure
Key management issues

Relating to Current Category Status

Brands currently owned/installed/used
Services currently used
Related product/services owned/used
Quantity purchased/used
Usage frequency and occasions
Satisfaction or dissatisfaction

Relating to Purchasing Process

Centralized or decentralized
Chain of authority
Purchase process (routine or search involved)
Criteria ranked by importance
Size of budget
Frequency of purchase/replacement
Time frame for purchase decision
Decision influencers
Information sources and media usage
Perceived risk in purchase decision

Awareness of your brand/service
Awareness of competition
Attitudes or perceptions of your brand/service
Attitudes or perceptions of competition
Purchase consideration for your brand/service
Purchase consideration for your competition

how good a customer? Is a company completely loyal to your product or service, or is it mixed in its purchasing? If a company does not currently own or use your product/service, is it a former customer, or a brand-new prospect? In what circumstances is the product used and for what reasons? A company that uses your product or service liberally across a wide range of occasions and for many good reasons is a different kind of target than a company that perceives the product or service from a more limited perspective. A satisfied customer is also a different kind of animal than a disgruntled customer.

Understanding a business's purchasing process is also critical in the segmentation process. Is the purchase or acquisition routinized or does it involve a specified search and evaluation process? What is the frequency of purchase and the time frame in which the purchase decision is to be made? Some organizations are very centralized in their operations, with all business or purchasing decisions made by one individual or at one location. Other companies tend to be more decentralized in their decision-making, having complex structures complete with purchasing agents within every department and at every location, in addition to hierarchies of personnel that become involved in the evaluation, review, or veto of various decisions. In this age of downsizing, many companies hire outside consultants to aid in the purchasing of products or services, and this is a critical piece of information to know when segmenting and communicating with your market. Management styles also vary with respect to their sophistication and strategic thinking. Most larger organizations have formal structures and procedures for acquisition of products and services, which of course should be understood by the business marketer. For the business marketer, the problem is that many customer organizations rely on informal structures and procedures that are not readily apparent and may be difficult to investigate via survey research. However, getting to know customers or prospects well enough to understand the subtlety of their organizations and procedures is difficult using any method.

Often, important segmentation variables are contained in the knowledge of what product or service features or benefits are considered most important to a company. For example, when considering what computer hardware or software to buy, organizations that have a high degree of internal technical expertise may have little or no interest in the services offered by a technology vendor, while those that have no internal expertise may look to the service aspect as the most important product characteristic. Knowing the awareness, attitudes, and preferences toward the various competitors in the product or service category in which you compete is also helpful. Are you automatically in the consideration set or will you encounter resistance from the start?

Survey research is the best and often the only way to obtain measures of variables like these. Once a customer database is developed to a point of having good information on all aspects of business related to purchasing, you have a richer understanding of the differences among those in your market and you are in a much better position to divide and conquer.

Product Introductions

Product introductions are a challenge for all marketing departments, whether consumer or business-to-business. With product failures the rule rather than the exception, market research is often utilized to try to identify potential failures before they happen.

Qualitative techniques are a good way to begin gauging the reaction to new product concepts and ideas. Because of the expense involved with a product, survey research is appropriate at the later stages of new product development.

Large-sample survey methods can be used in three ways to test a product introduction. First, a survey can be designed to thoroughly test the new product concept with the product or service itself being an abstract verbal description, artist rendering, or prototype. This use of survey methodology is still vulnerable to the problem of false positive responses, as discussed earlier. Respondents often will say they like a product idea or that they would definitely purchase such a product if it were available, whether they intend to or not. Therefore, basing an estimate of a product's success upon introduction into the marketplace on just the information contained within a survey is dangerous. Only if new product surveys are routinely conducted and there is a track record of how well survey response was related to actual market performance, should survey research be relied upon to predict a new product's success.

A second large-survey method is a mail survey. Such a survey can be conducted if a sample of the new product can be included in the mailing. With this type of research, respondents are given the instructions to either try the product or examine it. The respondent is then expected to complete a mail questionnaire or participate in a telephone interview evaluating the product. While the risk of overestimating positive response is still present with this survey method, at least the respondent has a tangible example of a product to react to. Unfortunately, in the business-to-business realm, many products can't be sampled in this way and so this method is not an option.

A third use of the large-sample survey is to follow-up on an actual new product or service purchase. In this case, once a customer has had experience with the new product, a questionnaire is administered. The new product might be available only on a limited basis, either in only some geographic areas or only to some customers designated as test customers or test sites. This type of survey is expensive and should be designed to accommodate any subsequent alterations or recommendations for the new product or service.

Measuring Customer Satisfaction

Certainly, the ultimate measure of customer satisfaction and service is repeat purchasing or use. But some markets are too competitive to afford the luxury of waiting to see if customers will repeat. All too often, by the time a marketer learns whether a repurchase is forthcoming, the customer has already moved to the competition.

One solution to this problem is to use survey methodology to track customer satisfaction with products and services. If there is a problem, you can identify it early on and have a chance to remedy it at a relatively low cost before it escalates and you lose customers permanently. It is much more expensive to win back lost customers or to win over brand-new ones than to keep a current customer happy.

You might argue, too, that a customer satisfaction survey is also a good way to maintain contact with the customer and continue to build business. By asking for a customer's input, you demonstrate that you care about their business and want to keep them happy. It is a good idea to make this a regular practice in your business.

Measuring customer satisfaction with products and service not only provides important marketplace information, but can also be used to reward employees and build employee morale. For instance, you can use the survey feedback to evaluate and track how particular personnel or branches are doing. Where satisfaction is high, employees can be rewarded; where there is dissatisfaction or complaints, steps can be taken to remedy the situation. By reporting survey results internally, and/or acknowledging achievements and progress, you can motivate continued performance.

Market and Sales Problems

Sometimes sales of a product may be either stagnant or declining, and the reasons may not be immediately obvious to you. There may be differing ideas as to why the sales problems are occurring and different solutions suggested to improve the situation. Survey research may help diagnose the real problem and prevent mistakes or solutions that make the problem even worse.

A survey done to diagnose market or product problems should almost certainly be preceded by qualitative research. Great care is necessary to avoid overlooking the real problems because of your own beliefs about the market and products. By first doing qualitative, exploratory research among a select few customers or sales personnel, you can identify possible causes and solutions that can be investigated further and on a larger scale in survey research. In this way, the real problems can be determined, rather than ignored or downgraded.

Large sample survey research is not always feasible for business-to-business marketers. Furthermore, understanding that results from small-sample qualitative research are not always sufficient for business decisions, there are times when quantitative analytical techniques can bridge this dilemma. Conjoint analysis and multidimensional scaling (or perceptual mapping as it is often called), two techniques explained in Chapters 10 and 11 respectively, are important techniques you should be familiar with, not only because they work very well with small samples, but because they yield incredibly useful, quantifiable information for a variety of business-to-business research situations.

Sophisticated Measurement and Sample Size

With survey research, generally the larger the sample, the better off you are, especially when your goal is to estimate with as much precision as possible the percentage of your sample that does this or that believes one way or another. Larger samples will decrease the sampling error, thereby adding precision, and will generate more stable, usable percentages.

However, larger samples mean that survey research can easily become quite costly. When you think about it, most of the cost in business-to-business market research surveys is in the fieldwork. And unfortunately, seldom is there much in the way of any economy of scale in fieldwork—a sample twice as large costs twice as much. If you mail your survey to 5,000 prospects versus 2,500, you pay twice the postage and twice the printing fees. If you telephone 1,000 customers instead of only 500, you pay for someone to be on the phone (long-distance charges as well as personnel time) for twice as long completing the necessary interviews. Furthermore business-to-business marketers are usually dealing with an executive customer base that is often difficult to reach, adding to the expense of accessing them and to the research overall.

In some instances, a business market may consist of a relatively small number of customers, and simply finding large enough samples on which to identify percentages of behavior or beliefs can be a problem in itself. Hence, there is a considerable incentive to find ways of doing research that yield effective results efficiently with smaller numbers of people.

One way in which you can overcome the problem of sample size is to use high-level measurement techniques in the research. The topic of levels of measurement has already been described in previous chapters, but you will remember that there are several "levels" of measurement that range from the simplest and lowest level—the nominal scale—to the highest level and most sophisticated ratio scale. The problem with many survey questionnaires is that they often have questions with nominal responses; in other words, questions are asked in such a way that responses are categorical, such as with yes/no or multiple-choice formats. Survey data is analyzed and then broken down by reporting percentages for each response category, i.e., the percent who answered yes and the percent who answered no. For percentages to be meaningful and stable, large-sample bases are necessary. A test of the stability of a percentage is how much that percentage would change if only one or a few respondents were switched to another category. Exhibit 6.2 illustrates this point.

If you have only 50 respondents in a particular group, the impact of shifting just two cases can greatly affect the results. In the example above, 34 people (or 68 percent) responded yes—they had purchased from catalogs. If 36 people responded yes out of the 50, the percentage changes by 4 percent to 72 percent. In fact, each individual represents 2 percent of the sample and any one can have great influence on the results. The same readjustment of two respondents in a larger sample of 500 does not alter the findings, as shown in Exhibit 6.2. The percentage responding yes remains 68 percent. Each respondent has less individual impact on the overall results, adding more stability to the numbers. The larger the sample, the more stable the percentages

Exhibit 6.2:
The Stability of a Percentage in Survey Research

Question: Have you ever purchased x from catalog or direct mail?

Results:		Sample Size = 50		Sample Size = 500	
		Number	Percent	Number	Percent
Yes		34	68%	340	68%
No		16	32%	160	32%
		Number	Percent	Number	Percent
Yes		36	72%	342	68.4%
No		14	28%	158	31.6%

because the less the impact any one individual will have on the overall results.

Over the years, the field of psychometrics has developed and improved the marketer's ability to measure psychological phenomena—such things as beliefs, attitudes, and values—with much more measurement sophistication. Today, rating scales are a familiar question form, designed to take advantage of a higher level of measurement. Rating scales ask respondents to express their attitudes or behavior along a continuum in terms of degree. Rather than a black-and-white agree/disagree response, *how much* respondents agree or disagree can be measured, as in a "strongly agree/somewhat agree/somewhat disagree/strongly disagree" scale. This allows you to describe smaller differences by comparing scale averages or means, rather than by reporting the simple proportion of those in agreement. This, in turn, allows you to be more efficient, using smaller samples in research.

Exhibit 6.3 once again shows the results from a question asking about catalog purchase behavior. In this case, however, respondents are asked to scale their behavior in terms of frequency. The average, or the mean, calculated on this data is a 3.2 in the first column. Again, two respondents are shifted from one point on the scale to another in the second column, yet the mean scarcely changes at all. With larger samples, the change would be even smaller. In this case, the small sample of 50 has yielded more stable results simply by using a more sophisticated measurement.

Multiple measures of the same or similar phenomenon also help with efficiency. For a complex topic, the more you know about the

Exhibit 6.3:
The Stability of a Rating Scale in Survey Research

Question: How often do you purchase x from catalogs and direct mail?

	Frequency	
Always	4	4
Frequently	7	7
Occasionally	22	20
Seldom	9	11
Never	8	8
Total	50	50
Mean	3.20	3.24

topic, the more ways you can measure the topic (for example, the more questions you ask), the greater your understanding will be. In a nonbusiness context, an example of this might be the topic of health. What is a person's state of health? If you asked whether someone felt they were in excellent, good, fair, or poor health, you'd have some indication. Such information would be far from perfect, but probably better than knowing nothing at all. If you also knew the age, you'd be in a better position to interpret the previous response. You might, for instance, presume that older people would tend to be less healthy than younger individuals. Add to your knowledge the person's weight, height, cholesterol level, blood white cell count, and blood pressure and your ability to estimate the health of that individual improves dramatically. The more that such measures are added, the better able you are to estimate relative health. In fact, how the variables relate to one another gives even greater insight and understanding—for example, how height compares to weight, or how cholesterol level compares to age.

In business research, this same idea applies: the more ways the same or similar phenomena can be measured, the better it is understood. If you are trying to understand a prospect's attitude toward your company, you can measure this with a simple scaling question from Excellent to Poor. But if you ask this prospect to rate your company across a variety of dimensions, say quality, pricing, service, and accessibility, you know much more about his or her perceptions. If you further ask these same attitudinal questions for your key competitors, you can relate their responses for your own company to those of others and have an even clearer picture of what this prospect's attitudes toward you really are. Again, the more you know and the more information you have to relate back and forth, the more confident you can feel that you understand the topic.

In general, you have two choices when it comes to conducting research: collect a lot of information from a few individuals or collect less information across more individuals. A rule of thumb to remember is that the more information you collect from any single individual, the fewer number of cases you will need in order to achieve a stable sample estimate. As you will see, both conjoint analysis and multidimensional scaling (described in more detail in Chapters 10 and 11 respectively) apply this concept by measuring a phenomenon systematically in every possible light resulting in the statistical stability without the large, expensive samples.

This issue of sample size should also be based upon how much diversity there is in the population or market and/or how many ways you will want to cross-section the sample in your analysis. If there is a broad range of attitudes or behaviors among your target group, then the more people you will want to survey in order to understand all these differing viewpoints or usage segments. If you want to compare those customers who never buy from a catalog, for example, to those who occasionally buy, to those who frequently or always buy direct, then you should have a healthy numbers of respondents in each of these subsegments to make any statistical comparison.

Communication Methods

Once you have determined that survey research is the best research design alternative, then the question of how the data will be collected needs to be addressed. Although this decision is not independent of the sampling issue or of the particular study information needs, this is a good starting point since so much of the discussion of sampling and questionnaire design relate to the communication method chosen.

In survey research there are generally three traditional methods that can be used to administer questionnaires: personal or face-to-face interviewing, telephone interviewing, and mail surveys. You can also now add computer-aided interviewing and the Internet to this traditional list of data collection methods.

Face-to-Face Interviewing

The personal interview has long been held as the standard by which other communication techniques are judged. When a well-trained interviewer personally administers a survey, you can be relatively certain that the survey questions are understood and properly answered. Usually when you are worried about gaining respondent trust and cooperation, a personal touch is helpful. In addition, you have the added benefit of showing respondents visual materials—complicated measuring scales, actual products, example advertising—as well as the ability to gauge reaction to such attributes as color, shape, design, texture, and size, all of which are difficult to discuss in the abstract. You can also involve other sensory dimensions such as touch, taste, and smell. From this perspective, then, personal interviewing affords researchers the most flexibility and thoroughness.

The problem of response bias, due to the interviewer's presence during the data collection, is typically downplayed in light of the preceding advantages. However, a poor personal interviewer has the power to inhibit or bias discussion of a topic. The fact that there is a face to the voice behind the interview heightens any respondent sensitivity to what is acceptable or normal in both a business and a social context. The demeanor, the dress, the overall appearance of the interviewer could irritate or intimidate, or even elevate, the respondent's sense of worth—and this will naturally spill over into how each person answers the questions put to them. Furthermore, the interview is administered, recorded, and interpreted through the eyes and expectations of the interviewer. Very small inflections in the interviewer's voice or slight alterations in the wording of questions, use of probes, and follow-up questions, can make a substantial difference in the data ultimately seen by the research analyst. Where the required sample is large, more than one interviewer is obviously necessary and the potential for this kind of interviewer bias is even more pronounced.

To help alleviate bias, the traditional wisdom regarding interviewers is that they should be as much like the respondents they are interviewing as possible. Yet, this rule of thumb often presents special problems for business interviews. It is difficult to find individuals like chief executive officers that are willing to conduct personal interviews. Using professional consumer interviewers, typically middle-aged women working part-time, to interview CEOs and businesspeople would ensure socially acceptable, but perhaps superficial, responses. In technical areas, the interviewer should ideally have some knowledge of the general business and specific industry jargon, but, again, this is very difficult to find in your typical consumer interviewer. It's not surprising then, that finding good business-to-business interviewers is an especially difficult problem.

One of the other disadvantages of the personal interview that is most frequently mentioned is the high cost. For personal survey research, you will end up paying more for interviewers than you would for telephone interviewers and, as the sample becomes increasingly disperse geographically, the cost rises because of the travel time involved. In business-to-business survey research, the costs are even greater because of the difficulty in scheduling businesspeople for an interview. The cost of a personal interview with a specified individual in a business organization is similar to the cost of a personal sales call. Busy individuals are difficult to reach and require considerable up-front effort to schedule. When the goal is to interview hundreds of business respondents, as is the case in survey research, this data collection method can become much too cumbersome and costly. It is not unreasonable to expect that the cost per completion would run in the hundreds. Consequently, surveys using personal interviews in business market research are relatively rare.

What is more feasible and much more common in business-to-business research is intercepting and interviewing respondents gathered at a central site, such as at a trade show or a professional meeting. However, although the interviewing costs may be dramatically lowered, the sample is clearly a convenience sample and not necessarily representative. There is also a possibility that the special atmosphere created by the event itself may bias the research conducted at shows and meetings. Events held at resorts are especially vulnerable in this respect.

Telephone Interviewing

Telephone interviewing has the clear advantage of being fast compared to other data collection methods. The actual field time will depend, of course, on how difficult respondents are to reach, how long the interview takes, how many interviewers are calling at one time, and how large the final sample needs to be. But a skilled interviewer can complete two to three short interviews per hour, and a small bank of interviewers telephoning during weekday business hours can generally reach and complete a brief five- to ten-minute interview among 100 business executives in one to two days. This allows relatively quick turnaround time on telephone survey research.

In some respects, telephone interviewing provides some of the same advantages of a personal interview. The interviewer can probe, seek clarification, or check the response. The interviewer may also be able to develop a feeling of rapport over the phone, which might generate richer response. Additionally, a telephone interview can overcome some of the disadvantages that plague personal interviews. For instance, geographical coverage is not much of an issue since travel is not required to make contact and almost any business has a telephone. Interviewer-induced bias, while still possible, is much reduced since there is considerably less interviewer exposure and more supervision and control over the interview itself. Questions are more structured in nature, and interviewers are instructed not to deviate from the questions as they are written on the questionnaire. Calling is usually conducted from one location, and, hence, supervisors can discreetly monitor the interviews and manage the process.

The most limiting factor for telephone survey research is the scope and flexibility of what can be accomplished over the phone. Time is limited, especially with a business respondent, which puts an immediate constraint on the volume and depth of information that can be collected. You lose the ability to show respondents materials and cannot, therefore, handle very complex tasks or topics that involve color, shape, and so on. Anyone who has ever tried to give someone directions over the telephone knows how much more difficult it can be to communicate without the benefit of the visual mode. Hence, the telephone interview must be limited to such items that can easily be communicated verbally. In a telephone interview you cannot ask the respondent to refer to anything, to check any source, or to do any work. You must rely entirely on the respondent's knowledge and ability to respond at the time of the interview.

On the other hand, telephone interviewing is an excellent way to obtain a respondent's top-of-mind or candid answers. Telephone interviewing is generally considered the best way to obtain accurate information on what respondents are doing at the time of the call since there is no memory lapse. If the survey topics are very straightforward and questions can be written in a structured yes/no or short multiple-choice format, telephone interviewing is probably the most time- and cost-efficient method of all. For instance, using a four-point frequency scale, you can very quickly and very easily collect quantitative information on how often they buy a whole list of items or participate in dozens of activities.

Costs for telephone survey research are not as expensive as personal interviews, but they are not *in*expensive. Excluding long-distance costs, telephone research may cost anywhere from $15 to $100 per completed interview, depending on the length of the interview and the time it takes to reach the appropriate respondents. If a sample is very geographically dispersed, telephone surveying makes infinitely more sense than personal interviewing, but the long-distance calls could raise costs to a point where mailing a survey makes even more sense cost-wise.

Telephone interviewing is much more common than the personal interview in business-to-business research. After all, the telephone is a ubiquitous presence in virtually every business office. The issue for business-to-business research that does not often arise in consumer research is how to reach a particular individual within a business organization. Finding the telephone numbers for key personnel or particular individuals can require considerable effort and sometimes the skills of a talented interviewer. Sample lists purchased from suppliers do not always include telephone numbers and, if they do, rarely are these numbers the direct lines of the named personnel on the sample list. Once the appropriate telephone number is known, the task becomes much simpler.

Another issue with respect to business interviewing that is not a concern with consumer research, is getting past all of the barriers that are put in place by businesses and businesspeople to keep outside distractions, such as unsolicited telephone researchers, away. Secretaries who screen all incoming calls have always been a problem; automated telephone answering systems and voice mail have created new complications that can make reaching a particular individual within a firm something like an epic quest. Add to this the growing popularity of telemarketing, which creates a cluttered inbound calling environment, and the telephone interview begins to look like a less attractive alternative.

In favor of the telephone interview, though, is a strong business dependence on telephone communication. Business executives generally expect to communicate by telephone, and most spend a significant part of their day engaged in telephone conversations. The business telephone interview requires both skilled and persistent interviewers to take advantage of this tendency and to overcome the barriers.

Mail Surveys

One of the most popular business survey communication methods is the mail. Obviously a mail survey involves the use of a self-administered questionnaire and will take longer to complete than a telephone survey because of the time it takes to mail a questionnaire. Minimally, a mail survey project should be allocated at least six weeks of field time.

Mail offers a number of advantages. Since a mail questionnaire can be completed at the discretion of respondents on their own schedule, both the participation and the thoughtfulness of the response might be improved. A mail questionnaire also allows respondents time to seek additional information if that is required—something that telephoning does not allow. And while you still lose much of the flexibility of personal interviewing, mail surveys can include visual material—such as pictures, advertisements, scent samples, and so on—with the questionnaire. Difficult measurement scales are easier when you can see them and rank-ordering or matching tasks are possible.

For complex or sensitive topics, a mail survey is more likely to be perceived as anonymous, thereby promoting a more candid response. This is important when you are trying to profile a company's demo graphics, such as revenue. In person and over the telephone, you are more likely to receive an inflated answer because of the urge to impress the interviewer, whereas there is no such urge with a paper questionnaire. In fact, a mail survey, in general, is considered to have the least amount of interviewer bias of all survey methods since no actual interviewer is present.

Of course, mail surveys have their disadvantages, too. Perhaps one of the most difficult issues involves the uncertainty of who actually completes the questionnaire, as there is no personal contact to ensure the identity of the respondent. An assistant could be given the assignment of completing the survey or the questionnaire could be handed off to someone else in the company who is perceived as having more knowledge on a topic. And there is always the chance that a questionnaire could be delivered to the wrong individual. In businesses, personnel and titles change relatively frequently and even the most up-to-date list brokers will not guarantee 100 percent the accuracy of the names, titles, and accompanying company information.

Because an interviewer is not present to probe further or clarify questions, it is even more important with mail survey research that questions be written very clearly and simply so that no misunderstanding can result. If a question is misinterpreted or a task is not completed correctly by a majority of your respondents, then the information is lost and the research effort is wasted.

Mail survey costs usually offer an advantage over either of the other two communication methods. Geographic dispersion will not affect the cost of postage the way it will affect the costs of telephoning. Mail costs are constant and predictable, based purely on the size of the sample to be mailed. Of course, the response to mail is typically not as high as it is for telephone research and more questionnaires will need to be mailed initially to offset this fact. This can have implications for the generalizability of the response you do get. That is why a great deal of effort is put into personalizing mail research, and, if the budget will allow, incentives and follow-up mailings to boost the response as much as possible. Yet, despite these extra efforts, mail survey costs are still frequently lower—substantially lower—than what telephone research would cost for equivalent final sample numbers.

Computer-Aided Interviewing and the Internet

Computer technology and the Internet have dramatically changed the face of market research data collection. Computers have been used to tabulate quantitative survey results for well over thirty years, so the use of computers in market research is nothing new. For about half that time, computer networks and stand-alone microcomputers have been used directly as data collection tools in the context of computer-aided interviewing (CAI).

CAI is most associated with telephone interviewing (called Computer-Aided Telephone Interviewing, or CATI). In this case, the telephone interviewer reads the questions from a computer screen and types in the responses as they are reported. In some cases, the computer will even do the telephone dialing for the interviewer. This kind of computer assistance certainly increases the speed with which an interviewer can administer a survey since the computer automatically accounts for any branching questions, presenting the appropriate follow-up question according to how previous questions were answered, and the interviewer is freed from turning pages and writing answers by hand. Keying the answers in real-time also eliminates the time-consuming task of converting the paper-and-pencil questionnaires into machine-sensible form by someone else keying it later. A data file is automatically created during the interview.

Computer assistance also adds a dimension of quality control to telephone interviewing as well—if an incorrect key is punched by the interviewer, the computer will bring your attention to the error immediately so that there are fewer data problems later on. If there are questions where the sequence of items should be rotated from interview to interview to prevent any order effects, this is programmed into the computer and happens automatically. If there are special quotas that must be met, as when you need to interview so many men and so many women, the computer will monitor responses and notify the interviewer when a respondent does not fit the remaining quota so that the interview can be terminated early. The computer will also note inconsistencies in respondent reporting or errors in completing a task, for instance, if a respondent reports a budget that seems inconsistent with the company revenue or a sum doesn't add to 100 as it should.

The complaint you normally hear about CATI is that it takes a considerable amount of knowledge and time to program the computer for a questionnaire using today's available software packages. It is difficult enough that many argue that for small one-time surveys, it is probably easier to administer the survey manually and key the data later than to handle it on a CATI system. However, for larger scale telephone surveys, especially those that are administered more than once, as in a tracking study over time, CATI is very cost-effective and worthwhile. Modern interviewing facilities should probably have CATI available.

Self-administered CAI is now also being used for intercept interviews at central site locations in place of personal interviewing. Here, the respondent sits at a computer and answers the questions on a computer keyboard as they appear on the computer screen. If the questionnaire is simple and friendly in its appearance, it is possible to interview many respondents in very little time with minimal human intervention. If several computers are set up, several interviews can take place at one time—something that cannot occur with a personal interviewer. Today, systems have been developed that do not even require respondents to type on a keyboard, but instead allow them to touch the appropriate box or letters on a screen to answer a question. This touch-screen capability simplifies the respondent task and improves respondent cooperation. Obviously, self-administered CAI offers all the same advantages of error and consistency checking, automatic real-time data entry, and automatic branching that the telephone CAI system offers. In addition, this technique works well for the small-sample analytical techniques, such as conjoint analysis, that are discussed later in the text.

Other uses of computing technology have been suggested, but are not as yet widely used. Simple telephone questionnaires could be completely automated with computer-generated and computer-recognized speech. Another option that has been suggested is to use the telephone touch-tone keypad in response to relatively simple closed-end response items. These automated techniques, given the level of available technology, would be easily accepted by most respondents.

Internet access is nearly universal in business environments. Respondents who already have computers and are networked could participate in a survey project through this network. It works much the same way as CAI. The Internet does have some of the problems of mail, that is being certain of the respondent's identity and the respondent making truthful and thoughtful responses. Nevertheless, computerized and Internet interviewing methods are becoming the dominant means of communication.

Other Survey Methods

At one time fax transmissions were relatively unique and attention-getting. Now they are commonplace and a business receives many unsolicited offers via fax, just as they do in the mailbox. The clutter-breaking advantage of the fax is now long past, although if used carefully, the fax retains the advantage of speedy communication.

The best use of fax communication in large-sample surveys is as a supplemental medium. It can make a good supplement to a telephone interview by providing visual material. It can also be effective for providing reminders or follow-ups. Increasingly today, businesspeople are refusing to answer questions over the telephone until they see the questions. Or they ask telephone interviewers to fax the questions simply due to their own time constraints on the phone. This is an interesting development and one market researchers will need to monitor if response rates continue to decline.

Overnight delivery services offer yet one more way to break through the communication clutter problem and get the attention of a business respondent. Anything sent via express mail is almost automatically deemed important and given priority over other mail. This shortens the data collection time considerably. Of course, the budget must allow for the extra expense of this communication mode. For smaller samples, or more specialized or important markets, the increased attention and response may well be worth the increased cost.

Market researchers need to be creative and keep abreast of any new opportunities to reach business samples as communicating with this population segment becomes increasingly difficult. There is little doubt that the cost of large-sample survey research will increase at a faster rate than most other kinds of research costs, due to the sophisticated communication barriers erected by businesses today. Research methods will have to take full advantage of new technologies in order to remain viable. And it is probably true that the future will see more large-sample business-to-business survey research tied to events and meetings than based on traditional random samples.

7 Fielding Survey Research

When the number of prospects within a particular market is extremely large, interviewing all of them (a census) is much too costly and impractical. Interviewing only a portion of the market, or a sample, is the obvious and accepted alternative. Yet, how you go about selecting a sample will most definitely affect the confidence you can place in the data that the sample generates.

The issue is one of sample representativeness. If you can't interview a census of your customers, then you want to be very certain that the portion you do talk to are representative of the whole group. That way, when you generalize the findings back to all your customers and make decisions that will affect the whole market, you aren't misjudging who they are and what their responses will be. This discussion of representativeness is most important in survey research because usually the goal of survey research is to estimate certain parameters of the population based on data from a sample. Furthermore, survey samples are usually quite large and expensive to interview. It is especially unfortunate to end up with data that is not necessarily indicative of your market. In qualitative research, less emphasis is put on generalization since the research is usually more exploratory in nature rather than conclusive, samples are smaller, and the monetary investment is much smaller.

Researchers use one of several systematic sampling procedures when selecting respondents in a sample to help ensure that the sample is representative. The choice of the sampling method is an important one.

Sampling Methods

There are two kinds of market research survey samples: random (or probability) samples and convenience (not random) samples. *Ran-*

domness means that a sample has been drawn in such a way that, as nearly as possible, every potential respondent is given the same opportunity to be included in the sample. In other words, there should be no biases or favoritism in who is considered or in who is ultimately selected. This affords the greatest probability of selecting a sample that represents and replicates the population as a whole.

While not every random sample will be a perfect mini-replica of the larger population, random samples allow the statistical estimation of sampling error based on probability theory. The statistical theory behind the calculation of sampling error is more theoretical than is needed for a practitioner's book and, thus, is not described here, but the sampling error statistic tells you about how much confidence you can place in the data collected. For instance, at standard confidence levels, if the sampling error is 5 percent and your sample data indicates that 60 percent of your customers are completely satisfied with your service, then you can conclude that there is a 95 percent chance that the actual percentage of all your customers who are satisfied is somewhere between 55 percent and 65 percent, or plus/minus the 5 percent. This statistic simply gives you a range, or a margin, of estimated error around your sample calculations based on the size of your sample and the stability of the sample estimates at that size.

If a sample has not been drawn randomly, there is no assurance whatever that your sample is similar to the larger population from which it was drawn. Even if you calculate an error statistic, the theory on which the calculations are based does not apply to samples that have not been scientifically selected. This makes generalization from nonrandom sample data more risky, and potentially dangerous, since the numbers could be misleading. The trade-off is that nonrandom, convenience samples are usually much less expensive to obtain, especially if a face-to-face interview is required.

Random Sampling

A random probability sample needs a well-defined methodology for the selection of respondents. In order to give everyone an equal opportunity to be selected, you must first know who *everyone* is. This means that everyone fitting the appropriate criteria for your particular market, the population, must be enumerated in a list. This list is referred to as the sample *frame* since it really frames the selection process. The sample is then drawn from this list in an unbiased way.

A *systematic* sampling method is the most common procedure for drawing a sample. By selecting a random starting point within the list and applying a skip interval, every nth name on the list is selected. As long as there is no systematic sequencing of the names within the list (as when company names are organized in identical sequences such as CEO/CFO/VP . . . CEO/CFO/VP . . .) that would correspond to the skip interval, the sample should be approximately equivalent to the entire list. Alphabetical lists are typically not a problem because those names selected will be directly proportionate to the frame, with more Ss and fewer Zs most likely. Lists generated by zip code or telephone prefix should not be a problem either since, if there are more customers in a particular zip code area, you would want to have more sampled from that zip code area as well. The skip interval is the same across the entire list. Most random market research samples, both consumer and business, and for mail or for telephone, are drawn in this manner. The problem is coming up with the appropriate list.

There are basically three sources of business-to-business lists. The first source is the telephone directory yellow pages. Telephone directories, available these days in digital form, are routinely reprocessed by suppliers for the purpose of survey sampling. Some of these suppliers attempt to enhance the telephone list with additional information from compiled business lists. The telephone list provides a good enumeration of businesses, since virtually all have telephones. But, often missing are the names of personnel working within those businesses. This is especially a problem for larger business organizations that do not have a direct retail presence in the local market. For example, the chief executive officer of Procter & Gamble could not be ascertained from the Cincinnati telephone directory.

Telephone lists can be a problem for consumer research because of the number of missing, or unlisted, numbers. Random Digit Dialing (RDD) methods are often discussed as a way to overcome this problem—where the computer randomly generates numbers. In business-to-business research, however, very few businesses would have unlisted telephone numbers, and randomly generating numbers would be wasteful since so many would ring up consumer households rather than businesses. Therefore, RDD is not an option in business research.

The second source of business market lists is traditional direct marketing response lists. These might be compiled from lists of subscriber names of various business publications or services, from the names on a particular cataloger's mailing list or house customer list, from membership lists of business associations, or even from lists of trade show attendees. Here you would have to learn which lists are available and match the characteristics of the names on those lists with the characteristics of your market. Almost anything that a list broker would have available for rent that might overlap with the market in which you are interested could become a candidate sample frame. If you rent several different lists with similar characteristics, you should compare them and eliminate any duplications (a process of merge and purge) to create a master list from which the sample can be drawn.

Special attention should also be given to membership lists provided by professional associations; these lists are often not maintained in a very sophisticated manner and require considerable manual effort in order to use them. Working with membership lists also adds some requirements that the traditional market researcher may not be used to. Frequently list owners want to examine the material that is to be compiled for lists they own. This adds an approval step before you can access the list. Also, membership list owners generally are not accustomed to providing their lists for research purposes, so they may be unwilling to sample the list for you and will charge you for the entire list regardless of how many names you actually use. If this is so, you will need to find a research supplier who can systematically draw a sample to your specifications.

Keep in mind that a sample frame must have as complete a list of those in your sample population as possible. If your intent is to sample from all readers of a particular business publication or from all attendees of a trade show, then these lists are complete and appropriate as sample frames. But when you are trying to generalize back to a broader target population, patching together lists to approximate that population is somewhat risky since you will probably miss a substantial number of people within that population who just don't happen to be on one of your chosen lists. This, of course, will affect the representativeness of your sample since the frame itself is incomplete and potentially biased.

Finally, a third source is the compiled list such as that prepared by Dun & Bradstreet (D&B). This is probably the most common source of business-to-business samples. This list is well maintained by D & B, and considerable effort is expended to ensure its accuracy. A compiled list often contains information other than company names, addresses, and telephone numbers. For instance, information on company revenue, industry type (SIC or the newer NAICS), or number of employees is also commonly known, allowing you to sample from companies meeting the specific parameters you set. Compiled lists may also contain the names of corporate officers—which makes it easier to personalize any contact made with the sample. But even the D & B list, probably the best available, should not be viewed as totally complete or reliable since the names, telephone numbers, and addresses within any business category change so quickly.

Generally speaking, although business population lists are far from perfect, they tend to be much more comprehensive and accurate than lists of consumer populations. Once you have identified a list source to provide the sample frame, instructing the supplier to select every nth name off the frame, or doing so yourself, is relatively easy. Usually these sample names can then be provided to you on computer disk, as a hard copy list, or printed on labels. It is always a good idea to get at least one hard copy of the complete sample for reference. If you are intending to survey through the mail, then having the names on disk will easily allow the personalization of envelopes and cover letters sent to your sample. If you are conducting the interviews over the telephone, then it is usually a good idea to have labels printed with all the pertinent information. These labels can then be stuck on separate telephone call sheets that can be distributed among interviewers.

Stratified and Cluster Sampling

Two other random sampling techniques are stratified sampling and cluster sampling. Stratified sampling can produce more representative samples with less sampling error than any other sampling technique, but it requires prior knowledge of the sample. If, for instance, you know the revenue of each company in your sample frame, and you believe that revenue is an important enough variable that you want to be certain that your sample exactly matches the population on this variable, you can *stratify*, or divide, your sample frame into meaningful revenue categories and randomly (systematically) sample within each. If you sample proportionately, your final sample should have exactly the same proportion of companies in each revenue category as the actual sample frame. In this example, you have not left the revenue distribution within your sample to chance; you have guaranteed representativeness on that one variable. You can stratify by more than one variable, obviously, but the process becomes more complicated and thereby more expensive. The key to remember, though, is that you need to have prior knowledge about the population in order to accomplish the stratification.

Cluster sampling simply implies that you randomly sample according to natural clusters, or groupings, of your population. Usually when a cluster is described, it is described in terms of physical, geographic areas, such as states or counties. But clusters can also refer to places (for example, metropolitan airports where businesspeople are naturally found in the course of business travel) where your population naturally congregates. The main reason for cluster sampling is that a sample frame does not exist or is not easily compiled and your population is geographically dispersed. Rather than trying to create a comprehensive list from which to randomly sample, you draw a series of samples, each one successively more targeted until you are at a point where you can derive a meaningful frame.

As an example, suppose you want to interview purchasing agents within businesses fitting particular SIC and revenue parameters but no lists exist to allow random sampling. It is simple enough to acquire a list of the fifty states from which you can randomly select a handful of states. For each state that is selected, you then compile a list of all the counties and draw another random sample of one to two counties within each state in which to focus your efforts. Finally, your geography is narrow enough that you can go about finding a list of potential businesses from which to draw a final sample. Cluster sampling is commonly used with personal interviewing in order to cut down on the number of places an interviewer will need to travel, since along the way, some states and counties have been entirely eliminated.

Clustering isn't necessarily limited to physical clustering. It can also be used to sample time. For instance, if you want to interview customers to a store or visitors to a particular location over an extended period of time, you can divide the total time into time blocks and then randomly select a few blocks to conduct interviewing. In this way, you have a random sampling of customers over time rather than a sample of customers interviewed at only one isolated time period or the expense of interviewers stationed on a continuing basis across time.

Although a cluster sample is random, it will not be quite as accurate as a stratified or even a systematic sample since, by virtue of the fact that it allows convenience to play a role in the sampling process, it is not as scientific. Yet, it is sometimes the only practical way to acquire a random sample. If a business-to-business retailer has hundreds of stores nationwide, each with its own customer base but no system in place to develop one comprehensive list of all those customers from which to systematically sample, then it only makes sense to randomly select a few of those stores to zero in on and create a sample frame based only on those few stores. It is both time- and cost-efficient to do so.

Convenience Sampling

Convenience samples, as the name implies, are samples found in a manner convenient to the market researcher. There is no assumption of randomness; therefore, no sample frame or list of potential respondents is needed. You simply find respondents that fit the sample criteria wherever you can and interview them. When you intercept people at a business meeting or trade show, or have sales reps interview current and prospective clients during a particular month's scheduled sales calls, you have obviously not taken the effort to make sure that every potential respondent has had an equal opportunity to be selected; you simply interviewed the first people you could find until you met your sample size requirements. When this is done, it is difficult to know how representative your sample actually is; technically you cannot even statistically estimate how much error there may be in your sample data. You simply do not have any way of knowing.

There are ways to attempt making a convenience sample more representative, as with quota sampling. If you know how your overall market is characterized on key variables that might impact the study results, you can screen those you interview on those variables and create a quota system where you sample so many respondents in each category. This is the same idea as stratification except that you are not randomly identifying the respondents based on prior knowledge of a sample frame. To use revenue as an example once more, you create meaningful revenue categories and set a quota for the number of companies that you want to interview within each category. Once a quota is filled, you screen out companies that fall into that category and instead concentrate on finding companies to fill the other revenue quotas. In this way, you ensure that you will have companies within your sample across the entire revenue spectrum. If you simply sampled at convenience, it is possible that you could end up interviewing all large or all small companies and bias the results needlessly.

A judgment convenience sample is one that is purposely hand-selected because you believe those in the sample are in the best position to answer the questions you have and to give you the range of information you need. You may even have a sample frame, but rather than randomly selecting names in a systematic fashion from the list, you scrutinize the list and pick out those that you think represent the population, much the same way expert witnesses are selected. An example of this technique would be if you wanted to assess reaction to a new product or marketing idea and you test the idea by interviewing a hand-selected group of your best customers or those customers who are on the cutting edge and have the ability to set the standards for the industry. There is great potential for biasing the study results if you are not careful since it would be easy to select those respondents you think will tell you what you *want* to hear.

In very specialized markets—again where a list might not exist to identify all potential respondents—another convenience sampling method can be very useful. A "snowball" sample uses referrals in order to find respondents fitting the specialized criteria. If you can identify even one respondent in the population of interest, that respondent will probably be able to refer you to one or more other people who are like themselves. Each of these people, then, can continue to refer more people, and so on until the numbers "snowball" and you have accumulated enough respondents for your desired sample size. Because only those who are fortunate enough to have been referred will have the opportunity to be a part of your research, randomness is absent.

All convenience samples, regardless of the technique used, have the same problem. They could be biased and, therefore, yield misleading or one-sided results. Convenience samples are best saved for exploratory research where you are not trying to generalize back to the greater population and accurately estimate particular parameters of that population.

Survey Response Rates

The *response rate* is a calculation of how many people actually responded to your survey as a percentage of all those you gave the opportunity to respond. When you think of response rates, you usually immediately think of those who have responded positively by completing an interview or a questionnaire. Technically, however, a response could be negative—meaning that the respondent refused to be interviewed or only partially completed the interview before terminating it. Someone who has actually refused to respond is different from someone you were never able to reach, or from whom you never heard anything at all. This is nonresponse. Therefore, you have response and nonresponse, and among those who responded, you have those who completed the survey and those who did not. The *completion rate* is the percentage of people who have actually completed a survey and can be included in a final sample count. While it seems as though this is only a matter of semantics, make sure you understand what is meant when someone talks about response rates—they may not mean what you assume they do. To be clear in this discussion, the terms *response rate* and *completion rate* will both be used so as to differentiate between the two.

Completion rates, the percent of all eligible subjects who completed a survey, vary by the method used to collect the data. Telephone completion rates tend to be higher than mail completion rates, and because the refusals are so high upfront on participating in a personal interview, completion rates for face-to-face data collection tend to be low as well. For telephone research, if high-quality field service agencies are used to conduct the interviews and collect the data, and enough time is allowed to make at least six callbacks to unreachable numbers, the completion rates can be as high as 70 to 80 percent. With mail surveys, the average return for business samples is only about 10 to 15 percent, but with proper follow-up procedures and incentives, completions can double. With extensive pre- and post-procedures and multiple mailings, you can obtain mail completion rates equivalent to those of telephone surveys.

The issue of completion rate is an important one because, of those who are contacted (either via phone or mail), the higher the percent who do *not* complete a survey, the more suspect is the final sample in terms of its representativeness. All those potential respondents who did not respond could be different in some way from the ones who did. Hence, your data could be skewed to represent the minority rather than the population as a whole.

Ideally, completion rates would be 100 percent, with everyone who is randomly sampled completing an interview. But this is impossible. You will never receive 100 percent completions among a business market—no matter how small—just due to scheduling and time constraints. Still, you must strive for as high a completion rate as possible to alleviate concerns of sample bias.

Reaching busy business personnel, however, has become an increasingly difficult task. Response and completion rates for all survey methods have visibly declined over the years, especially in more recent years when the amount of unsolicited telemarketing and direct mail has increased so dramatically. The resulting clutter has made it especially difficult to reach businesspeople.

The problem has actually been made worse by the recent spate of downsizing and personnel shifting. Now that many organizations have fewer employees, it is even harder to get the attention of the remaining employees who are busier than ever. As a defense mechanism, many organizations have become less accepting of outside communications. In an attempt to reduce mail room costs, some businesses, for example, will not deliver anything to their employees but first-class mail. Some businesses even claim they will not deliver first-class material if they get a substantial number of similar envelopes, in the belief that these are really solicitations. The point is that if you cannot get through to respondents in the first place, your response rate suffers as a result.

Obviously, a well-constructed, easy-to-complete questionnaire is a must if you want to encourage participation, but for now we will assume that is a given. Specifics regarding questionnaire construction will be discussed in more detail later. Depending on the communication method used to collect the data, there are other ways to increase response if time and budget allow.

Telephone Response

The first thing a respondent hears in a telephone interview is the interviewer explaining what the study is about. In this introduction, it is important to establish the credibility of the study and the interviewer and gain the respondent's interest without delaying for too long the actual interview. The longer a respondent sits on the other end of the phone listening and not actively participating, the more likely it is that he or she will lose interest and hang up. Therefore, it is best to keep the introduction very short—the interviewer should briefly identify him- or herself and the research company with which they are affiliated and explain the general purpose of the study and who is being interviewed. Then, without asking the respondent's permission to continue, launch right into the questions and involve him or her in the subject matter of the interview.

Once the interview has begun, hopefully the questionnaire itself will maintain interest. Length will affect how many respondents actually complete the interview, however. While longer interviews are, of course, possible if a telephone appointment is set up between the interviewer and respondent at a mutually convenient time, they should be discouraged in business research. The shorter the interview, the higher the completion rate will be. Certainly an interview should take no longer than ten to fifteen minutes, but five-minute interviews will be all the more successful if completion rate is the criterion.

In telephone survey research, what will affect the completion rate as much as anything is how the sample telephone numbers are managed. If every call sheet is distributed among the interviewers and called once, then every one of those numbers must then be included in the base on which completion rate is calculated. A high number of those attempted contacts will result in nonresponses (no one answering or a secretary informing the interviewer that the respondent is not available at the moment and to please call back). If there is sufficient time and budget allotted to call each of these numbers until either a positive or negative response results (completion or refusal), then this is not a problem.

However, schedules and budgets do not always allow indefinite calling. In this case, it is best to distribute the call sheets more conservatively, waiting until the active numbers are used up (completed, refused, or called a minimum of six times with no answer) before distributing new call sheets. Managing the process this way keeps the total sample pool smaller and holds the proportion of nonresponses to a minimum, thereby boosting the response figures and the representativeness of the final sample. The only caution is to be sure that call sheets are randomized before they are distributed. If the numbers were printed in a particular sequence, such as state by state, and the call sheets are passed out from the top of the pile, the states toward the bottom of the pile may never make it into the sample and this would create bias instead of reducing it.

Exhibit 7.1 shows a final breakdown of the final disposition of the calls made for an actual telephone survey. The response rate here is 73 percent if you include refusals as well as completed interviews. The completion rate is 61 percent. Notice that almost one-third of the numbers in the sampling pool were not called and that this reduced the total sample base. Ineligible numbers reduced this base further, resulting in a valid sample of 1,815 from the original 3,000 numbers purchased from the list broker. It is on this valid sample base that calculation of responses or completions is made. Ineligibles included numbers that (1) were not working, (2) were for companies that had gone out of business, (3) were not businesses, (4) had changed without a new number reported, or (5) had no one who spoke English. Numbers where the respondent was unavailable during the interview period, or where an interviewer could never get through to anyone, were coded as a nonresponse.

Exhibit 7.1: Disposition of Numbers in a Telephone Survey

Total sample pool	3000	
Numbers unused	926	
Total numbers called	2074	
Ineligible numbers	259	
Valid sample	1815	100%
No answer	237	
Respondent not available	245	
Total nonresponse	482	27%
Refusals and partials	225	12%
Completed interviews	1108	61%

Mail Response

In mail surveys, there are several points at which response could be lost. To begin, the mail needs to be delivered to the correct respondent. Invariably, even the best of lists have addresses that are outdated or incorrectly/incompletely specified and the mail is returned undelivered. If the survey is addressed to a particular individual and that individual is no longer working at that company or that address, the mail is usually just tossed by someone at the company and, because you never even know it was not delivered, it becomes part of the inevitable nonresponse error.

Assuming the survey is delivered to the right office and the right person, the mail sometimes goes through an intermediary, such as an assistant or a secretary who screens out the "junk mail." It is possible that the survey could get screened out at this point before it ever reaches the respondent. Even if the secretary does pass it on and the respondent does receive the survey, the envelope needs to be opened and the cover letter read. Some businesspeople, especially higher level executives such as CEOs, dump more than half their incoming mail into the wastepaper basket without a second glance. If the respondent does actually read the letter, the letter and attached survey must pique their interest enough for them to complete it or set it aside to complete later. If the survey is set aside, there is a good chance that somehow in the course of the day or the week, the survey will get forgotten and never completed.

Finally, assuming the survey is completed, it must be returned in the mail back to the sender. Even at this stage, the survey may not make it to the mailbox. It could sit around for days or months until finally someone finds it and tosses it away, or returns it too late to be included in the final sample analysis.

The trick with mail surveys is to get past all of these barriers. Personalizing the envelope with the individual's name and correct address will help to get it to the right person. A personal look to the outside envelope (name typed/printed/handwritten on the envelope rather than a label; a real stamp rather than a bulk mail insignia; quality paper stock (or perhaps a slightly smaller or larger envelope size to draw attention, etc.) will go a long way to getting the envelope opened. Additionally, incentives usually help to keep the survey from being immediately tossed and may even encourage participation, and well-written cover letters are a must to spark enough interest to keep the momentum moving. A pre-addressed and stamped return envelope helps to assure the questionnaire's safe return.

The research evidence on incentives, by the way, shows that cash incentives work better than freebie trinkets or promises of gifts upon receipt of the survey and that the amount of the cash incentive is irrelevant. A one-dollar incentive works almost as well as a ten-dollar incentive. The real purpose of the incentive, especially in a business environment, is to keep the questionnaire from being immediately discarded. It is attention- getting to find a crisp one-dollar bill in an envelope. (No, the dollar does not compensate the respondent for his/her time, and it is not intended to do so. Often in the cover letter reference will be made to the incentive in terms of "buying a cup of coffee.") Placing two quarters in a small envelope and stapling it to the survey has also proven successful. Again, the amount of the incentive is not really the key issue. The bulky fifty cents will definitely catch someone's attention and prevent the survey from being discarded or screened out from the respondent, whereas sometimes the dollar can be missed. While the amount or form of incentive is not always critical, the inclusion of an incentive is; incentives almost always increase mail response.

Cover letters, like telephone interview introductions, should be kept as brief as possible, but since there is no one to answer any questions, a bit more explanation as to how the respondent's name was obtained and why it is so important for the respondent to complete the survey is needed. The critical ingredients in a cover letter are:

- Personalized greeting with name spelled correctly.
- Brief sentence or two about the purpose and importance of the study.
- Explanation of who is being sampled and how names were selected.
- Plea as to why it is so important for the reader to respond.
- Promise of anonymity and confidentiality (if true).
- Mention of return envelope or any other specifics you need to draw their attention to, such as an incentive.
- Sincere thank you and closing.

A generic cover letter is shown in Exhibit 7.2.

What will also boost response is a second mailing to those who have not responded within the first couple weeks of the fieldwork beginning. Either a complete package can be sent, including another questionnaire and cover letter and maybe another incentive as well, or a postcard reminder can be mailed to prompt those who have just forgotten or are sitting on the survey. If you have a system in place for tracking those who have responded and those who have not, you need only send the follow-up mailing to those who you have not heard from. A postcard reminder is shown in Exhibit 7.3.

In the same way, you can precede the survey mailing with a postcard alerting respondents that the survey is on its way and asking them to look for it in the next week. If the postcard and the main mailing follow each other within days, you should see a bump in the response because of the extra attention you have drawn to the study. Of course, a postcard before, along with a postcard after, will add extra expense to your research. But if response is critical, these are proven methods to help increase your final sample size.

The calculation of response and completion rates is the same for mail as it is for telephone survey research, the only difference being that there are no unused numbers since everyone in the sampling pool is mailed a survey. You will have undeliverable mail, though, and ineligibles will still result because there will be companies that respond and tell you that they have since ceased to be in the relevant business, or that they are not who you think they are—a wholesale distributor, for instance. Generally, the nonresponse percentage will be higher in mail than with telephone because without following up

Exhibit 7.2: Example Mail Survey Cover Letter

August 4, 2005

Mr. Kenneth Doe
President
Doe Manufacturing
333 Main Street
Saint Paul, MN 55109

Dear Mr. Doe:

I hope you can help me. I am involved in a research effort to better understand the opinions and perspectives of executives like yourself in the manufacturing industry. The items on the enclosed questionnaire focus on you, your company, and the effect that industry trends are having on how you run your business.

I cannot emphasize enough how critical your timely response is to the success of this study. I am not selling any product or service.

You were randomly selected from among a list of manufacturers within a ten-state Midwest region. Your company is, therefore, one of only a few in the manufacturing industry that I have involved in this study, making your participation tremendously important. I assure you that any information you provide will remain anonymous and completely confidential—responses will be analyzed only in combination with others.

I appreciate the fact that you have a busy schedule and may receive requests for information such as this often. However, I hope you will take a few minutes to respond. A dollar doesn't buy much today, but I believe it will still buy a good hot cup of coffee here in the Midwest! Have one on me while you fill this survey out.

Thank you in advance for your participation. The information you provide will help illuminate the difficulties that manufacturers like yourself are facing to remain competitive in today's tougher business climate.

Sincerely,

Tamara S. Block, Ph.D.
Block Research, Inc.

P.S. I really need you, the key decision maker of your company, to complete this survey. It is your perspective and opinions I am interested in.

Exhibit 7.3: Example Reminder Postcard as Follow-up to Mail Survey

About a week ago, you received a survey regarding XXXX. If you have not already completed this important survey, would you mind taking just a few minutes now to complete the brief questionnaire and drop it in the mail to us? Since you are one of only a few to have been included in this study, your response is critical to us. If you have already returned the survey to us, thank you!

Sincerely,

Tamara Block
Block Research, Inc.

P.S. If you have misplaced the survey, we will be happy to rush you another copy. Please phone at your earliest convenience (xxx-xxx-xxxx).

on those who do not respond, you have no way of knowing what their actual disposition is. Telephoning businesses, you usually can screen out the ineligibles even if you never speak to the actual respondent since, with enough callbacks, someone will answer the phone and you will be able to determine whether they are appropriate for the sample or not. Exhibit 7.4 is a response rate table typical for a mail survey.

Sample Size

The issue of sample size is typically much less clear cut than that of which sampling method to use. Sampling method is often dictated by the budget and the available lists. Determining how large the sample should be is more complicated. First of all, you need to distinguish between the size of the sampling pool and the desired final sample size. The final sample consists of those respondents for whom you have completed an interview, start to finish. Along the way, you will encounter numerous potential respondents for whom you will not be able to complete an interview for one reason or another. Therefore, you need to have a pool of respondents from which to call or to whom you will mail, which is larger than the desired sample. Work backward, first determining how large you want the final sample to be and then estimating the size of sample pool needed to generate that number.

Exhibit 7.4: Disposition of Sample for Mail Survey

Mailed sample	3000	
Undelivered mail	47	
Total numbers called	2953	
Ineligible numbers	18	
Valid sample	2935	100%
Nonresponse	2016	69%
Refusals and partials	86	3%
Completed interviews	833	28%

The final sample size is based on a couple of factors: how much error is acceptable and what kind of analysis will be done on the data. Sample size is inversely related to the sampling error. Larger samples are typically more generalizable because they have less error. Smaller samples, while less costly to survey, will have greater error and be less representative. Smaller samples also limit the kinds and extent of analysis and comparisons that can be done. For instance, if the analysis will involve dividing the sample into geographic regions or industry types for comparison purposes, or by other characteristic categories such small versus large companies, then the samples need to be larger. Think of each category that is to be broken down for comparison as a separate mini-sample and increase the sample size accordingly. If you segment one sample too many ways all at once, the size of any given cell or category will become too small to analyze at all and the research will not yield the information necessary.

While there are statistical answers to the question of sample size, there is a tendency to rely on rules of thumb and to continue to use the same sample size that was used the last time. One rule of thumb is to use samples of at least 100 when you are planning to percentage any response. Most of the commercial communications research companies use standard sample sizes of about 150. If you plan to divide the sample by size or industry or gender, estimate at least 50, but preferably 100 for each subsegment. Regardless of how big your actual market is, samples of more than 1,000 or so are usually unnecessary. The sampling error does not decrease enough to warrant larger samples at this point.

Once you have an idea of how large you would like your final sample to be, estimate what you think the completion rate will be for the communication method you are using to conduct the survey. If you are mailing the survey, for instance, you might estimate a completion rate of 20 percent. If the final sample needs to hit 500, then you would consider mailing to 2,500. If your list is not very clean or is outdated at all, you should probably boost this figure to account for mail that will never be delivered. If you are interviewing respondents over the phone and you estimate you can achieve a 50 percent response or better, then you'll need to have 1,000 numbers to complete 500. If the *hit rate*, or the percentage of numbers that are working, is expected to be low, or the criteria for inclusion in the sample are rigorous, then you'll need to adjust this figure even higher. As an example, if you want to speak with businesses that have only IBM or IBM-compatible computers installed, you'll need to estimate the share of IBM/compatibles in the market in order to know how many businesses you'll have to call to find one that fits the criteria. If you determine that three out of four have the desired computer platform, then 25 percent of the numbers will be screened out as ineligible and the sampling pool needs to be increased by that much to offset this. If only one in four will meet the inclusion criteria, then you should multiply the sample size by four times.

Questionnaire Construction

Exhibit 7.5 shows the basic steps involved in constructing a questionnaire. Preceding this first step, of course, the research objectives and information needs must be clearly understood and written down, since it is from this list of information needs that the content of the questions is derived. The key thing to remember here is that every question should have a purpose that directly relates back to the research objectives and the analyses that are anticipated. Questions that address details that are interesting and nice to know, but irrelevant to the research goals, are very expensive since they take up space and/or an interviewer's or respondent's time.

You should also ask yourself whether or not the particular respondent will have the ability to answer the questions based on what they know. If they can't immediately access the information needed, the likelihood is that they will skip the question or toss the whole survey.

Exhibit 7.5: Steps in Questionnaire Construction

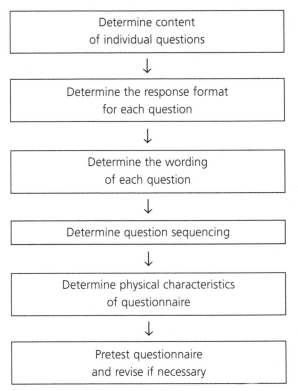

Determine content
of individual questions

↓

Determine the response format
for each question

↓

Determine the wording
of each question

↓

Determine question sequencing

↓

Determine physical characteristics
of questionnaire

↓

Pretest questionnaire
and revise if necessary

Even if respondents are informed on the topic and have the information you want, you must also consider whether they will share that information with you. Confidential company data is not something that many responsible business executives will divulge to anyone, let alone a stranger. Company revenue is probably not a problem since this is not confidential and not a personally sensitive issue; however, if you ask your respondent what his or her personal income is, you may have trouble.

Before actually sitting down and writing questions, you must have already decided what communication method you are going to use to administer the survey. A telephone survey is somewhat different in terms of how the questions are worded, what response formats work best, and its physical appearance, as compared to a mail survey. Personal surveys would be written similarly to telephone questionnaires since an interviewer will be reading the questions aloud. However, a personal survey can take on certain characteristics of a mail survey in that you have the visual medium and "show cards" can be developed to allow the respondent to see the response choices. This means that you are not as limited in what you can do as you are on the telephone. For the purpose of this discussion, only telephone and mail will be detailed since they represent the mainstay of most business survey research.

Rules for Writing Survey Questions

There is somewhat of an art to writing good survey questions, but the basic rules of thumb from which all questions are written are pretty straightforward. There may be no one right way to phrase a question, but there are definitely better ways. It may seem like a small point, but the way a question is worded and the response format you use will influence the kinds of answers you get back. Change the wording or the format, and you will probably get back different information. When you are close to a topic, it is very easy to let a question slip by that is double-barreled, or leading; therefore, use the following list of rules as a reminder of what constitutes poor question writing.

1. Keep question vocabulary and sentence structure simple.

   There are three levels of vocabulary: (a) core vocabulary (words most people are very familiar with and use in their everyday speech), (b) words that are recognized but not commonly used in common speech, and (c) vocabulary that is not recognizable either because it is jargon that is unfamiliar or because it is so infrequently seen or read that most people do not have a clear understanding of what is meant. Even with a business audience that is probably more educated and fluent in their vocabulary than the population at large, it is better to stick with core vocabulary when writing survey questions. Instead of asking, "Are you cognizant?," ask "Do you know?" Respondents will be able to comprehend faster and more likely to complete the survey.

   In general, it is a good idea to stay away from specialized jargon. Even phrases such as "information technology" or "Total Quality Management" or "ISO 9000" (worse yet, their acronyms: IT, TQM, etc.) that may seem very obvious to you may not be as familiar to others who are not as close to the topic. Customers are described in terms of characteristics rather than demographics; computers have memory and speed rather than RAM, ROM, bytes, and megahertz.

However, if you are surveying a market in which you are relatively certain that all your respondents will be familiar with particular terms that are relevant to the topic of study, using well-known jargon in an appropriate manner is acceptable. In fact, there could be some instances where, if you did not use the obvious jargon, respondents may believe you do not understand the industry and may be less likely to cooperate.

Complex sentence structures with dependent clauses, multiple parts, and potentially confusing antecedents should be avoided. If you need to ask a long question, do your best to break it up into several sentences leading up to the question, rather than stringing it all together into one long paragraph query.

2. Avoid ambiguity. In any survey research, you must be sure that all respondents will clearly understand and interpret the meaning of questions the same way. Therefore, use terms that have a common meaning to everyone, or clarify a term more concretely if there is concern. When the pronoun *"you"* is used, for example, be sure that it is clear from the question whether it means (a) "you," the respondent, (b) "you," the company with which the respondent is affiliated, or (c) *"you,"* the respondent grouped along with his or her co-workers. Words such as generally, often, regularly, and occasionally should be given a common frame of reference for everyone where possible. In other words, specify that *regularly* means that the respondent read at least three out of the last four issues, or that *often* means once a month or more frequently. What one respondent considers often in terms of needing service or repairs for their truck fleet may be much less frequently than someone else who claims to need service often.

Similarly, when you ask for company profits, be sure to specify the time frame (annual) and whether you mean before or after taxes.

3. Avoid double-barreled questions. Every question should have only one reference or one idea. A double-barreled question is one that contains two or more question items. This can cause the respondent to become confused, especially if the answer to each item is different from the other. These types of questions can sneak up on you if you are not careful. Whenever you see a conjunction, such as *and,* in a question, two things

are being joined and probably should be split into two separate questions.

For instance, in the question, "Does your company track sales and profits?" you have asked both about sales and about profits. The company may track one and not the other, making this question difficult to answer the way it is asked. "What is your evaluation of the price and convenience offered by catalog showrooms?" Obviously, this question is asking two things, the respondent's evaluation of price and their opinion about convenience. There is no obvious conjunction in this next double-barreled question, however: "How would you rate the quality of the office equipment you have purchased over the last two years?" This is potentially multiple-barreled since there could have been multiple equipment acquisitions, some of which may have been of high quality in the respondent's opinion and some of which may have been of poor quality.

4. Avoid leading or loaded questions. Leading questions are those that lead the respondent to answer a particular way or choose a particular response more often than other responses. Sometimes this can happen because the question itself suggests one possible response without suggesting all the other alternative responses as in the following example: "What information technology acquisitions, such as computers or telephones, have you made in the last six months?" Here, computers and telephones will be considered first by everyone and probably mentioned most often. Other IT expenditures that are not suggested in the question will be less frequently mentioned, even if they were more frequently purchased, simply because the respondent must think of them on his or her own. And if a respondent confirms that the company has indeed purchased either computers or telephones, the tendency would be to stop and think no further since one to two items have already been mentioned and should suffice for an answer. Another example of a leading question is one that starts with, "Don't you see . . ." rather than, "Do you see . . .," since it has already expressed a bias in the affirmative direction.

Loaded questions include some subtle or not-so-subtle undertones that influence the answer and make it difficult for a respondent to answer honestly. "Do you use insecticides that are environmentally safe?" "Would you say that your company is up-to-date in their manufacturing processes?" How can a respondent say no and feel good about their company?

5. Avoid overgeneralization or overspecificity. Be careful of asking respondents to generalize their behavior or attitudes too much, yet be wary of asking for such a precise answer that the respondent is not able to respond at all. To avoid overgeneralizing, include a limited time period in which the respondent can frame their answer: "Of the last ten business lunches you have eaten outside the office, how many did you eat at fast-food restaurants?" This is better than asking, "What percentage of the time do you go to fast-food restaurants for business lunches?"

Asking "How many times exactly" may prove to be too specific and difficult to answer and if you ask too many questions like this, respondents will simply stop trying and hang up. A precise number such as fifteen or thirty also gives the analyst no idea of the opportunity base. In other words, three out of thirty opportunities is much different than three out of three opportunities. Ask instead, "How often" and offer categories that provide more comfortable, less precise ranges that respondents can easily place their behavior or attitudes in, and that give some kind of reference point.

How often do you use your business discount at XYZ Store?

❑ Always
❑ Frequently (more than half the time)
❑ Sometimes (less than half the time)
❑ Never

Response Formats

In addition to choosing the wording of a question, you must choose the form in which the responses will be measured. Response formats can be open-ended, multichotomous (multiple choice), dichotomous (only two alternatives), or scaled. The format chosen will depend to some degree on the question content and how the question can most suitably be answered, and it will depend on the method of data collection.

Open-ended, unstructured questions in which the respondents can answer any way they please, using their own words and thoughts, are usually reserved for qualitative research or for personal interviewing on a limited basis. They should be eliminated altogether or kept to a minimum in telephone research and the same is true, to a lesser extent, in mail surveys. Open-ended questions take more time to administer and record, and in a telephone survey where time is of consequence, the time spent on an unstructured question can preempt the time spent on other questions, or prompt respondents to terminate the interview. Open-end queries are also the most difficult kinds of questions to quantify, requiring special effort and attention that adds to the time, complexity, and cost of a study. If they are used, they should be used sparingly, be phrased as fill-in-the-blank type of questions whenever possible ("What brand did you buy?" "Name three booths you visited at the XYZ trade show"), or used as quick, pointed probes for elaboration on a prior response ("Why?" "Why not?").

Multiple-choice questions are fixed alternative questions that offer a choice among several response categories. Two rules apply:

1. The response list must be all-inclusive or exhaustive. All possible alternatives should be presented so that a respondent isn't forced into selecting a compromise response that doesn't really reflect his or her disposition. Prior exploratory, qualitative research should have already identified the range of alternatives. If the list is too long or some of the items are too specialized to be itemized, an "Other" category should be available to give the few respondents who need it the option of writing in an answer. Even these should be kept to a minimum if possible since the open-ended nature of the "Other" response will also complicate the coding process.

2. The response categories must be mutually exclusive. In a multiple-choice situation, respondents are instructed to check only one "best" response. Therefore, the response categories should not overlap or coincide with one another, forcing respondents to guess at which one they should check. The most common violation of this is when ranges overlap:

    Please check the category that best represents your firm's annual revenue.

Incorrect:	Correct:
❏ $1–$5 million	❏ Less than $5 million
❏ $5–$25 million	❏ $5–$24.9 million
❏ $25–$50 million	❏ $25–$49.9 million
❏ Above $50 million	❏ $50 million or more

Dichotomous questions are fixed alternative questions with only two response categories from which to choose, as with True/False, Yes/No, More/Less, Male/Female, Do/Don't Own questions. Sometimes a series of dichotomous items are grouped together as a check-off list:

> Please check any of the following business publications that you regularly read (that is, read 3 of every 4 issues)
>
> ❑ *Business Week*
> ❑ *Newsweek*
> ❑ *U.S. News and World Report*
> ❑ *Forbes*

Scaling questions all take the form of a valued continuum, consisting of continuously ordered categories along which respondents can position their attitudes or behaviors. Scales offer a higher level of measurement and more precision than any of the preceding question formats and for this reason, should be used whenever possible. Keep in mind, however, that complicated scales cannot be easily administered over the telephone.

There are some key issues that arise in scale construction that will affect the results you get:

1. How many scale intervals should there be? In practice, you most frequently see scales of four to seven intervals. Ten-point scales are used since people are accustomed to thinking in tens. The more intervals on the scale, the more precisely it will measure. However, a scale that becomes too big or contains an awkward number of intervals (for example, 13 points) is difficult to administer, especially over the telephone. Related to this is the issue of whether you should have an odd or even number of scale intervals. The real question is whether or not you should give the respondent the choice of a neutral point, as with an odd-number scale, or force them into a positive or negative position, as with an even scale. Depending on the situation, one alternative may bias the outcome more than the other.

2. How should you anchor the scale? Do you use words, numbers, pictures, or some combination of these to portray the scale? Do you simply anchor each end of the scale, or do you anchor every interval along the scale? Graphic depictions will

help if language can present a problem for some special audiences. If words are used, select them carefully so as not to ruin your scale with ambiguity and subjectivity. Numbers offer the most precision and least ambiguity.

3. Should you use a comparative or a noncomparative scale? A comparative scale is one that asks the respondent's attitude for one brand relative to another brand, as when you ask them to rank order their preference. A noncomparative scale treats attitudes toward the competitive brands as independent. The decision of which scale to use depends on what you are trying to accomplish with the research.

4. Should the scale be direct or summated? When only a single item is used to measure an attitude, it is direct. When several items work together to measure the overall attitude, as when you have a scale to assess multiple aspects, this would be considered a summated scale. One special consideration for a summated scale is that if several individual scale items are used, there should be a balance between the ones that are worded positively versus the ones that are worded negatively. You might also consider changing the direction of the poles so that the positive adjective isn't always anchoring the same end.

5. Have you created a ceiling effect? A ceiling effect occurs when the categories in a scale do not differentiate among respondents because they all mark the same position. Usually this occurs because a category is too broad or because the scale isn't sensitive enough in one end or the other. Since the notion behind scaling is to differentiate among respondents, a ceiling effect undermines the value of a scale.

Too many different scale types exist to enumerate here. A few of the most common are described to give you a feel for the variety in which they come.

A rank-order scale is an ordinal comparative scale. Respondents are forced to decide which they prefer among alternative items. The number of items to rank should be kept to a minimum to keep the task manageable. Ranking is difficult over the phone with any number of items; for example,

Please rank the following three brands in terms of your likelihood of purchasing each. Write a 1 next to the brand you would be most likely to purchase, a 2 by your second choice, and so forth.

    Brand A ____
    Brand B ____
    Brand C ____

A bipolar adjective scale is one anchored by adjectives at each end of a continuum. Often several scale items are used together in a series. Scales can be odd or even, intervals along the scale can be anchored with boxes, numbers, or even words. It is important that the poles (ends) be anchored by adjectives that are clearly opposite in meaning so as not to bias the scale in a favorable or negative way. Three variations on this are shown in Exhibit 7.6.

A Likert scale is one that asks for respondents' agreement or disagreement on a series of statements. Statements should be evenly balanced in terms of those that are favorable and unfavorable. Usually Likert scales are saved for measurement of attitudes that cannot be easily transformed into adjective scales. An example of a Likert statement is shown.

The XYZ Corporation serves its customers well.

___Strongly Agree__ Agree__Neutral__Disagree__Strongly

A constant sum asks the respondent to divide a fixed percentage or number into component parts to show the relative influence or size of each; for example:

What percentage of your business is:

    Wholesale   _____ %
    Retail   _____ %
    Manufacturing _____ %
    Other   _____ %
                  100%

The two things to remember about selecting question response formats is (1) it is best to provide higher level measurement (for example, scales) wherever possible to aid in the analysis that can be done later, and (2) variety is more interesting and involving than using one type of response format throughout the questionnaire.

Exhibit 7.6: Bipolar Scale: Three Variations

Using the 5-point scale shown, please rate XYZ publication on the criteria shown by circling the number that most closely represents your opinion.

XYZ Company

Relevant	1	2	3	4	5	Irrelevant
Technical	1	2	3	4	5	Nontechnical
Informative	1	2	3	4	5	Not informative
A good value	1	2	3	4	5	Not a good value

Listed below are several issues other companies have identified as important to their operations. Please indicate the extent to which each is a problem for your company.

	Extremely Important				Not at all Important
a. Cutting costs	1	2	3	4	5
b. Finding labor	1	2	3	4	5
c. Expanding globally	1	2	3	4	5
d. Increasing service	1	2	3	4	5

As a new customer, please indicate your opinion of XYZ product on each of the following . . .

	Better Than Expected		About What Expected		Worse Than Expected
a. Quietness	1	2	3	4	5
b. Quality	1	2	3	4	5
c. Ease of use	1	2	3	4	5
d. Reliability	1	2	3	4	5

Sequencing Questions

It is a good idea to think of the questionnaire as having three major parts: an initiation to the topic, a body, and a conclusion. The introduction and the first few questions set the stage for what is to come and suggest the kinds of questions or tasks that will be sought during the remainder of the survey. Therefore, you want to involve everyone very early with questions that are easy and quick to answer and have questions that are applicable to all respondents. Usually you ask more general questions up front because they ease a respondent into the study topic. Questions then become progressively narrower and more specific in scope. This is often referred to as a funnel approach. It works in journalism and it works in survey instrumentation.

The body of the questionnaire contains the bulk of the questions and the main substance and detail of the survey. As you move into the body of the questionnaire, you must be careful to organize questions in a logical, conversational manner, continuing to move from the more general to the more detailed questions. By doing this, you will obtain more thorough and accurate information because the sequencing has gradually led the respondent deeper and deeper into the topic and it becomes easier for him or her to dredge out the detail that is desired.

Typically, questions within the questionnaire body are organized or grouped into several smaller sequences. If several topics are being covered, questions for each can be grouped together with transitional verbiage between the topics. For ease of administration, usually question items that are similarly scaled are put together, so that instructions need not be repeated over and over again for isolated items here and there. For instance, if you have a series of Likert agree/disagree statements, present them all at one time before moving on to the next response type. As questions begin to get more detailed and specific, some are apt not to apply to all respondents. Branching questions can then be used to divert respondents to the appropriate follow-up questions or to skip them through the questionnaire to the next topic. In this way, if a respondent responds that he or she does not eat lunch outside the office, the interviewer does not continue to ask questions about how often, where, and with whom they eat out. The caution here, though, is to keep the amount of branching to a minimum. Too much skipping around can confuse respondents or interviewers, and the data quality will suffer as a result.

The questionnaire conclusion is the last page or so of items that close the interview. By this time, the main substance of the study should already have been addressed. What remains are usually the biographical or demographic-type questions that are used to classify respondents and their companies. These are saved for last because they are the least interesting type of questions and the fastest to complete. Questions that are more risky/sensitive/confidential in nature are typically saved until the end as well. By the time the end of the survey approaches, respondents may be less skeptical and more cooperative; hence, this kind of information may be easier to get. Questions about budgets or policies that are confidential in nature are often found toward the conclusion of a survey in the hopes that the earlier part of the interview or survey had established some rapport, trust, respect, or at least familiarity with the topic that eases the respondent through these questions more smoothly.

While the market researcher has the ability to sequence the questions in a logical and appropriate manner, the communication method will determine exactly how much control over the sequencing there actually is. With a telephone interview, there is very good control. Respondents hear the questions they are asked in the order the questions are read to them by the interviewer. This becomes an important issue when later questions could influence earlier questions.

For instance, if you want to know top-of-mind awareness or other attitudinal information on your brands and the competitions', this should come before any specific questions on your brand alone. Should a respondent be cued to either the purpose of the study or the identity of the sponsoring organization, their subsequent response may be strongly biased or influenced. In telephone research, respondents have no way of knowing what questions and what specific brand probes lie ahead in the interview and cannot speculate or be influenced. This is why telephone recall methods are popular.

With a mail survey, respondents often will read through the entire questionnaire before sitting down to complete the survey with pen or pencil. Therefore, later questions can easily influence the answers given in the beginning questions in a way not possible with the telephone. For this reason, unaided awareness questions cannot be used in the mail survey if brands are listed elsewhere in the questionnaire. And in order to get candid responses on any one brand, other brands are usually included throughout the questionnaire as well in order to disguise who the real sponsor of the study is.

In summary, when you are sequencing questions:

- Use a funnel approach
- Create questionnaire sections
- Use logical sequence within sections and overall
- Use branching conservatively

Physical Characteristics of the Questionnaire

The physical appearance of the survey instrument will greatly depend on the method used to administer the survey. Since a telephone questionnaire or a personal questionnaire is never put in the hands of the respondent, it does not need to be written and designed with the same attention to cosmetic details that would be required with a self-administered questionnaire. The appearance of a mail survey, on the other hand, is critical to the completion rate. A mail questionnaire that looks unprofessional, cluttered, or difficult will not likely motivate people to respond. This is even truer in business-to-business research than with consumer research.

There are differences in what is considered appropriate for a telephone instrument compared to a mail instrument. A telephone questionnaire should be neat and easy for an interviewer to understand and to follow, but it does not need to be typeset or spaced in an especially visually appealing manner. There does need to be some means for an interviewer to record a response (lines, boxes, numbers to circle) and enough room to write down verbatim responses on open-ended questions, but again, how visually appealing these features are is not an issue. In fact, responses on a telephone questionnaire should be precoded with numbers and column field positions (data entry information) wherever possible for faster, easier coding and processing later on.

Any instructions for the interviewer are usually shown stylistically in a manner different from the questions and words that are to be read aloud during the interview. Traditionally, this has meant that interviewer instructions were printed in ALL CAPS, while actual questions were printed in uppercase and lowercase formats as in a book. However, as long as the style is consistent throughout the survey so that the interviewer knows which is meant to be read aloud or which is meant for their silent use only, instructions can be designated in a number of ways—boldfaced, bracketed, printed in a different color or typeface, and so on. Interviewer instructions should be very clear in meaning so that questions are administered consistently. Although interviewers should always be carefully trained on the questionnaire— its questions, appropriate probes, branching, and so on—it is always a good idea to include important instructions on the questionnaire as a reminder.

A mail questionnaire needs to look neat, spacious, professional, and even fun. White space should be used liberally, and the typeface should be large and easy to read whenever possible to create the illusion that the questionnaire is short and simple. Even the response mechanisms that are used will make a difference in the perceived difficulty with the questionnaire—boxes look and work much better than lines to write on or numbers to circle. Plenty of lines, spaced liberally, need to be allotted to open-ended questions to allow the respondent the room to write freely and amply; if lines are too cramped or too short, very few respondents will bother to write anything at all.

One common mistake in mail questionnaires is to put coding information on it, such as numbering every response and including information on how the data should be keyed and processed later. This makes the questionnaire seem colder and more impersonal, as well as potentially adding to a more cluttered and less professional appearance. The phrases "for office use only" or "do not write here" should never be seen on a mail questionnaire as they are potentially insulting to respondents.

Some argue that typesetting the questionnaire improves its appearance and will increase response. Experience has shown, however, that as long as the questionnaire is neat and professional, typesetting is not mandatory as it does not add as much of an edge as believed. Typesetting can have the effect of making a questionnaire appear cold and impersonal. There is something to be said for a survey that is not as slick looking; it sometimes has the effect of creating a more personal aura that encourages participation, since there is the illusion that each respondent is more important to the overall success of the study.

In many surveys, there are conditional questions that need only be asked if a previous question was answered a certain way. In a telephone interview, as long as the branching is clearly noted in instructions for the interviewer, this sequencing of questions is acceptable. In a mail survey, such branching should be discouraged as much as possible because it is too easy for respondents to get confused and to execute the branching incorrectly.

Questionnaire length is not an issue for a telephone survey except as it relates to the time on the telephone. As mentioned earlier, telephone interviews should be limited to five to ten minutes whenever possible. If questions are written in a structured format and sequenced well, the large number of questions or pages that can be completed in this time period will sometimes surprise you. With mail, shorter questionnaires generally work better than longer ones, but questionnaire length by itself is not necessarily a problem. It is possible to mail an eight- to ten-page questionnaires and still get more than a 30 percent response. Again, the trick is to make the questionnaire look easy to complete. A questionnaire in the form of a stapled booklet looks easier and more fun to complete than several pages, printed front and back and stapled at the top. Questionnaires longer than eight to ten pages begin to appear and feel unwieldy, and the completion rate begins to drop off. However, even a one-page questionnaire will be discarded if the questions are poorly written, unorganized, and hard to read.

Pretesting the Questionnaire

The test of the questionnaire should always be how well it obtains the desired information. Certainly careful consideration of question wording is necessary from the beginning, but ultimately the questions need to be administered to people to test for their clarity and effectiveness. You will often find that questions that may work well in a self-administered form, do not work over the telephone, and vice versa. Even questionnaires prepared by the most experienced researchers should be pretested. In fact, an indication of the experience of the researcher is the strength of his or her insistence on a pretest. It is just good research practice.

Fielding a Survey Research Project

The two major kinds of survey research—by phone and by mail—share many similarities, but they also have different requirements, which are discussed below.

Telephone Research

When you embark on a telephone survey research project, you should probably consider getting several bids from alternative field service agencies to perform the actual fieldwork. Not every field service agency has the capability to handle telephone interviewing on a large scale. Other facilities can be quite sophisticated, complete with CATI capabilities in place. Telephone interviewing facilities are available throughout the country and can always be found in larger cities. The geographic location of the facility is really only important to the researcher that may wish to monitor the fieldwork personally. There are several other considerations that *are* important in selecting a facility for business-to-business research.

Given the choice, all telephone interviewing should be conducted from a central and supervised location. Decentralized telephone interviewing, where interviewers call from their own homes or multiple locations, may look attractive in terms of cost, but the quality and consistency of the research will suffer. Fielding all calls from a central site allows a trained supervisor to oversee the calls and call sheets, monitor any quotas that need to be filled, and immediately make adjustments or modifications to questions or procedures if problems occur. Follow-up calls are easier to make when they are part of a coordinated effort. This kind of supervision is critical to the quality of data and the response rate, and is usually packaged in the services and costs of the field facility.

The experience and character of the interviewers are especially important in business-to-business telephone interviewing, as discussed previously. Most telephone interviewing facilities have extensive experience with consumers and will have interviewers with that background. However, these same interviewers may not do as well with business subjects. A business interviewer must be able to establish rapport and communicate in the language of the respondent. It is probably not sufficient to take experienced consumer interviewers that normally work at night and over weekends and have them make business calls during the day; interviewers with real business-to-business experience are more desirable.

Conventional wisdom says that the interviewer needs to be as like the respondents as possible. This suggests that a predominately male sample would respond better to a male interviewer, and a predominately female sample would respond better to a female interviewer. A male interviewer, for instance, would probably be more effective interviewing welders, and a female interviewer would have more success interviewing nursing supervisors (given today's gender compositions). A female voice, however, is more universally accepted across both genders and is more likely to elicit cooperation among the widest base of people. The widespread use of the female voice on automated telephone systems is evidence of this. Speaking from personal experience, however, the skill and background of the interviewer far outweigh the gender issue.

When getting bids from alternative telephone field agencies, you should be aware that there are important differences between a research-oriented telephone interviewing facility and a telemarketing facility. Professional interviewers are trained to obtain cooperation and information from their respondents. Telemarketers are trained to solicit sales. Telemarketers are much less likely to appreciate the subtle nuances of the interview, and if you attempt to use them for this purpose, you'll be putting the quality of the interview in jeopardy. Telemarketing centers may be used for reminder or supplementary calling, but not for market research.

When you approach a field service agency, you will no doubt be asked two questions: How long is the questionnaire? and How difficult is it to reach the respondents? Most telephone interviewing centers calculate their costs in terms of the number of interviewer hours necessary to complete the required sample size. The number of calls that need to made in order to reach the appropriate respondents, as well as the length of time the interview takes, are both important in estimating the number of interviews that can be completed per hour. Business samples often require multiple calls to identify and reach the appropriate individuals, and this will affect the cost estimate you are given.

Telephone interviewing facilities are most likely to bid on a per-completion basis. Therefore, the higher cost per completion for business-to-business samples, along with the need for experienced interviewers, will probably make business-to-business telephone interviewing costs somewhat higher than consumer interviewing costs. Today a typical fifteen-minute telephone interview with an adult consumer sample would cost about $50 per completion. Per-completion costs for business samples would be more, probably more than $100 per completion.

Mail Survey Research

As with telephone interviewing facilities, there are mail market research organizations that can handle all of the tasks necessary to field a mail survey. These companies are a little harder to find than telephone facilities because there are not as many. A marketing directory, such as the American Marketing Association's *Membership Directory*, is a good source of companies. References from others that have done mail survey research is another recommended way to find a good supplier.

The tasks involved in fielding a mail survey are relatively straightforward but numerous.

1. The stationery and envelope stock need to be ordered and printed.
2. Business reply envelopes need to be printed.
3. The questionnaire needs to be printed, collated, and stapled.
4. Incentives need to ordered (banks sometimes need time to acquire enough new dollar bills to accommodate large survey projects) and attached to the survey.
5. Cover letters need to be individually laser-printed if they are to be personalized.

6. The mailing needs to be assembled in the proper order—including any necessary folding.
7. The outside envelopes need to have respondent names and addresses printed on them or laser-printed labels attached.
8. The inside contents need to be matched to the name on the outside envelope.
9. Identification numbers need to printed on materials, if respondent tracking is to be done.
10. The postage needs to be applied.
11. The surveys need to be sorted and mailed.

Many businesses believe that because they have the in-house capability to typeset, print, and mail, that it will be more cost-efficient to prepare the mailing themselves. This is probably unrealistic. Almost always there is a timetable attached to completing the study and rarely is a business prepared to handle expediently the volume of tasks a large mail survey requires. It is often far better to pay a service to coordinate all these details for you.

If you were to get bids from several mail houses, you will probably not find as much difference in the cost estimates as you would in a telephone project. Questions of interviewer experience and training are not relevant. Costs are usually bid on a total project basis given the size of the mailing, incentives, and particular details needed in the assembly of the piece. While scheduling can always be an issue with any field service operation, mail houses are extremely busy during certain times of the year, such as the fourth quarter, and you should be careful not to assume that a sizable mailing will assemble and mail itself overnight. Finally, quality control is just as important with mail research as it is with interviewing.

Survey Analysis and Reports

Any number of marketing research texts detail the statistics involved in research analysis: how to calculate sampling error and how to perform statistical tests such as t-test, chi-square tests, analysis of variance, regression, and so forth. This has not been the focus of this book. Issues of measurement have been discussed as they relate to sample size and type of research design, and Chapter 5 provided a refresher on descriptive statistics such as means and standard deviations that are useful in summarizing survey data. In addition, Chapter 5 briefly reviewed the various analyses that are often applied in segmentation research, which, of course, is very relevant for the analysis of survey research since surveys often provide the backbone for most databases.

Analysis of survey research is usually confined to simple descriptive procedures that report the means and percentages for question responses as well as simple cross-tabulations of data along key demographic groups, such as revenue or industry type. Rarely would more than two variables be analyzed in relation to one another. In many cases, for the research purposes, this is all that is really necessary to glean the appropriate information out of the data. The key to analysis is to make sure that the research objectives have been met.

Unfortunately, the analytical strategy for many is to run virtually every variable by every other variable so that if there is ever a question in the future, it could perhaps be answered. This strategy tends to make research reports thick and heavy, difficult to read, and for the most part meaningless. Without relating the numerous tables and tabulations to the objectives of the study, most of this will go unread.

While cross-tabulation has its place in analysis, most studies deserve more. The analysis should be guided by the statement of problems and objectives, and the analytical technique should be selected that best fits together the measured variables with those objectives in order to answer the research questions. This may mean that a simple cross-tabulation of two variables will do. In other instances, a more sophisticated analysis looking at various combinations of multiple variables may be more appropriate. This is what segmentation is about and is the subject of the next chapter.

The best approach to analysis is an iterative one. Those responsible for formulating and implementing the marketing strategy should see the results of the study in a simple, descriptive, and comprehensive manner. By reviewing this, invariably more questions arise that can be answered by additional statistical analysis. The final report will be much stronger and have greater utility if this kind of involvement and interaction can occur between the analyst and those who are using the research to make decisions and learn about their customers.

8 Qualitative Research Methods

Qualitative research plays an important role in marketing and business-to-business research. Many of the techniques that fall under the umbrella of qualitative research are borrowed from psychology and psychoanalysis and, when applied and adapted to marketing problems, have in the past been labeled *motivation research*. The reason for this label is that the goal of in-depth qualitative research has always been, and still is, to probe for and understand the nature of the attitudes and motivations that people have and how these feelings influence behavior. The key is getting close enough to people to learn what motivates them. You need to go beyond asking the same standard questions of everyone and allow people to express themselves in their own way in much more detail.

In-depth methods are based on the fundamental premise that if you provide respondents with an ambiguous cue or open-ended question, they will respond in a way that reflects their true personalities, inner feelings, sentiments, motivations, or other psychological characteristics. The goal of the in-depth interview, then, is to provide a sequence of verbal cues or questions that respondents can project themselves into.

In-Depth Methods: Key Characteristics

In-depth methods include focus groups (or group interviewing), and one-on-one interviews (interviewing individuals rather than people collectively in groups). In both instances, the information collected consists primarily of verbal answers to questions or conversations among people. Of course, words are only one means of expression.

Posture, facial expressions, and tone of voice—these are all keys to understanding what is being said, along with the words.

No two in-depth interviews will ever be the same, and the information cannot be easily quantified. The analysis of in-depth interviews to a great degree relies on the subjective judgment, interpretation, and insights of the research analyst. It is the open-ended and flexible nature of in-depth research that is at once its biggest strength and its primary weakness.

Flexibility is a major advantage of in-depth qualitative research because interviewers do not adhere to rigid schedules or question formats. They typically work from a discussion guide, which is more or less a list of topics to be addressed. The order in which the topics are discussed, the amount of time spent discussing each, and the exact way in which a topic is introduced can vary considerably from interview to interview.

A good interviewer will listen carefully to what is being said (or not said) and react accordingly, sometimes probing either directly or indirectly for more information, sometimes framing new questions as new information or ideas arise, often making corrections in the course of the discussion as necessary to yield the most useful insights from the interview. This unstructured format allows respondents to participate with the same degree of latitude and flexibility. Therefore, qualitative research will always yield more richly detailed information than quantitative research.

Because the interviewer has such close personal contact with respondents, he or she is able to take advantage of "show and tell" by showing or demonstrating things and soliciting reactions from respondents. This allows a wide variety of techniques to be used in conjunction with in-depth interviewing that are not available with other more structured and less personal research methods. For instance, you can demonstrate or have participants actually participate in using a new product prototype. Or you can pass around or show print brochures or advertisements for participants to read and evaluate. You can even use small-group quantitative techniques, such as conjoint analysis or perceptual mapping (described in more detail in Chapters 10 and 11), in the course of an interview.

Another advantage is that there is not only close interaction between the interviewer and interviewees, there is more involvement and interaction on the part of those interested in the research results. In most cases, those interested in the results can view interviews through one-way mirrors, watch videotapes, or listen to audiotapes of the discussions. You can see with your own eyes and hear with your own ears what is going on. In the research report, actual quotations excerpted from the interviews can reinforce the findings or insights and make them come alive in a way that statistical and numerical tables cannot. This personalization of the information is sometimes the best way to convince either management or a sales force that what you say is true.

Despite the obvious pluses that in-depth research provides, there are two major weaknesses. First, as already mentioned, the information is subjective in nature and open for bias. Responses are difficult, if not impossible, to quantify. Questions are rarely asked in the same way. The interviewer can easily influence the responses, and the findings themselves are open to more than one interpretation in some cases.

A second, and potentially more critical, weakness of qualitative methods is that they are not projectable. In-depth qualitative research is suggestive rather than definitive. You should always keep in mind that the numbers of people interviewed, either individually or within groups, are typically quite small. While these small numbers can mean that studies can be conducted for less money and in less time (two more clear advantages to this type of research), they also mean that the results should be applied with great care because they have considerable potential for misuse.

Qualitative research is not quantitative, and if numerical summaries or percentages are reported, they are probably biased and not meaningful. Since samples are small and not scientifically (randomly) selected to be representative, the findings may or may not represent the larger market and should not be generalized. If the goal is to describe and project the attitudes or behaviors of a larger population group, qualitative research should be used in a supplemental role to other quantitative research and should never be allowed to serve as the sole basis for the statement "our research shows."

How Qualitative Research Can Be Used

With the previous caveats in mind, there are research situations where qualitative methods are the most appropriate to use. Qualitative research can be the only research tool when the nature or content of the response is not entirely predictable. Some typical business-to-business situations include generating ideas, understanding the buyer by learning more in-depth motivational information, evaluating marketing or communications strategies and tactics, expanding on quantitative research, and developing quantitative instruments and protocols. Each of these five situations is described in turn next.

Generating Ideas

In-depth interviews or focus groups are commonly the source of new ideas, suggestions, and problems that you may not have considered before. In the course of a group of potential or current users discussing a product with one another, for instance, they may begin to list what it is they do not like or what the product doesn't do that they wish it did, followed by a wish list of suggestions for improving the product or service. This kind of discussion can provide the input for product refinements or even new product ideas that can be further developed and tested.

Some companies will purposely schedule groups on a regular basis with the goal of picking their customers' brains and generating fresh ideas. However, you should be warned that many customers are not very creative at conceiving of new product ideas, especially products that meet needs or solve problems they may not have thought much about or even realized they had.

Ideas and suggestions for marketing and communications strategies—including packaging ideas—can also arise from in-depth interviewing. It is true that everyone thinks they are an advertising expert. When you put a group of customers together and show them examples of creative executions, they will critique them with a vengeance. Ask them how they would improve a piece, and they usually have answers. And sometimes through this kind of creative brainstorming session, they will generate some workable ideas. Sessions such as this are often used, for example, to generate product brand names.

The fact is that after working with and selling a product or service one particular way for a long time, you can sometimes become less objective about, or even insensitive to, new ideas and ways of doing things. You simply are too close to a situation to be fresh and creative. Talking to customers or prospects, putting new minds to work on the problem at hand, can often help get you out of the trap of traditional thinking. In one session with a group of small business customers, a participant suggested that he would be more likely to pay attention to and read information that was sent to him on computer diskette rather than as direct mail print material. This proved to be a communication idea that one business-to-business marketer ended up testing further and using.

Understanding the Buyer

All business-to-business marketers would probably say that they understand their customers, yet most would no doubt say they could know more. In-depth methods are especially valuable for learning more about your customers. Even with all the syndicated data available and past research that may have been conducted, unless you periodically educate yourself by listening to customers firsthand, you can become distant or detached from them. Even salespeople, who are frequently in contact with customers and who believe they know everything there is to know about their customers, often come to realize that they have been so busy selling that they are surprised to hear what customers are really thinking and talking about. In-depth group discussions can serve to revive and/or revise your perceptions about the marketplace.

Understanding the buyer and the buying process is especially challenging in the business-to-business situation. In many businesses, your prospective client may be subject to multiple organizational influences and roles, which can make understanding your buyer a complicated task. Simply identifying who the buyer is in many organizations can be a difficult task. Examining an organizational chart will reveal the formal chain of command among personnel, but this will usually not reveal the critically important *informal* linkages that might influence a purchase decision. Focus group interviews are a very powerful tool in revealing organizational customs, along with the treatment and importance of a particular product category to that organization. Critical issues facing the buyer group, those things occupying its time and energy, usually surface in a focus group interview as well. It is a good idea to conduct periodic in-depth research with buyer groups for no other reason than to understand their current problems and concerns.

Often qualitative research will help to generate or refine hypotheses about customers or prospects, which can be confirmed and validated with quantitative research. For example, you may believe that the price competition within your customers' industry is driving them to become more price-oriented themselves, leaving you to wonder if you need to consider new pricing strategies to this market. By conducting some in-depth research, you may learn that you were correct in your premise that the industry has become price driven to a great degree, but you may also learn that this price sensitivity has not as yet transferred over to your particular service or product. This, of course, could and should be validated with quantitative research on a more projectable basis, but the in-depth research allowed you to explore your hunches and modify the way you might ask the questions on a survey.

Evaluating Marketing Concepts, Strategies, and Tactics

Perhaps the most common application of in-depth techniques is to refine and evaluate product or marketing concepts, strategies, and tactical executions.

Almost all new marketing ideas—new product ideas or positioning, ideas for product or packaging alterations, new distribution strategies, or alternative creative ideas—can be described as *concepts* early on in the development process, even before the specifics and finishing details have been produced. The notion behind a *concept test* is to assess the general reaction to the idea in order to direct creative efforts or to refine the concept further, reducing the risk that it may eventually fall short of expectations. If a concept is still in rough, unfinished form, quantitative research is not really warranted, but in-depth research, which offers clues about customers' objections, can be very useful. You should always evaluate a concept among potential customers before fully committing resources to it.

While the initial reaction may be revealing, more important are the reasons behind a customer's particular reaction. If they like the idea, *why* do they like it? If they hate the idea, *why* do they hate it and what could be done to change their mind?

It is these insights that are important, not the head count of how many are positive or negative on an idea. Remember, in-depth methods will not provide projectable numbers; but they will usually uncover potential problems and barriers to acceptance, if they exist, that might be avoided through concept modification.

As an example, let's say you have a new product concept for a desktop organizer that would combine the functions of several types of currently marketed organizers into one. Through in-depth research with various office personnel, you find that several people comment on how awkward one particular aspect of the organizer is compared to what they are using now. One person really likes the efficiency of the organizer but bemoans the fact that she wouldn't be able to use it because her company has a clear desk policy—nothing can be left unlocked on top of desks at night due to security precautions. From this, you go back and redesign the one misplaced element for easier use and at the same time readjust the proportions of the organizer so that it can fit into a standard desk drawer. Further in-depth research confirms that these alterations improve the response—nearly everyone interviewed prefers it over what they currently have.

While the positive response in this example is reassuring and most likely has improved your chances of success with the product, you should still be wary of overestimating the acceptance based on these initial product tests. Keep in mind that, as with many research methods, there is the likelihood of generating a false positive reaction within an individual or group interview situation. If a respondent is willing to grant an interview, then he or she probably is motivated at least partially by a desire to help the interviewer. This well-intended desire to help sometimes drives the respondent to give an answer that he or she believes the interviewer either wants or needs to hear. Because it is also much easier in normal social intercourse to say "Yes" or react positively, potential buyers, when asked if they would purchase a hypothetical product, will often indicate yes.

As concepts are refined, further qualitative research is usually warranted to evaluate the final tactical executions. In-depth methods are often used to evaluate communications tactics, such as printed advertising materials or brochures, television commercials, and the like. These executions can be shown and discussed in order to gauge whether or not they are actually meeting communications goals, such as communicating key points clearly without confusion or misunderstanding or conveying a particular mood or product positioning. It is surprising how easy it is to be so close to a creative tactic that you lose perspective and objectivity. This is especially true when working with humor or anything that might be considered attention-getting or out of the ordinary. For instance, you may believe that your customers will think your attempts at humor are humanizing and memorable, but in actuality, the joke might be entirely lost on many. Instead, the main takeaway may be that your message was irrelevant.

Sometimes, it is a matter of one word or phrase, or even a particular visual element in a piece, that can unintentionally create a negative, even hostile, reaction by communicating something different than what you intended. Presenting the execution to a group of customers can check for any potential miscomprehensions and associated marketing problems that might result if the tactic were implemented. This diagnostic capability is usually well worth the extra time and effort. Qualitative methods provide good disaster insurance.

Developing Quantitative Instruments and Protocols

Qualitative research is always a good idea when fine-tuning quantitative research procedures and designing questions and their wording for a survey questionnaire. In this situation, qualitative research is used for pretesting the protocols and instruments.

In-depth qualitative research gives you the chance to try out a research procedure to see if it will be understood and logistically possible. If you are planning an observational study to monitor warehouse or in-store operations, for example, it would be wise to interview some personnel to be sure that when and where you intend to observe is appropriate, is representative, and will not interfere with the operations you are trying to evaluate. If you intend for a survey to be administered by the sales force during customer calls, how will the sales personnel react to the length and content of the survey? Will they be embarrassed to ask for customer cooperation and, therefore, only solicit cooperation from certain types of clients? Will they feel that the survey brings meetings to an end on an awkward note and, as a result, refuse to assist in the research at all?

In-depth research helps in a variety of ways in developing quantitative questions for a survey. Interviews conducted over the telephone must be very succinct and standardized; questions that are confusing or complicated to the respondent will result in refusals or hang-ups. With a mail survey, you have no ability to clarify any misunderstanding; hence, any problems need to be worked out before the survey is mailed out. If not, the response rate could deteriorate or those questionnaires that are completed could be of little use.

There are several specific uses of qualitative research in survey research:

1. Qualitative research can ensure the use of appropriate language in a questionnaire by familiarizing you with the way in which customers talk about products or topics of concern, and by eliminating jargon.

   It is easy to forget that customers do not always talk the same language or know the technical jargon that you use. While some business-to-business audiences may be more familiar with basic marketing vocabulary than a consumer audience might be, they cannot be expected to understand terminology used to describe products or strategies or markets that has grown up within your company. Furthermore, not everyone is up-to-date on the latest expressions in the industry. Even what seems to be very basic, standard industry vocabulary can be misunderstood or unfamiliar to the most sophisticated product users. The technology industry, for instance, is constantly grappling with the problem of finding a simple, understandable way to describe certain types of technology. Computer classifications, such as mainframe and LAN, or common applications, such as spreadsheets and "online" services, are not universally understood and survey respondents may misclassify the equipment and software installed in their company unknowingly. "Total Quality Management," "business process re-engineering," and "just-in-time delivery" are concepts used frequently in the business press today, but these, too, will mystify many businesspeople.

2. Qualitative research can generate descriptive statements of attitudes or behaviors that can be used in attitudinal segmentation studies.

Often in survey research, the goal is to quantify certain attitudes or behaviors and perhaps use this information to classify respondents into different segments. Only through in-depth discussions with your survey audience will you learn the true scope of all the various attitudes or behaviors that exist. And only through in-depth research will you learn how to express those attitudes and behaviors in a way the audience can understand and relate to. If you are a business-to-business marketer that sells through direct mail or catalogs, knowing the needs, attitudes, and barriers associated with catalog buying, especially within your product category, is potentially important to understanding various customer and prospect segments. In-depth research will aid in developing these kinds of question items for quantification.

3. Qualitative research can generate a comprehensive list of response categories or confirm that a multiple-choice question provides an exhaustive list of alternatives to respondents.

While open-ended questions, those that ask a question without any corresponding response alternatives, are intuitively desirable, they more often than not result in less-than-desirable responses in survey research. Many respondents will not have the time—or will not take the time—to think about and answer a question in words and sentences; they would prefer to simply check a box or circle a number. Those that accept the invitation to write in their thoughts, often end up venting on, or veering off to, an unrelated topic without fully answering the question. Therefore, it is preferable to convert such questions to close-ended formats wherever possible. To do this, however, means you must know what the response alternatives should be. Any viable category that is inadvertently left out can bias survey results.

4. Qualitative research can prevent response ceiling effects by finding the most representative range of response categories. When you ask a survey respondent to indicate the level or number of something by checking one of multiple categories, you must be sure that the range of categories you provide is representative of and differentiates among those in your audience. Company revenue is a good example. If everyone surveyed checked the highest income category due to the fact that the revenue range you provided was too low, then this study variable has created a "ceiling" effect and has not differentiated among anyone's revenue base. If you are trying to learn frequency of use and the lowest category in the question starts the scale with "monthly," you will lose the fact that there is a segment of customers who buy the product or use the service once or twice weekly.

5. Qualitative research can pretest understanding of long or complex questions and scaling techniques, as well as branching patterns.

Do respondents understand the directions for a question, and will they complete it correctly? If not, you have lost the opportunity to gain valuable information. Some scales can be a bit tricky for some audiences if the scales have an awkward number of scale points, or if you are asking for percentages that add to 100 percent. Questions that have multiple parts or that require different successive questions for those who answer yes versus those who answer no can be confusing if not explained properly. Sometimes, whether or not the response categories are shown across the row or down the column can greatly impact a respondent's ability to understand and answer even a simple question.

Expanding on Quantitative Research

Qualitative methods also can be used to help provide insight into quantitative research results. Sometimes the findings of quantitative analysis seem contradictory. Further qualitative research can shed some light in this situation and perhaps resolve the apparent conflict or provide the necessary insight to understand the numerical evidence. Quantitative research will sometimes reveal a trend or finding among customers that is completely unexpected and hard to explain. Presenting this finding to a sample of your customers and asking them to explain what they believe this means or what factors are contributing to the trend is an easy solution that may, in fact, bring new insights that would have been overlooked from the use of the quantitative research alone.

Focus Group Interviews Versus One-on-One Interviews

In one-on-one interviews, or in-depth interviews, an interviewer directs questions to an individual respondent and probes for in-depth answers and explanations. Ideally, highly trained interviewers with expertise in psychological probing techniques will conduct the interviewing. The experience and training of the interviewer is of great importance because the one-on-one setting affords that interviewer a great deal of control and influence over each individual interviewed and without the proper skills, the potential for interviewer bias is high.

The fundamental idea behind a focus group or group interview is to use the dynamics of small group interaction to your advantage by allowing group participants to stimulate in-depth discussion on a topic. The interviewer in this case becomes a discussion moderator who has the responsibility of focusing and guiding the discussion on the topics of interest, rather than interrogating or "interviewing" participants. Good moderators are equally important; however, the skills are different since the group dynamics to a great degree substitute for the interviewing expertise of the moderator.

There are those researchers who believe that any in-depth interviewing should be handled as one-on-one interviews, while another contingent of researchers strongly encourages the use of group interviews instead. There is probably a place for both and, in many cases, either method would probably work given the tasks at hand. A discussion of the benefits and concerns with each method is probably warranted before we look at each in more detail.

One-on-one enthusiasts point out that interviewing individuals provides more detailed information on each individual than a group situation could provide. When highly involved or complex, step-by-step behavioral patterns are needed, one-on-one interviews are definitely of more benefit. In some cases, more stimulus materials can also be presented and discussed one-on-one than with a larger group, allowing greater flexibility and input. There is also more flexibility with respect to changing protocols, adding or subtracting questions, or redirecting the sequence of topics based on the experience in early interviews. The first focus group is always a learning experience for a moderator and, if a guide has been poorly designed, can be less productive than subsequent group sessions. In the equivalent number of individual interviews, adjustments could have been made several times if necessary to perfect the interviewing style and make more interviews productive.

All answers and ideas produced in a one-on-one interview are generated by the one respondent without any peer pressure or influence from other participants, which is always a factor in a group setting. For example, in a group discussion there might be a domineering participant who, if not curtailed by the moderator, could potentially squelch participation or candor from a more timid respondent; in an in-depth interview that kind of dominating personality would not be a factor at all. The concern is that if some views prevail while others are not heard in the group, the result will be less diversity or a narrowing of the discussion or opinions expressed. This is of special concern to those who have a vested interest in the outcome, such as when in-depth research is used to evaluate concepts or creative tactics. Here, it is argued, the negatives expressed by one group member have the potential of negatively influencing respondents who at first might have been favorably inclined.

For some sensitive or very personal topics, people might be more likely to talk freely with a single supportive interviewer than in front of a group of peers or judgmental strangers. Much more relevant and important to business-to-business research, however, is a situation where confidentiality and anonymity with respect to the information given by a respondent is required. In this case, one-on-ones are the best alternative. For instance, if confidentiality is promised, CEOs of companies may be more likely to reveal information, such as current pricing or promotional strategies, in the company of one professional interviewer than to a group of potential competitors. In fact, a group of CEOs within a given industry would not want to discuss pricing strategies together, since this would violate antitrust laws.

A last reason to use one-on-one interviews is simply a logistical one. If you want to interview a particularly exclusive and small respondent group, perhaps top executives or medical professionals from around the country, gathering a group together at one time in one common place may be impossible. In this case, you may need to travel to those respondents in order to reach them and squeeze an interview into their busy schedules.

Focus group supporters, on the other hand, are quick to point out the time and budget efficiencies of group interviewing, since more than twice as many people can participate in a focus group as can be interviewed individually in the same time period. By way of comparison, a single in-depth interview will usually last anywhere from half an hour to just over an hour, whereas the standard group interview lasts approximately two hours. When a quick turnaround is needed, it is possible to conduct several groups across one or two days with a couple of weeks' notice. Even very elite groups can be gathered if the incentive is worthy and the pool of potential respondents is large enough to draw from. Where the pool of respondents is small, today's video teleconferencing capabilities are opening up even more economical ways of bringing geographically distant and hard-to-reach participants together.

What a group may lack in detailed individual participant attitudinal or behavioral profiles it gains in the breadth of discussion and the increased productivity that group stimulation and interaction provide. An in-depth interview relies solely on the interviewer to stimulate and provoke the respondent to think and find ways of expressing him- or herself. In a group, there are multiple people stimulating and reacting to each other, with the moderator playing a much less dominant role. This group interaction can often produce a synergistic effect, where the result is actually much more than you would get from all the same participants interviewed alone. In other words, more often than not you gain greater discussion on a topic; more diversity of perspectives, opinions, and behaviors; increased numbers of suggestions and ideas; and perhaps more detail on the subject matter at hand. This is the best distinction between the two methods, and the best reason for choosing groups over individual interviewing.

Additionally, there is less potential for a moderator to bias a group discussion than there is for an interviewer to bias individual interviewees. The moderator's role is to be as unobtrusive as possible without losing control of the group. If and when a participant starts to dominate the discussion and becomes a possible biasing factor, a good moderator will step in to remedy the situation. Managed well, a group setting will stimulate added diversity rather than squelch it and will not bias the proceedings. One of the contributing factors to the relative objectivity of a group over individual in-depth interviews is the greater tendency for group discussions to be observed directly through one-way mirrors, facilitating client participation. Depending on where one-on-one interviews are conducted, direct observation may or may not always be possible. Focus groups will be discussed more completely in Chapter 9.

One-on-One Interviews

One-on-one interviews are typically conducted when a group in-depth interview is not possible or practical. They should be done with extreme caution as one-on-one in-depth interviews are among the most likely to provide misleading results. As mentioned , individual interviews will not be plagued by "group think" or by dominant group personalities. But what is not understood as well as it should be is that in a one-on-one interview the interviewer becomes the dominant personality.

Generally speaking, experience shows that the dominant personality is less of a problem with business groups, probably because every group participant is a somewhat dominant personality, canceling the effect. It is also true that dominating and authoritative personalities rarely are able to have the kind of influence in business groups that they might in consumer groups. Therefore, the dominant personality theory *alone* is probably not the best reason to do one-on-one interviews.

Advertising agencies are especially fond of one-on-one in-depth interviews, which are commonly used to evaluate creative tactics. A well-trained interviewer can also most certainly come back with the desired results, and the agency can claim that research supports their enthusiasm for the particular program. Agency use of this technique is especially dangerous to a client marketer when the agency is either in a competitive situation with other agencies, or is defending or attempting to expand a spending budget. The lesson here is that one-on-one in-depth interviews should not be placed in the hands of those with a vested interest in their outcome.

The quality of the in-depth research results depends on the skill and training of the interviewer. Most one-on-one in-depth interviews are not conducted by interviewers who would have training approaching that of the psychoanalyst. A trained face-to-face interviewer may be able to administer a questionnaire very ably but not necessarily an in-depth interview. There is a different level of skill and training required to get respondents to project themselves into the ambiguity. Sometimes the use of the term "one-on-one" to describe the research really means research that was poorly done with a sample that would otherwise be judged to be too small.

In business-to-business research, group interviews can break down when it becomes too difficult to recruit a sample of people who are not already familiar with one another. In one geographic area, or in a particular field or category that is somewhat specialized, many businesspeople will already be acquainted.

Other problems with groups can occur when the topic concerns information that might be considered proprietary. Some businesses may be reluctant to discuss some topics with their competitors present. Some may be uncomfortable just being in the same room. Furthermore, you may not be able to gather together in one place a group of individuals with such busy schedules. In this case, it is simply easier to go to them rather than expect them to come to a central location. This, then, is where one-on-one in-depth interviews play an important role.

Selecting the Sample and the Site

The sample for one-on-ones, while it could be randomly drawn, is usually selected nonrandomly using judgment and quota convenience samples, much the same way as focus group respondents are recruited. Screeners need to be developed in order to recruit the right kinds of people, and incentives are usually needed to encourage interest.

Often one-on-one interviews are conducted using the same type of central site facilities that are used for focus group interviews. This makes it easy to both audio-record and observe the interviews behind two-way mirrors.

Protocols and Questionnaires

One-on-one question guides are similar in form to focus group discussion guides. The questions should be primarily open-ended and asked in a logical order to help the respondent provide the detail you are looking for. A one-on-one question guide requires more careful planning and attention to possible probes than does a focus group guide because the dynamics of small group discussion are absent. The interviewer must provide the cues to keep the participant talking.

If it is necessary to show the respondent material, such as an advertisement, then the one-on-one format offers the advantages of the personal interview. One-on-one interviews are popular means of gauging reaction to advertising and related material. The interviewer can be sure that the respondent has seen the material because it is shown during the interview. The respondent can provide their reaction to the material in their own terms, and the interviewer, through the use of probes, can help develop the response. The problem is that a quantitative measure of performance is not obtained, making it difficult to compare responses to other similarly evaluated material. This is true of group interviews, however, as well.

All qualitative research should be used with the greatest care. Qualitative results cannot be generalized to the entire market and are almost always very subjective in their interpretation. While qualitative research can provide an invaluable insight into many marketing problems and opportunities, it should rarely, if ever, be the only element in a research program. Instead, qualitative research should be done in conjunction with quantitative research. In fact, the opposite situation is equally as true; quantitative research with no qualitative components may be just as questionable.

If carefully planned and executed, qualitative research can be a most useful tool for the business-to-business market researcher.

9

Focus
Group
Interviews

The most common form of qualitative research is the in-depth focus group inter-
view. Conducting focus groups properly involves considerable effort
and numerous considerations.

Focus Group Interviews

When designing a qualitative research study using focus groups, several decisions need to be made. Most of these decisions will be made
with whomever you have contracted to conduct the groups or with
the facility, unless, of course, you are moderating and conducting the
sessions yourself. These steps are listed below. Keep in mind that
many of these decisions are made simultaneously since they are interdependent. Therefore, do not interpret the list below as a hierarchical
process. The decisions and their surrounding issues, as well as additional background information, are discussed in more detail in the
following sections.

1. Select a moderator.
2. Decide who is to be interviewed and develop a screener.
3. Determine the number, composition, and location of the
   groups.
4. Recruit group participants.
5. Write the discussion guide based on research objectives and
   develop any necessary materials.
6. Schedule the facility, food, and videotaping (if desired).

Selecting the Moderator

When launching a focus group project, selecting the group moderator is a critical first step. Many organizations will have their own focus group moderator on staff if they do enough of this kind of research to warrant one. In addition, most advertising agencies and marketing research firms will have moderators either on staff or with whom they regularly contract for their clients' needs. Focus group facilities will also sometimes have an experienced moderator on staff to serve your needs or have recommendations of moderators in the area that you can use. A research directory, such as the American Marketing Association's *Membership Directory & Marketing Services Guide*, or even the telephone yellow pages, will always have a listing of research consultants or firms that specialize in qualitative research. Because of the demand and the somewhat specialized nature of group interviewing, you will often use independent research consultants who exclusively engage in moderating groups.

The experience, skill, and style of the moderator are obviously key factors in selecting one. Being a group moderator is not as easy as it might first appear to a casual observer. There is a technique to keeping a discussion open and flowing without allowing it to venture too far off course to where it becomes irrelevant to the research goals. There is also technique involved in soliciting participation from as many individual group members as possible, while at the same time controlling or managing those who aggressively intimidate or dominate the discussion. It takes at least a year of moderating groups to become reasonably good at it.

It is also critical that the moderator understands your business and has experience moderating the kind of respondents you will be recruiting. Moderating consumer groups is very different from moderating CEOs or very specialized professionals, such as doctors. If there is technical language and jargon associated with your business, a moderator needs to feel comfortable directing questions to and fielding answers from respondents. In order to know how to probe when necessary, a moderator needs to understand what is being discussed. This issue is a particularly difficult problem in many business-to-business areas.

It is also important that a moderator fit your style. Since you will spend a great deal of time working with the moderator, using him or her much as you would an advisor, you need to feel comfortable interacting with the moderator you select.

In many cases, the moderator is also the discussion analyst who drafts the discussion guide and writes the final research report. In fact, it is probably preferable to have one individual do both. It is crucial that the moderator and whoever analyzes and summarizes the discussion clearly understand the objectives for the group discussion and have the ability to relate the discussion to those objectives.

Moderating Style

There are a wide variety of moderating styles that range from being very "directive" to "nondirective." The term *moderator* connotes a more nondirective, "less is more" approach. From this perspective, the less time you spend listening to the moderator, the better. A good moderator gets things started and then participates only to prevent the discussion from meandering off the topic, redirect the discussion if a topic has not been sufficiently addressed, or moderate or encourage the participation by others in the group where necessary.

A directive style leans more toward that of an interviewer or an interrogator than a moderator, where the discussion is pointedly kept moving in a particular direction with less room for spontaneous conversation and discussion. Moderators of this style will have a more dominant presence in the group, asking more questions, directly probing individuals, and sometimes even provoking individuals to respond. Some moderators will use their own presence through the use of body gestures or movement to elicit response by moving around the room and pointing at participants to get them involved. An aggressive moderating style can be effective unless the moderator's behavior intimidates or, by playing such a dominant role, compromises the quality of discussion from the participants.

Every moderator will have his or her own personal style, and the question is how comfortable you are with that particular style. The most important considerations are that the moderator be pleasant and professional and appear sincere, supportive, nonjudgmental, and neutral on the subject matter being discussed.

Moderating Techniques

A moderator should rely heavily on the dynamics and interaction of the group to generate topics, pursuing them to their fullest. Occasionally, though, the moderator must probe in order to get the depth of information required. The discussion guide should provide the moderator with the necessary topics to cover and probes within each so that his or her personal opinions are not interjected into the discussion.

The following is a list of some of the more common probing techniques:

1. Why? "Why?" is the most important probe because it steers the discussion toward the reasons behind voiced opinions.

2. Uh-Huh. This provides a neutral continuity by indicating the moderator is listening without implying approval/disapproval or agreement/disagreement.

3. Silence. An inexperienced moderator will rush to constantly fill the lulls in the conversation. However, silence can be an effective tool to generate further discussion since the discomfort of silence forces respondents to speak up. Caution should be exercised to not overuse this routine obviously as it could interfere with the spontaneity of the discussion.

4. Sophisticated Naiveté. In this scenario, the moderator positions him- or herself as the seemingly uninformed or naive moderator and invites being educated by the group. For example: "Could someone explain to me what you mean by that?"

5. Reasons. Sometimes reasons that might explain opinions don't arise spontaneously, and, at some point later, the moderator will need to redirect attention back to the topic and ask for more information to fill in the gap. A useful probe might be: "You previously mentioned X. Could you tell me a little bit more about what you meant by that?"

6. The Playback Routine. Here, the moderator repeats the respondent's last words with a slight voice inflection to imply a question. This encourages the respondent to explain with more clarity.

7. Gestures. Gestures can often help encourage or discourage participation by a group member. For instance, a moderator might raise an eyebrow to show interest and encourage continued discussion, lean toward a shy person to get them more involved, look away or slightly turn away from a domineering or talkative person to dampen their enthusiasm, or shrug to reconfirm neutrality when a respondent looks or asks for a moderator's approval.

There are some additional, more general things to keep in mind during a focus group interview.

1. If the group gets too enthusiastic and interrupts a speaker, the moderator should be careful of stopping the discussion because this will interfere with the spontaneity of the session. The moderator should let the interruption run its course and then return to the original speaker and topic.

2. The moderator should avoid overtly answering any respondent's question, instead encouraging them to answer it themselves. For example, reflecting the question back to the respondent by saying, "What do *you* think?"

3. When the moderator feels the discussion has digressed from the topic at hand, he or she should gently steer the discussion back to where it was prior to the diversion. Abrupt transitions can have the effect of throwing cold water on a conversation.

4. When the group's opinions appear too homogenous, the moderator should probe with, "Does anyone feel differently?" or "Do you all agree?" to indicate that dissenting opinions are acceptable. In some instances, a group member, acting like an authority figure, creates this apparent homogeneity by intimidating anyone else from speaking up lest they appear ignorant. Here the moderator might actually be more aggressive in soliciting opposing opinions by instructing another group member to play devil's advocate and think of any arguments that might contradict what has been said. By doing this, the moderator has given the group the freedom to speak up without appearing to personally disagree with the authority figure.

While these subtle techniques can be used to handle and manage most discussion flow problems, there is the occasional group that unfortunately includes someone who dominates the discussion to the point where others simply give up and say nothing. There are even times when the dominator will go so far as to reinterpret what others have said: "I think what she really means is. . . ." Domination by one group member can greatly dampen anyone else's desire to participate and can quickly derail a group if not stopped early on. When the more subtle moderator techniques, such as avoiding eye contact or physically turning away from the talkative person, do not work, sometimes more direct methods are necessary. The moderator can pose a question and ask each respondent around the table to answer in turn, beginning on the opposite side of the table from the dominant personality. A moderator can stop an especially long discourse by interrupting and asking of someone else "Do you agree with what he is saying?" or "What is *your* opinion?" or "I understand completely what it is that John is saying, but let me hear what some of the rest of you think." If a dominator becomes especially overbearing, other group respondents will usually come to the aid of the moderator given any opportunity.

Deciding Who Is to Be Interviewed and Developing a Screener: Group Selection and Recruiting Methods and Criteria

When considering who to interview and how to design the groups, the following questions usually arise: Who should be interviewed? How many groups, participants, or locations should be included in the study? How should the groups be composed—who should be included or excluded from a group? Again, these are not independent questions. They must all be considered before a final decision on any one can be made.

Who Is to Be Interviewed?

The first step in any research project, even before it is determined that qualitative research methods and, specifically focus groups, will be used, is the statement of the research problem and objectives. From these, then, the determination of who the target audience is for the research should come relatively easily. However, you need to be able to spell out the exact criteria for inclusion in the group(s) and this is not always as clearly specified in the research objectives as it might be.

If you are trying to learn more about your current customers and what you can do to improve your services or how you can better communicate with them, then recruiting groups from a list of those key customer contacts is obvious. You probably already have quite a bit of information that can be used to select those customers who will best serve the interests of the research. You need to ask yourself if there are particular restrictions on the overall sample characteristics, or if there are subsegments that you wish to delineate in designing the groups. For instance, are you going to sample only from those customers who have purchased in the last year or who are of a particular size or purchase volume? Or are you going to distinguish between recent and lapsed customers, big businesses and small businesses, large volume customers and smaller volume customers—including both?

If you are not planning to interview current customers, and you do not have the information on potential respondent characteristics in a database as you might with customers, Dun & Bradstreet or similar industry database suppliers can most likely supply a list of individual names and titles from companies, along with key company demographics, such as SIC. Still, you will need to construct a screening device to ensure that you are recruiting the appropriate kind of respondents.

The screener—the instrument used to specify and implement recruiting criteria—is a brief questionnaire or series of questions used to classify potential group members and determine respondent eligibility. Without revealing information that might be considered biasing and that might alert respondents to how and why they are being selected, you need to sort out those who fit the study parameters from those who do not. Exhibit 9.1 shows an example of what a basic screener may look like when the criteria for selection are:

- CEOs, presidents, and owners
- hardware and general merchandise stores
- that have been in business at least ten years
- employ between 5 and 100 people
- and have revenues either in the $10M to $49M bracket (Group 1) or the $100M to $149M category (Group 2)

Note that in this case, the respondent name and title are known beforehand, as is the retail SIC code. Note also that while years in business and employee size are broken down only enough to isolate the appropriate group specifications, revenue is delineated more than it actually needs to be for selection purposes. This is intentional; the additional revenue information can be tracked and kept for those who are finally recruited into groups. Special care must be taken to write questions in a logical manner and sequence to facilitate the recruiter's decision of whether to recruit or terminate a respondent. Behavioral or subjective perceptual questions can also be asked as a means of selection, such as, "Have you purchased any paper products for your business in the last year?" or "How comfortable would you say you are with computing technology?"

The decision about who should *not* be included in the research is

Exhibit 9.1: Focus Group Screener

SIC: _____ (Only call SICs beginning with 52 or 53 and vary across range)

Title: _____ (President, CEO, or owner only)

Hello, my name is _____ and I'm calling from XYZ Research in Evanston, Illinois. May I please speak with _____.

We are calling a select number of retailers in the Chicago area to participate in an important research study. I have just a few questions to ask you about your business in order to classify your company with other retailers.

1. Approximately how long have you been in business? (WRITE IN ACTUAL NUMBER OF YEARS)

    _____ Less than 10 years—TERMINATE
    _____ 10 years or more

2. About how many full-time people do you employ at your store? (WRITE IN ACTUAL NUMBER OF EMPLOYEES)

    _____ 5 or less—TERMINATE
    _____ 6 to 100
    _____ Over 100

3. Does your business's annual revenue fall below or at or above $100 million dollars?

    BELOW . . . 1   AT or ABOVE . . . 2

And, in which of the following categories, then, does your company's annual revenue fall? Is it . . .

BELOW $100M	AT or ABOVE $100M
_____ Less than $10M—TERMINATE	_____ $100M–$124 Million
_____ $10M–$24 Million	_____ $125M–$149 Million
_____ $25M–$49 Million	_____ $150M or more—TERMINATE
_____ $50M–$99 Million—TERMINATE	
(RECRUIT FOR GROUP 1)	(RECRUIT FOR GROUP 2)

important as well. It is standard practice to eliminate anyone whose profession is marketing research or who has a market researcher in his or her family. First, anyone working in the research field is more likely to understand the moderating techniques and guess what it is that the research sponsor is trying to do with the research and manipulate their answers accordingly. There is also some concern that conflicts of interest could occur when someone related to a group respondent does research for a competitor of the group sponsor. It is also customary to exclude anyone who works for a direct competitor—for the same conflict of interest rationale. If group members are being exposed to new product concepts or creative tactics for your company, you do not want that information being leaked to your competitor down the street.

The professional focus group participant is another concern, although it is probably more unusual to find a business-to-business participant who would attend focus groups on a regular basis than in a consumer sample. Still, in some industries or special ethnic groups, it might be possible to find people who have been repeat participants. Many focus group facilities that regularly recruit respondents have lists of people who have participated in groups before or who have been expressly screened beforehand to learn if they would be interested in participating in future groups. When clients call on short notice, these prescreened lists prove useful in recruiting the needed numbers of group respondents quickly, especially for special segments, such as women executives, small business owners, or Hispanic businessmen. Good focus group recruiters also have a rule of thumb to be careful not to call, or to screen out, anyone who has participated in a group within the last six to twelve months (or perhaps even longer) on a similar topic or for the same client.

Determining the Size, Composition, and Location of Groups

The next stage is to decide on how many people, how many groups, and how many locations are needed.

How Many?

The next step is to determine the size and scope of the project. Invariably, the question "How many groups should we conduct?" is asked. There is no black-and-white, standard answer to this question because the number of groups really depends on the number of variables that need to be addressed by the study. With more variables or sample subsegments to be included, the number of groups naturally increases. The more heterogeneity or variation in behavior or attitudes that is expected across your sample, the more you should consider scheduling additional groups.

A typical qualitative study will consist of somewhere between two and six groups, although larger studies are sometimes warranted. Usually, you find that each successive session produces less and less new information and more and more redundancy of ideas. By the time you have conducted six groups, the net gain in useful material is probably not worth the incremental cost of doing additional groups. Doing larger numbers of groups in order to increase the sample size and, hence, increase the generalizability of the information, is wasteful and naive. No number of focus groups will produce the kind of projectability that a scientifically sampled survey project would. Groups are simply not meant to be generalizable, regardless of how many you do.

If you wish to compare two or more different subsegments of the market, for instance, comparing CEO views to those of company employees, or the perspective of the purchasing agent to those of the end-user, usually several groups are needed. While sometimes different segments can be combined into one session, there are often reasons why they should not be (as discussed in the next section on group composition). You should remember, however, that the goal of qualitative research is to explore the range of ideas or views across the various segments, not to quantify and compare them to one another on the specifics. Every group is different, and no one group will be representative of a given segment.

Most researchers will agree that it is inadvisable to conduct only one focus group session, except when there are extreme time and budget constraints that preclude more sessions from being conducted. The reason for doing more than just one group is that there is a learning curve to group interviews on the part of the moderator and client. The first session serves to test the question guide and acquaint the moderator with the audience and is usually the least productive of all sessions. Furthermore, while no number of groups will give projectable results or guarantee representativeness, one group will assuredly offer less diversity than two or three groups would. And despite careful screening and planning as well as expert moderating, there is bound to be the occasional group that simply flops—it rains and too few show up, the guide doesn't capture key information after all, or the group dynamics are such that they fail to spark or sustain a productive discussion.

Related to the decision of how many groups to conduct is the issue of how many different interviewing locations should be included in the study. Most studies will include more than a single location for the sole purpose of getting a wider range of views, the assumption being that there may be regional differences or influences in the way people think or behave. Again, the goal is not to quantify and directly compare the east to the west, or a metropolitan area with a more remote area, but by including both, you increase the chances of gaining new insights and being cued into potential differences that could be tested quantitatively in later research. If geographical diversity is warranted, usually conducting a couple of groups in each of two to three locations is sufficient for this purpose. Of course, if you are a business-to-business marketer selling only locally, there is absolutely no need to have geographical dispersion unless you are worried about "tainting" potential local customers by allowing them in your groups to evaluate rough creative or product concepts. In this latter situation, you may choose to relocate your research to another similar community where you do not currently do business.

The question of how many participants should be included within each group is a bit more straightforward. While some groups are conducted with as few as six respondents, the rule of thumb is to keep groups to between eight and ten respondents. Groups that are smaller than eight tend to produce a more limited discussion because the range of opinions, and the chance of opposing views emerging to spark discussion, is less. In addition, smaller groups generally tend to get "talked out" more quickly. Larger groups, on the other hand, can actually inhibit discussion by swamping small group dynamics. The chance that the moderator will lose control of a large group discussion is much greater. Since there is more distance between moderator and participants, the corners of the table (even round tables!) will tend to hold their own conversations off to the side. And it is not possible for the moderator, or the audiotape for that matter, to track every conversation and keep the discussion moving in the proper direction. Once the group splinters in this way, it is difficult to get everyone's attention back to center stage and on the topic at hand. There is also greater potential for some group members to not participate at all since it is so easy for them to sit and say nothing when everyone around them is talking.

On this note, it is important to stress that when recruiting participants, it is wise to overrecruit in anticipation of some failing to appear. In other words, if you would like two groups of eight to ten respondents, at least ten to twelve should be recruited for each. That way, if several do not show, or show up too late to be included in a session, there are still enough participants to assure the group's success. Invariably, there will be times when everyone who is invited attends. Rather than overcrowd the interviewing room and potentially undermining the goals of the research, it is usually a good idea to only invite ten and dismiss two with thanks (and incentive money). Sometimes it is possible to scan the group or preview the sign-in sheets to make a determination of who you think will be the best and most representative participants of those available.

Group Composition

The issue of who exactly should be included in a group comes down to whether you believe diversity within a group will lead to greater depth and range of discussion, or inhibit discussion. Generally speaking, relatively homogeneous groups, where members have a common, shared background or interest that can serve as the base from which discussion is derived, are most effective. Once members in a group recognize their mutual behavior or interest, they each have a greater sense of security and confidence to speak up within the group and share their experiences with those they know will understand. Homogeneity also eliminates the possibility of tensions or inhibitions caused by differences.

Segregating groups by gender, for instance, is a common practice. In other words, when you have both men and women in your target sample, you might conduct one session with only men and another with only women. Especially on topics that have undertones of a personal nature, embarrassment or vanity might prevent men and women from talking freely within a group. However, in business-to-business groups with company executives, mixing genders is not as much of a problem as you might think. Women managers are every bit as vocal as their male counterparts and usually do not become submissive to men when they are included as equals in a group of working professionals.

Another common practice is to segregate by race or ethnicity. Again, this tradition has little merit in business-to-business research unless race is accompanied by other differences that might provoke antagonism or intimidation, such as economic differences. Usually, the reason to recruit an all African American or an all Hispanic group is to purposely focus on their particular behaviors, beliefs, or opinions as a customer segment.

Economic, social class, or professional differences carry far more weight in determining group composition than other kinds of differences. Economic or educational differences and the related social class issue can prove to be a troublesome barrier to open discussion because of the status implications. For instance, a very small businessperson may be less likely to disagree or speak up in a group where there are CEOs of major corporations. Similarly, it is best to keep a group homogeneous with respect to professional level or status. Company presidents contribute best in a group with other company presidents. Purchasing agents contribute more when among other purchasing agents. Mixing secretarial staff and management in one group is not advisable even when both may have valid contributions to make on the topic of purchasing office supplies.

When it comes to professional disparity, there can be very real differences in the backgrounds, training, experience, and even the lingo of individuals in different personnel groups or levels of management. In specialized industries, groups should be recruited so that participants have a common understanding of industry jargon and similar levels of business sophistication whenever possible. Mixed groups, in this case, will yield more superficial discussion and will probably fail to adequately develop the topics of interest because the differences create a gap that is too broad to overcome in the space of an hour or two.

A last point: the group discussion should be based on the topics presented by the group moderator and not on the basis of previously established relationships. This means that group members should not know each other. If employees and their bosses attend the same group, they will bring with them the same dominant/subordinate roles that dictate their behavior outside the group. If group members are peers within a company or within in an industry who have socialized or worked together in the past, whatever relationships have been established prior to the focus group session will hinder equality of discussion within the group. Finding participants who do not know each other, or of each other, can be very difficult when recruiting business-to-business groups located in the same geographic area. Businesspeople tend to belong to associations, attend trade shows, and interact through the normal course of doing business. In fact, this is a special problem with business-to-business research compared to consumer research.

If it is apparent that the pool of potential participants will most likely know each other, then a focus group is probably not the best research approach and one-on-one interviews should be conducted instead. Focus group interviews probably would not be the method of first choice for qualitative research among employees of a single company, for example, unless that company was extremely large and the probability of group members knowing each other was greatly reduced.

Recruiting Participants

The actual recruiting of focus group participants is usually completed by the focus group facility at which you are conducting the interviews. In fact, the cost of recruiting is usually bundled with the fee for the room. Recruiting costs may be higher for more difficult-to-reach groups. With business-to-business research, this is typically the case since business executives are not as easy to reach or schedule as are consumers. Usually a cash incentive is paid to participants in return for their willingness to spend two hours in a group session. Again, the amount of the incentive will vary depending on the type of respondent, the location of the facility, and the length of time for which the session is scheduled. Facilities are not shy about recommending an incentive level. They are the ones who are responsible for recruiting the cooperation of enough respondents to make the group a success.

The Discussion Guide

As in all market research, almost nothing can substitute for a well-conceived problem definition to ensure the overall success of a project. This is certainly true for focus group research. The study objectives get translated into the focus group discussion guide—a list of topics—that the moderator works from. A good discussion guide should reflect the thought that went into the planning of the group discussion.

The guide is not a list of predetermined questions, and it looks nothing like a survey questionnaire. It is a set of notes that outlines the important areas to be covered during the focus group session. It is usually a good idea to write down at least the bare bones of some well-worded probes that, by their wording, will require in-depth answers from the participants and, at the same time, reduce moderator bias by eliminating the potential for the moderator to phrase a question in a way that leads respondents. However, a good moderator who is very familiar with the research objectives and with the topics on the guide will not need every question and probe written out fully. Because he or she needs to have the freedom to address topics in the order in which they arise in the natural course of the group discussion, a moderator must be able to see clearly from the guide what the key topic areas and probes are so as to be able to skip around easily. Full-length questions can hinder this to some degree.

Actual questions and probes used in the guide should be of the unstructured or semistructured type. Unstructured questions are stimulus and response free, meaning they do not specify exactly what the respondent should be focusing his or her attention on and they do not specify answer options. The respondent is completely free to answer any way he or she pleases about any aspect of the topic presented. An example would be: "What is your reaction to this advertisement?" By way of comparison, a structured version of this question would be: "Does this advertisement communicate low price to you?" In this instance, the respondent is being asked about a specific copy point and is essentially given the choice of answering "yes" or "no," with no invitation to follow up with any explanation. Structured questions do not promote discussion by their very nature and, therefore, should be avoided in in-depth research studies.

Semistructured questions provide a bit more structure by focusing on a particular aspect, but they still leave much room for freely answering in an in-depth fashion. Examples would be: "What did you learn from this ad that you hadn't known about facsimile machines before?" or "How did you feel about the little genie magically making the network distribute the facsimiles to the different individuals?"

Completely unstructured questions are most often applied in the opening stages of a group discussion, while semistructured questions are most typically used at a later point when productivity is waning. Semistructured questions can also be used as a follow-up probe to an unstructured question to hit on certain key points if and when no one in the group addresses this point spontaneously on their own.

The most common way of sequencing questions or topics within the guide is to direct the flow of conversation from a general topic area to progressively more specific subtopics and details in a "funnel" approach. This has two advantages. By starting with a broad topic that everyone can relate to, all group members can become involved in easy discussion early on and acclimate themselves to speaking up within the group setting. This makes everyone feel more confident about talking freely throughout. The funnel approach also orients the group by focusing their thoughts on the general topic before a moderator starts probing for details, making those details come to mind more quickly and efficiently when this does occur.

Any questions concerning your product or services should be left until the end. If you have any interest whatsoever in learning about the topic in a general way or about the competitive dynamics within the particular industry, you will compromise your ability to do so immediately upon the mention of your product. This is another reason for beginning generally and progressively narrowing the focus of the discussion to specifics, such as details on a given brand. When the group participants know or think they know who is sponsoring the research and what the goals are, especially with the knowledge that someone from that company is sitting on the other side of the two-way mirror, there is a tendency to be less candid about that particular sponsor and its products/services. As a result, the discussion often immediately narrows to that brand or company and its subset of attributes or problems. In fact, it is very difficult to go back and pick up on a broader topic area without someone in the group relating everything back to the sponsoring brand. Other competitive information will be lost or at least compromised.

To just give a brief example of how you might structure a focus group discussion guide, consider the following example. Let's say you are marketing your hotel chain to corporate meeting/event planners and have scheduled groups among the appropriate personnel. To find out more about their behavior and selection criteria for event locations and to understand their attitudes toward your hotel versus the competition, you might loosely organize the guide as shown in Exhibit 9.2.

One slight deviation from this general sequencing rule is to direct a relatively narrow, structured question to the group and starting with the first person to the left or right of the moderator, to encourage each and every group member in turn to answer. This serves as a kind of introduction for each member to the group and forces everyone to speak, again with the intent to make them feel more comfortable with contributing throughout the session.

The question can, in fact, be handled strictly as an introduction and have little to do with the main group topic. With business-to-business participants, for instance, a moderator might ask everyone

Exhibit 9.2: Sample Discussion Guide

I. General Behavior and Decision-Making

  A. Describe the *kinds of events or meetings* that are typically held off-site within their company.
    —Sales meetings
    —Fun, employee appreciation events
    —Honorary awards programs
    —Client pitches
    —Routine business meetings

  B. *Who plans* or is involved in the decision of where to go? Who makes the final decision?

  C. Are different off-site locations used with every event, or do they return to the same site routinely?

  D. What *criteria* are used in selecting the off-site location? How important are:

—Cost/Discounts	—Decor or ambiance
—Size	—Convenience or proximity
—Food	—Seclusion from other guests
—Service	—Entertainment or activities available
Pool	—Babysitting services

II. Competition

Where does your company typically hold off-site events? Why? Likes? Dislikes? How could they improve?
    —Hotel A
    —Hotel B
    —Resort A
    —Restaurant C

III. Attitudes Toward Your Hotel

  A. How would you rate Hotel X as an event site and why?
  B. How could Hotel X better serve your needs?

IV. Evaluation of Creative Concept(s)

  A. SHOW CONCEPT(S)
  B. What is your reaction to Concept A? Why do you say that?

to say where they work, how long they've worked there, and what their key responsibilities are within the company. Or if CEOs or small business owners are being interviewed, ask each to say a little bit about their business and how they came to own or head their own business. However, if time is short, you might get more directly to the point and have each give a kind of status report (what they have or what they normally buy) on the general topic area. For instance, if the topic is computers, ask each business owner to say what their business is and describe the kind of computers they have installed within their company. After this, however, unstructured questions should follow to generate more in-depth explanations about these behaviors.

Here are just a few summary pointers on preparing the discussion guide:

1. Begin the session in an unstructured way on the general subject area. Then start to funnel the discussion into more specific areas of interest, leaving any questions that identify the research sponsor until the end.

2. Group questions that pertain to one subject area together and be sure to exhaust one subject before moving on to the next. While the actual discussion may wander in and out of a particular area of interest, or spontaneously arise in a different order than you anticipated, putting all the probes and questions for one topic together makes it easier for the moderator to make a mental check that the key points have been covered at some time during the session.

3. As a way of prioritizing topics and pacing the session, estimate the amount of time that you think should be adequate to cover the area and put a suggested time period on the guide. Most moderators will do this anyway, making their own "clock" notes on the guide to serve as cues to remind themselves of when to move on since it is their responsibility to make sure everything is covered in the time allotted. However, an open discussion of timing among all those involved will help to clarify for everyone what the priorities are.

4. Many of the same general question-writing rules apply here that apply in survey research. For instance, avoid questions that may embarrass respondents or place them on the defensive. If a potentially sensitive topic needs to be addressed, save it for later in the session. Also, avoid phrasing questions in a leading way so that respondents feel more inclined to answer one way as opposed to another.

5. Keep the guide as simple and uncomplicated in form as possible. Keep the language as simple and conversational as possible.

6. Do not overload the session with too many different topics or

tasks. A typical guide might be one to three pages in length (including ample white space).

This last point is especially worth reemphasizing. There is always the tendency to try and cram everything that you ever wanted to know about a topic or about a target audience into this one two-hour session. The logic goes something like this: "We've gone to all this effort and spent all this incentive and research money to gather these customers together, why can't we just ask this one extra thing or two? It won't take very long." Before you know it, the guide becomes longer and longer, and the number of tasks to complete or creative pieces to pass around increases to expand the time geometrically.

Remember that each question on a focus group guide is not the same as a question in a survey research project. You are asking a group of eight to ten individuals, all of whom you want to hear from, to think about, speculate, and answer thoughtfully and in detail each and every question, with time for follow-up questions as well. While some questions will naturally take longer and encompass more, any question will take longer than it appears on paper. In general, the fewer the topics, the more detailed input on any one topic you will receive.

It goes without saying that the moderator should be thoroughly familiar with the outline and the research objectives. However, he or she needs to freely cover topics as they come up naturally in the discussion. The most important thing that a moderator can do is to listen to what people are saying and follow up on new points as they are raised, rather than feel obliged to lumber through the questions as they exactly appear on the guide.

Often, a client new to qualitative research will become very worried when it seems as though a moderator has skipped questions or has allowed the conversation to wander off to another topic before all the questions have been answered on the current topic. There is seldom a reason to worry. If the key points have not arisen naturally in the discussion, usually at some point a moderator will direct questioning back to those points that have been bypassed. In the meantime, the likelihood is that much more has been learned on a topic by allowing the group dynamics to work their own natural course. Always remember, the discussion guide is just that—a *guide* and only a guide.

You should think of the guide as being a research tool that is dynamic; it should be allowed to change when it becomes necessary, based on experience using it. Almost always, changes are made to the guide in successive group sessions. For instance, greater priority and time may be given to certain topics in order to explore them further and in more detail. At the same time, other discussion areas may be demoted to a secondary role, either because the discussion proved to be less productive than anticipated or because it was so productive that further discussion does not seem as warranted. The sequencing of topics may also change in order to accommodate these new priorities, or because the natural discussion progression seemed to be different than originally anticipated, or it was found that earlier questions seemed to bias or alter the discussion on later questions in an unexpected way. This is one reason that is it preferable to have some time between groups for the moderator and the client to have a chance to discuss and make any necessary modifications.

Scheduling and Conducting Sessions

While many of the decisions involved in scheduling a facility will be handled by your moderator and the procedures used in conducting the interviews will be determined by the chosen facility, it is worth knowing what these decision points or procedures entail because they can influence the kind of groups and discussion you get.

The Interview Site

Whether you are planning one group in one location or six groups across three to four locations, the issue of where to conduct the group interviews is an important one. Some moderators will work right out of their homes, inviting respondents to an informal gathering in their living room or dining room. It is also an option, perhaps, to conduct the interviews out of your place of business, in a company conference room for instance. However, most groups are probably held in a research facility somewhere, designed purposely for this kind of event.

An off-site location provides a neutral setting for more open and candid discussion. Even when groups are being conducted among your own employees, it is often a smart idea to have them meet somewhere other than the office or company headquarters. It gives the impression of more objectivity and allows them the psychological freedom to vent or talk honestly without fear of being watched or overheard by their superiors. A home setting may interject bias because the more respondents know about a moderator, the more they can change their answers to fit with what they expect the moderator would like to hear. With business-to-business research, especially, a home setting probably does not fit with the professional image you'd like respondents to have about your company when they leave the session.

Most metropolitan areas will have at least one focus group research facility you can contact. Smaller markets sometimes will not and you will have to consider locating your groups to the city or suburb nearest your desired location. Research companies specializing in qualitative research will usually have facilities in several markets across the various regions of the country to allow you the ability to work with just one company to do all your groups.

Facilities will vary greatly. While some are housed in separate office buildings or suites within an office building, some locate themselves in shopping malls. One of the key characteristics to evaluate is how conveniently located and accessible the site is for respondents. How close is the facility to where the bulk of your respondents live or work? How difficult is it to get to the place through traffic at various times of the day? How easy is the facility to find? Is the address clearly noticeable from the street? Is there ample parking? Two benefits of a facility being in a shopping mall are that it is an easy landmark to find, one most nearby respondents will be familiar with, and there is always parking available.

When you are traveling out of town to observe a focus group session, it is also a plus to have a facility that is close to restaurants and hotels for easy meals and lodging before or after group sessions. For this reason, some research facilities have rooms in airports or hotels near airports.

Another consideration in choosing a facility is its layout and how it is equipped. A facility will usually have a guest reception/waiting area where respondents can be received and remain until the appropriate session time. The interviewing room should have a client observation room next door to it, equipped with a two-way mirror along the adjoining wall so that clients can view unobtrusively, and quality audio equipment so that discussion can be clearly heard by clients and cleanly taped for later transcription or review. It is preferable for these rooms to be visually separate from the waiting area so that clients can move about freely without being noticed by group participants who are waiting to be admitted. Both the interviewing and observation room should be insulated from outside noise and distractions (windows can actually be a negative factor) and should be relatively spacious so that respondents and clients alike do not feel jammed into the room.

Most facilities equip their focus group rooms with a large conference table that allows comfortable seating for about eleven to twelve people. A round or oval table is preferred because this allows respondents to make eye contact with the moderator and encourages equal participation, as well as facilitating interaction among the respondents themselves. Observation rooms are often configured with long tables running the length of the room and tiered in elevations to allow the back row to see as well as the first row.

Of course, in addition to the logistical considerations, a major requirement for any site used for focus group interviewing is that it have an atmosphere that encourages respondents to feel at ease and comfortable, and it not inhibit respondents from openly and honestly reacting. A difficult-to-find site with noisy, cramped, stuffy quarters will cause unnecessary distractions and deter productive discussion.

While observation rooms and audiotaping are standard for any group session, videotaping the session is also an option. Videotaping, however, is not a routine procedure and adds an incremental cost for the equipment rental, tape, and the photographer.

Group Scheduling and Recruiting

Interviews can be scheduled mornings, afternoons, and evenings, during the week or weekend. They can be sandwiched between meals, or scheduled over a meal, with food being brought in for respondents as an extra courtesy. Often, when several sessions are necessary at one location, they are scheduled one after the other on one day, or in the evening of the first day and the morning of the next. There are days of the week and times of the day that are more productive than others, depending on the audience. What works well for consumer groups may not be desirable for business-to-business groups.

Given work schedules, it is very difficult to schedule business-to-business groups during the day. Unless the group participants have especially high-level titles, such as CEO, most business executives have obligations to their employer during regularly scheduled office hours. Evening sessions are more productive, running from 6 to 8 P.M. and 8 to 10 P.M. or perhaps a single session from 7 to 9 P.M. Saturday mornings can also work for those who have a hard time getting away during the week. Another alternative that works for business-to-business research, is to schedule groups over a mealtime, incorporating the meal into the session. A breakfast meeting, for instance, can work well for executives because it can take less time from the day's activities than a luncheon session. It is also less susceptible to end-of-the-day, last-minute details that can deter getting away on time for an early evening session.

Every facility will have their own scheduling and recruiting procedures that they follow and can offer their recommendation on how best to schedule particular groups based on their past experience in their given area. For instance, a facility coordinator will be able to recommend an evening start time given the traffic conditions during rush hours, or days of the week that tend to be most productive. You can, of course, schedule a group at almost any time if you have enough time to recruit, enough names to draw from, and pay enough. It is common for city sites where traffic and parking are problematic to offer higher incentives for participation than suburban locations. It is also common to offer higher incentives for weekend versus weekday sessions. Facilities usually require a minimum of two weeks to a month prior notice in order to recruit the number of respondents necessary.

Once a respondent has agreed to participate, he or she is usually sent a confirmation letter with the date, time, place, and directions to the facility. Respondents are then regularly called within twenty-four to forty-eight hours of the scheduled day to be reminded and confirmed. Because even those with the best of intentions can forget or have an unexpected appointment crop up, facilities will always over-recruit participants.

Session Proceedings

Upon arriving at a focus group facility, respondents are usually asked to sign in at the reception desk. From the sign-in sheets and the prior screeners used to recruit the group, a list can then be compiled of the actual group attendees and any key information that was collected during the screening interview. This list can prove helpful if too many respondents show up and you need to select someone to excuse from the session. If a session is scheduled very near a mealtime, often respondents will be asked to come a few minutes early in order to eat beforehand in the reception area.

Once everyone has arrived, respondents are invited into the interviewing room by a host. Each will have a name plate or tag to identify them to the moderator and to each other. Usually only first names are used in order to maintain anonymity and an informal atmosphere.

The moderator's opening remarks will set the tone for the entire interview and are, therefore, very important. Several key points need to be covered at the beginning of every session:

1. An explanation of why the interview is taking place, emphasizing the importance of the respondent's role. Mention of the general category is sometimes helpful, such as "you are all presidents of manufacturing companies."
2. Encouragement to speak out honestly and openly about what they feel.
3. Assurance that negative as well as positive comments are welcome.
4. Casual mention of the tape recorder and that the session is being recorded, with a request that participants speak up one at a time to facilitate taping. If a session is being videotaped, this too should be mentioned.
5. Reference to the two-way mirror and that there are observers who are purposely being kept in another room to minimize the distractions to the discussion.

After the initial remarks the moderator can consult his guide and begin the interview.

Analysis and Reports

A focus group report should summarize the full range of responses or discussion coming from the group. The final report should correspond to the initial discussion guide and relate back to the original purpose and objectives of the research. The detail provided in the report will depend to some degree on the taste of the organization initiating the research and the style of the analyst. Some organizations prefer very terse and concise reports that relate the principal findings without elaborate explanation or illustration. This is probably sufficient when groups are used to evaluate product or creative concepts and the outcome is generally very to the point. When the client has participated by observing all the interviews, a short summary is sometimes all that is really needed.

Other organizations prefer reports that liberally include a full range of excerpts from the discussion to clarify and illuminate points and make the findings come alive. This requires a transcript of the proceedings to be typed, so that quotations can be transcribed in full context for use within the report. Even here, the quotations should be selected with care so as not to overload a report with redundant or unnecessary quotations. In many cases, the analyst and report writer may summarize a particular discussion point without quotations because there may not be any one response that states the idea as efficiently as the analyst can.

In analyzing the discussion and writing the report, (1) the sequence in which issues or discussion points are raised by respondents and (2) the length of time spent by the group on a particular point—or the intensity of the response to a question or display materials—should be considered as well as what was actually said. On the one hand, a single respondent could say hesitantly that they had relatively good feelings about a company, accompanied by several other nodding heads, and on the other, the group as a whole could unanimously and excitedly volunteer exclamations of approval. Knowing who said what can be helpful in the analysis, too. For instance, if a negative comment here and there arises, it would be good to know that all these negatives came from the same person who admitted at some point in the discussion that he had had a bad experience with the company in question and refused to have anything ever to do with it again. Unfortunately, unless a response is identified as coming from a particular respondent, this kind of insight is lost.

Because groups are relatively small, nonrandom, and nongeneralizable, quantifying information is rarely meaningful and descriptive statistics such as percentages should not be used. Statements such as "Seventy percent of the participants agreed" or "Three out of ten liked the product concept" are potentially misleading since percentages assume at least 100 respondents. However, most of the time, a client will want to know some measure of intensity or agreement on a subject. In this case, it is better to use words that describe the frequency of response or respondent actions without stating particular percentages or ratios. Adverbs such as "infrequently" or "widely used" are more acceptable.

One of the greatest dangers in qualitative research comes from placing the interpretation of a focus group discussion in the hands of obviously biased parties. There are times when you might be inclined to hire a moderator to conduct the sessions but then have someone from within your company attend the sessions and write up their analysis of the discussion, foregoing the formal analysis and report by the outside supplier. This should be avoided. After all, part of what you are buying in a moderator is an objective outside ear and the expertise to organize the pieces and parts into a cohesive, comprehensible whole. Yet, the same danger can exist even in an outside researcher if he or she is seeking support or affirmation rather than attempting to gain new insight. It is most interesting how two individuals with different predispositions can listen to the same qualitative discussion and have completely opposite interpretations. This situation, incidentally, is not that as unusual as you might think.

The Focus Group Budget

There are really four broad cost components to consider in budgeting for a focus group:

1. Focus group facility and recruiting, including respondent incentives
2. Moderator/analyst professional time
3. Travel costs
4. Incidentals (food, photocopying, videotaping, etc.)

By far, the largest cost component is the first—facility and recruiting expenses. While facility costs will vary slightly from area to area, the major determinant of expense here (other than how many groups you conduct) is how difficult respondents are to recruit. The more elite, specialized, and/or elusive respondents are, the harder it is to solicit participation. More time will need to be spent on the phones calling a broader base of potential participants and this obviously adds to the recruiting expense. Also, higher incentives will probably be needed to encourage respondents to attend. It is not uncommon to pay $200 or more per participant (including any who are dismissed due to overrecruiting) when business executives or professionals, such as CEOs or physicians, are recruited in larger metropolitan areas. This is four to five times as much as would be necessary for an ordinary consumer participant. Obviously, in business-to-business research, the recruiting and incentives will be more expensive than for consumer marketing research just because of the nature of the respondent.

A moderator/analyst usually bills on a fee basis, either for an entire project or per group. This would include time spent with the client defining the research goals; time spent writing the discussion guide, screeners, and any other research materials; the actual time spent moderating; and the time taken to analyze and write the final report. When more than one group is to be conducted, the per group rate is probably reduced since the incremental cost per group is mainly the time spent moderating and traveling.

Exhibit 9.3: Sample Focus Group Budget

Facility and recruiting $2,700
Incentives 2,200
Video playback equipment and recording......... 450
Food and refreshments—Respondents...............150
Food and refreshments—Client 100
Travel expenses...1,400
Moderator professional time and report. 3,000

TOTAL BUDGET $10,000

The third cost component, travel, is only a factor when the moderator needs to travel to the respondents. In this case, the travel expenses for airline tickets and hotels can increase total project costs, especially if several groups are conducted and each is in a different geographical location. Client travel costs will add to this expense as well.

Other miscellaneous expenses have been grouped in the incidental category. This would include videotaping costs when this option is chosen, respondent and client food for meals and refreshments, and copying charges if materials need to be produced for the group.

Exhibit 9.3 contains a sample of a focus group budget for two groups conducted in two separate out-of-town locations, each with ten participants and one extra recruit. The participants, retail managers, are each being paid a $100 incentive. Videotaping is added and sandwiches are provided to participants in the earlier group as well as to the attending clients, in addition to refreshments during the group sessions.

10 Conjoint Analysis

Conjoint analysis is a technique used to quantify people's preferences, or priorities when choosing the most preferred alternative from a set of products or services. It is often labeled *trade-off analysis* because in making such a decision, you usually must trade off one brand for another or one brand's set of characteristics or benefits for another brand's features. Obviously, this parallels a purchase situation: customers typically evaluate the various features of any given product or service and decide which features are more important and, therefore, which product/service he or she will buy/use.

While conjoint analysis can apply to situations other than a product purchase, it is perhaps easiest to understand the technique in this context. For example, a customer evaluating and choosing a personal computer would need to consider features such as brand name, type of monitor, amount of memory on the hard drive and in RAM, operating system, price, need for and the ease of attaining service, software that might come as a package with the computer, and so on. The assumption is that the buyer is facing various combinations of these characteristics or features when deciding to purchase computer A or computer B and that in selecting one particular computer, he or she is consciously trading off, or putting less priority on, characteristics not present in the preferred computer. By quantifying the importance of these various features (based on how often each is selected or traded off), you can predict your customers' preference for a particular brand (either new or existing), or even produce a product or service that reflects the most preferred combination of features.

Conjoint Applications

Conjoint analysis (CA) has been applied across a very wide range of products, services, and markets. It is a research tool that can effectively and efficiently answer some of the following questions:

- What value does my customer or the market put on the various features of my product?
- How could I improve my product or service? Or, how *would* I alter the competitiveness of my product or service if I changed this or that?
- If my competitor changed this or that aspect, how might the market respond?
- What is the price elasticity for my brand? What is my brand name worth?
- How can I segment the market based on differences in what people think is important?

Since conjoint analysis measures people's priorities by deriving a quantifiable value for each and every product feature, it is quite useful for identifying the most important product attributes. This makes it especially applicable to designing new products or redesigning existing ones. New conjoint analysis computer models even allow you to set up "what if" scenarios, changing characteristics of your brand or your competitors' brands, to simulate how these changes will affect consumer preferences. If it is found that different groups of people value different features or feature combinations, CA can serve as the foundation for a segmentation scheme.

Once a buyer's priorities are identified, or various segments with different priorities are found, CA can also aid in the development of marketing communications strategies to the appropriate target and be used to test the relative importance of tactical alternatives. Where a marketer is not certain of the value of a product's brand name and image in setting price, or is not certain of a brand's price elasticity, conjoint analysis is one of the few techniques that can quantify and estimate this without elaborate and expensive field experimentation.

While CA has had wide application across a variety of markets, it is especially applicable in the business-to-business world because of the decision process that most companies must go through in selecting a vendor, a product, or a service. Conjoint analysis lends itself best to products and services that are multi-attribute in nature, or in other words, stimuli that can be easily and realistically broken down into a basic set of features that are recognizable and important to the buyer.

Therefore, CA is most often associated with products or services in which the buying decision is more rationally and/or economically based—higher ticket, less routine items. The higher the stakes, the more shopping around and comparison of features is naturally done and the more elaborate the evaluation and decision process is. Hence, industrial products, capital expenditures, and services—these are all categories that would work well with CA.

Conjoint analysis is most appropriate in situations where the decision-making is dominated by a single individual because the research technique is conducted among individuals. In business-to-business marketing, often the decision is based on input from a committee or multiple persons. In this case, CA can be effectively used to understand the differences in priorities and preferences of these different individuals within a company. For instance, three different executive officers within one company may be involved in the final decision of what vendor to use or what personnel candidate to hire. Each officer might prefer someone different from the others. Conjoint analysis, in this situation, can help these executives better understand their own and each other's priorities in order to derive a workable solution in the end. But, even better, if you know what is important to each constituent, you can tailor your selling effort to target and satisfy the different concerns of each decision-maker involved—emphasizing reliability and serviceability to the department head, for instance, while stressing technological superiority and innovativeness to the CEO.

Just some of the areas in which CA has been used are shown in Exhibit 10.1. As you see, these fit the criteria of being multi-attribute in nature and of higher economic or emotional risk.

Exhibit 10.1:
Typical Situations Using Conjoint Analysis

Airline travel	Freight train operations
Automobile insurance	Health insurance
Automobile and truck tires	Information-retrieval/on-line computer services
Bank services	Laptop computers
Carpet cleaners	Lawn chemicals
Car rental agencies	Long-distance telephone services
Copying machines	Medical equipment
Credit cards	Printing equipment
Employment agencies	Telephone services
Facsimiles	

Conjoint Basics

Conjoint analysis involves presenting respondents with alternative choice situations and having them rank the alternatives from most to least preferred—a relatively simple task. Then it is a matter for the computer model to *decompose* these preferences by analyzing what features have been consistently present or traded off in the way choices were rank ordered. Those features that have been traded off more frequently, are assumed to be of less importance than features that are nearly always present in the more preferred alternatives. The output of the model is a set of numerical values associated with every feature and feature level that portrays the relative importance of each to the individual.

For example, in evaluating laser printers, you might consider the following features: whether it has color printing; is network capable; how fast it prints; how long is the warranty; and price. Various combinations of these features would be presented to respondents in a systematic way for them to rank-order or indicate preference. The resulting output, using just a few of the above features, is shown in the hypothetical example in Exhibit 10.2.

In this laser printer example, the analysis resulted in computer-derived scores for each selected level of each feature. These are typically called *utilities*, or *partworths*, because they represent the value, or utility, of a given feature to the respondent. In other words, each score shows what a particular feature level is worth, relative to others, in its contribution to the respondent's overall preference choice. Higher scores indicate more importance, of course. By adding together the utilities for each feature of an actual laser printer you would theoretically have the overall preference value for that particular machine. Comparing this to the total utility of another laser printer would tell you the relative preference for one over the other.

Referring to Exhibit 10.2, then, for this one individual, price and print speeds are the most important feature in the purchase decision and the lowest is the most preferred price point. Network capability and warranty have less impact on preference because the utilities are much lower for these features.

Exhibit 10.3 shows minidiagrams of the partworths, or utilities, for each feature. From these diagrams you can easily see that a change in price from low to high greatly reduces preference, and with the high a price point, preference dips considerably lower. The difference between the highest and lowest utility is an indication of the impact of this feature on overall preference. Note that the elasticity of the network capability feature is small and relatively flat. In other words, a change in the network capability of the printer does not appear to influence preference much one way or another; whereas the price elasticity is steep—a change in price has an extreme impact on preference.

These elasticities can be quantified as weights, or percentaged, against the total to show relative influence. These percentages are shown in Exhibit 10.2 and can be interpreted here as meaning that for this individual, low price is most important and faster print speed

Exhibit 10.2:
Hypothetical Conjoint Output for a Laser Printer

	Partworths	Difference	Relative weight
Color Printing			
Yes	.8		
No	.1	.7	13%
Network Capable			
Yes	.8		
No	.5	.3	6%
Print speed			
Slow	.1		
Average	.5		
High	1.8	1.7	33%
Warranty			
One Year	.2		
Two Year	.5		
Three Year	.9	.7	13%
Price			
Low	2.2		
Medium	1.2		
High	.4	1.8	35%
Total utility		5.2	100%

is next most important. The network capability and warranty contribute relatively little to the overall preference for this person.

The ideal laser printer, in fact, for this respondent is one that has color printing, network capability, high print speed, a three year warranty and a low price. Raising the price would have the almost same effect on preference as slowing the print speed, or of removing color printing, network capability and shortening the warranty to one year. Note that the overall preference would be about the same.

Price is an interesting feature present in most business-to-business, as well as consumer, purchase situations. It seems obvious that someone would want to pay the least amount possible for an item given their choice; hence, the higher utility for the lowest price does not come as a surprise. However, the importance of price to the overall purchase decision, or the steepness of the elasticity curve (the part-worth diagram), could vary from person to person or product category to product category. This is why it is so critically important to use price points that are realistic and possible. If there were an option of receiving a laser printer free, the curve would most likely be even steeper in this laser printer example—but artificially so since free is never really a realistic option. If the machine were free, then any consideration of what other features it did or did not have would take a back seat; after all, what would these other features matter if the machine were free!

What is just as important is how price as a feature overall relates to other attributes. If a respondent always ranks the lowest price the highest and the highest price the lowest, then regardless of what any other feature is included or not, that respondent would be considered extremely price sensitive and the only way to sell to that respondent would be through price. If, however, the respondent sometimes ranks other attributes or attribute combinations as more or less important as the price changes, then price is less dominant in the decision and another selling strategy may work better.

While price was shown to be important in the laser printer for this one individual in Exhibits 10.3 and 10.4, you may find that other individuals undergoing the same conjoint exercise might place greater importance on the brand or print speed. Differences such as this allow for the application of conjoint analysis as a market segmentation tool. Individuals who are extremely price sensitive can be grouped together as a market segment, while those who are more brand conscious and less price driven, can be aggregated as another important segment.

Exhibit 10.3:
Partworth Diagrams for Hypothetical Printer Example

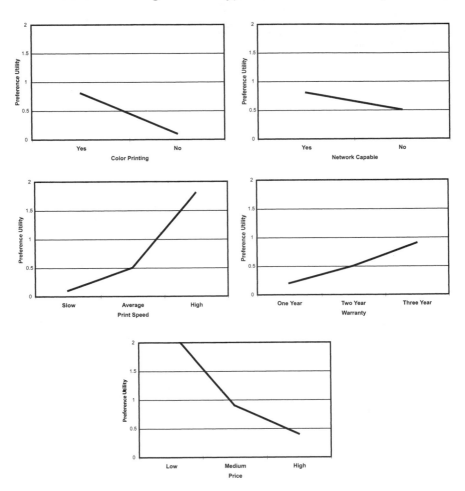

Obviously, an important first step in any conjoint exercise is to determine the appropriate features to test and the levels for each feature. The number of features and/or the number of variations on each feature will greatly impact the complexity of the respondent task. The more detail that is included, the more combinations of features there are to be tested and hence, the more alternatives to rank or choose among for the respondent. Therefore, features need to be selected with care, including only those that past research (perhaps qualitative focus group discussions) has shown to be important in the purchase decision.

Exhibit 10.4:
Relative Importance of Various Printer Attributes

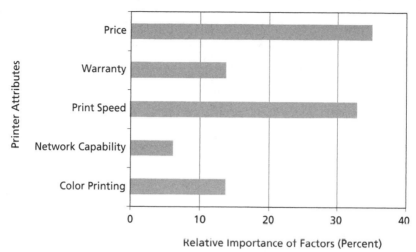

Relative Importance of Factors (Percent)

Once features are selected, there is the task of deciding how many levels to include for any given feature. In some cases, this may be obvious and straightforward, as with the presence of color printing or not (black and white) in a laser printer. Another example would be when the levels have little or no relationship among them, such as a feature like warranty length. In other cases, it is not so simple. Price is one of those variables that can be difficult in this respect—even more so because it is usually such a critical variable to get right. There are literally hundreds of price points that could be tested. You need to apply whatever insight or assumptions about the way price operates in the category in deciding how many and what price points will be selected to test. For instance, if you believe that the market responds to price in a straight linear fashion—the higher the price, the less preferred; the lower the price, the more preferred—then you really only need two price points to represent the entire price spectrum and determine the elasticity. On the other hand, should you believe that there is a curvilinear response with a lower threshold price level that your product must be priced above in order to be considered and under which it will be presumed cheap or defective, or a high price point beyond which preference will not continue to increase, then more price points need to be tested to document these pricing assumptions. The diagrams in Exhibit 10.5 demonstrate the difference between a linear and curvilinear elasticity curve. The implication is

Exhibit 10.5:
Determining Feature Levels for Conjoint Analysis

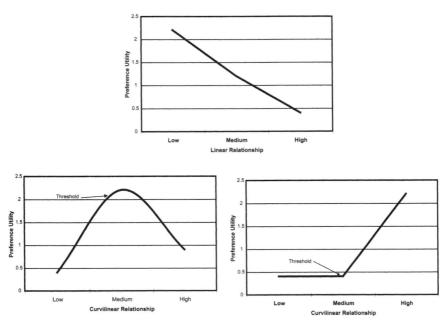

that only two price points are needed in the former example while three or four price points are minimally needed in the latter example. This discussion obviously applies to other continuous variables as well, such as print speed, length of warranty, and so on.

Trade-Off Conjoint Analysis

Trade-off conjoint analysis, or the *two-factor approach*, is the term applied to the form of conjoint analysis that requires respondents to make choices about every combination of feature levels. It is this necessary but sometimes intense data collection task that adds to the stability of the utilities for even those samples that are on the small side. The task is made easier for respondents by presenting them with a series of combinations based on only pairs of features, or two features at a time. Two by two, then, all features are paired off and their various combinations ranked in terms of preference. The prevailing assumption of this approach is that an individual is capable of evaluating features independently of one another; in other words, preference for an item can be expressed given only two features and without knowledge or consideration of all the other possible features.

To illustrate this approach, think back to the laser printer example earlier. In this example, there were five features to test or trade-off against one another. To keep the numbers simple, let's consider only three of these features here: print speed, color printing, and price. In a two-factor approach, all pairs of these three features would need to be considered separately, or three pairs in all: (1) speed and color printing, (2) speed and price, and (3) color printing and price. Each pair would be combined to create a set of alternative combinations based on how many levels exist for each feature. Pairing off print speed with the handset option results in six choices for which the respondent needs to rank their preference (3 print speeds × 2 color printing conditions).

Exhibit 10.6 shows one common way of presenting these options on paper—in a matrix or table format where the rows are the levels for one feature and the columns are designated by the levels for the second feature. In this way, six cells result, which represent the six possible combinations of the two feature levels. The task, then, is for

Exhibit 10.6: Trade-off Conjoint Matrices

Color Printing		
Print Speed	Color	Black Only
Low		
Average		
High		

Price			
Print Speed	Low	Medium	High
Low	3		
Average	2		
High	1	4	

Price			
Color Printing	Low	Medium	High
Color			
Black Only			

the respondent to consider each cell as a choice and rank these alternatives from most preferred to least preferred. Each time a favorite cell is chosen, the respondent is left with the remaining alternatives and forced to pick their next most favorite choice. This continues until there are no options left.

If you consider the second table in Exhibit 10.6, there are three levels for each of the two features, or nine cells in the table. The most preferred choice would probably be the same for nearly everyone, a printer with the highest print speed at the lowest price. You would indicate this by marking a "1" in that box. Then you need to make a decision—do you opt for a slower print speed and keep the low price, or do you pay more to keep the faster speed? If you choose to trade-off print speed in favor of price, you mark a "2" in the box as shown. This is the first indication that you may be price sensitive, at least relative to print speed. Then once again, you are faced with the decision of whether to trade-off print speed to the slower level or pay more to have double the print speed. A price sensitive person would continue to select the low price over speed; someone who is less price driven might select the latter option by marking the bottom box of the second column instead. And the choices continue.

Note that the task is relatively straightforward and simple when only two features are involved. If price in this example is always the number one feature for an individual, then the ranks systemically follow the columns. If another feature takes precedence over price entirely, the ranks would follow the rows, for instance, always the fastest print speed regardless of price. In many instances, price may be traded-off selectively, as when someone is willing to compromise on print speed to eight ppm but not to the point of the slowest printer speed; here, the ranks will jog around a bit throughout the table. Still, the task is simple and fast.

The difficult part is accomplished by the CA computer model, which then attempts to systematically evaluate what trade-offs have been made and how often for each feature across all tables in order to derive utility values. These, of course, represent the priority placed on any one feature level as revealed by the initial preference ranks.

It is easy to see how even a slightly more complicated problem would dramatically increase the number of choices or cells that would need examination. If there were four price levels and four print speeds instead of three for each, the table would contain sixteen choices to rank instead of nine. If four features were evaluated rather than just the three, the number of separate tables would double from three to six. Therefore, you should be cautioned to scrutinize and select features and their respective levels carefully before plunging into a conjoint analysis.

The trade-off approach works well when features do not interact with one another, or in other words, the preference or utility of one variable compared to another does not depend on the circumstances of a third feature. If the decision cannot be made independently of that other variable, then there is likely a statistical interaction between them that a two-by-two approach will not be able to measure. For instance, considering the laser printer example again, if the decision of which print speed is best is completely dependent in a buyer's mind on an evaluation of color printing or network capability, then a two-factor approach will not suffice since print speed always is evaluated in the context of memory.

Full-Profile Conjoint Analysis

A second approach to using the conjoint method is called *full-profile*, or *multiple-factor*, approach. Today, with computerized models to facilitate the process, this has become the dominant method used by researchers. As the name implies, the difference in the procedure is that respondents are presented with complete profiles of alternative products, each alternative profiled in terms of information on each and every feature of interest. Rather than considering alternatives that are defined by only two features at a time, an individual is confronted with many alternatives for which he or she must consider all the various features before indicating a rank- ordered preference among them. The reason this method is so popular is that it most parallels an actual decision or purchase situation. A brand or service is defined by all its features, and a decision to buy one over another is made in that context. While it is true that this may be a more difficult evaluation process for the buyer, especially when there is a lot of information on which to base a decision, it is also the more realistic process.

Again, all possible combinations of features and feature levels need representation and rank ordering in order for the computer to systematically assess what is being traded-off. Consider the example from before where the laser printer was limited to three features. The total number of profiles created by combining these three features is eighteen (3 print speeds × 2 color print levels × 3 price levels). These eighteen product profiles are outlined in Exhibit 10.7. Each profile

Exhibit 10.7: Product Descriptions in a Full-Profile Conjoint Analysis Example

Card	Print Speed	Color Printing	Price
1	Slow	Yes	Low
2	Slow	Yes	Medium
3	Slow	Yes	High
4	Slow	No	Low
5	Slow	No	Medium
6	Slow	No	High
7	Average	Yes	Low
8	Average	Yes	Medium
9	Average	Yes	High
10	Average	No	Low
11	Average	No	Medium
12	Average	No	High
13	Fast	Yes	Low
14	Fast	Yes	Medium
15	Fast	Yes	High
16	Fast	No	Low
17	Fast	No	Medium
18	Fast	No	High

would be presented on a separate card so that the respondent would have a stack of eighteen cards. The task is to rank order the cards from most preferred to least preferred.

Verbal descriptions presented on a card or on a computer screen are perhaps the most common way profiles are presented. However, paragraph descriptions, pictorial representations where features are prominently displayed, or, sometimes, actual products or mock-ups of products can be used as well.

Regardless of the presentation format, if the number of alternatives is too many and the task too great to accomplish in one simple rank ordering, a two-step (or multiple-step) sorting process can be used. In this case, respondents first separate the eighteen profiles into two or three piles—for instance, those they definitely like, those they definitely do *not* like, and those that fall somewhere in between. Then, they proceed from the "definitely like" pile, rank ordering just these from most to least preferred, to the middle pile doing the same, and finally to the "don't like" pile where they rank order those so that in the end a complete rank ordering is obtained.

Just as with the trade-off approach, the greater the number of features and/or feature levels, the greater the complexity of the task since there will be many more profiles in the pile. Adding just the one extra price point would increase the number of profiles from eighteen to twenty-four (3 speeds × 2 colors × 4 prices); adding another printer feature with just two levels doubles the number of profiles from eighteen to thirty-six (3 speeds x 2 colors × 3 prices × 2)!

At some point, the number of combinations can become too numerous and complex to reasonably handle without fatiguing a respondent. There are ways to statistically weed out some of the combinations that have mostly redundant information in order to keep the number of alternatives smaller. The trick is to make sure that all of the necessary comparisons are retained to properly assess trade-offs on the main features. Most of the conjoint analysis computer programs have routines that will do this for you and dictate the best profiles to include in the analysis. In the previous example, instead of eighteen profiles, you could get by with only eight (3 + 2 + 3). This is just a fraction of the original number, and any good experimental design book or chapter that discusses "fractional" factorial designs can amplify this process. It is usually a good idea to include some repetitive comparisons, referred to as *holdouts*, to check for reliability.

Typically when a fractional design is used, what is lost with the elimination of some profiles is the measurement of certain interactions among the larger set of variables. Remember that an *interaction* means that two or more features cannot be evaluated independently from one another because the preference will behave uniquely in combination. Since a full-profile method tests combinations in their entirety, all interactions are automatically measured if they exist. By sacrificing some of the profile combinations in order to simplify the burden to the respondent, some of these interactions will not be fully tested. Because interactions can greatly complicate a conjoint analysis, many commercial conjoint research suppliers ignore them altogether anyway; therefore, practically speaking, this issue of interactions is academic. However, in the instance where interactions do exist, ignoring them can yield inaccurate preference measures.

Alternative Measurement Techniques in Conjoint Analysis

The discussion thus far has been in terms of rank-order judgments made by the respondent. While it is easiest to understand the technique by imagining respondents making these types of judgments, other formats can be used in conjoint analysis and computer-aided interviewing has become a popular way to handle these.

The Paired Comparison

In either the trade-off approach or the full-profile approach, you can simplify the rank ordering process even further by only presenting two alternatives to a respondent at a time. For instance, two of the cells from one of the tables in the two-factor approach, or two of the profiles from the stack of profiles in the full-profile method, can be shown at once and the preferred one selected of the two. Obviously a series of pairs would need to be shown, but the decision of which is the favorite from only two options is so much simpler and faster that it is often used. From this kind of paired comparison procedure, a final rank order can be statistically estimated.

Rating Scales

A rank ordering of preference can also be estimated using the full-profile method if each profile is independently rated using a scale. Pro-

Exhibit 10.8: Example Conjoint Presentation

WHICH LASER PRINTER WOULD YOU PREFER?

Printer X:
   Color Printing
   Network Capable
   Three Year Warranty
   Average Print Speed
   High Price

Printer Y:
   Color Printing
   Not Network Capable
   One Year Warranty
   Fast Print Speed
   Medium Price

CHOOSE A NUMBER TO SHOW YOUR PREFERENCE

Strongly Prefer Left	1	2	3	4	5	6	7	8	Strongly Prefer Right

files could be rated in terms of how much each is liked or disliked on a scale, how likely it is that each would be purchased, or some other criterion appropriate to the study objectives. The problem with rating scales is that ties can occur, where one profile may be rated exactly the same as another. Paired comparisons and rank-order judgments force the respondent to compare and choose. When ties occur, it is more difficult to estimate trade-offs in priorities since none are made.

Exhibit 10.8 shows an example of a paired comparison that also uses a rating scale to measure preference.

Computer-Aided Interviewing

Because administering a conjoint analysis procedure can become a complex task needing supervision and explanation, computer aided techniques have been increasingly employed as a tool in CA. Many of the software packages have well-developed computer-aided interviewing routines that respondents can complete on their own. Since presentation of features or profiles on a computer screen must be simplified to function well, the task is sometimes easier for respondents than a similar presentation on paper.

In addition, with the computer aiding the process, the exact presentation of features and feature levels for a product choice situation can be adapted and tailored to each individual based on some initial parameters set by the respondent, such as budget range, which might impact the range of price points that are most realistic, or the set of brands with which a respondent is familiar since he or she could not properly evaluate brands that were unfamiliar. Furthermore, if the computer detects a pattern of priorities in a respondent's choices, then later comparisons can be altered (and perhaps some eliminated altogether) in order to evaluate the most difficult trade-offs in more depth. A market researcher administering CA would have a tough time keeping track of a respondent's choices in this way and knowing how to tailor the response set. Yet, for a computer, this is relatively simple.

Computer-aided techniques reduce respondent fatigue and can improve the data quality. They have been in use for more than twenty years. Typically, a computer is set up in a research facility somewhere in a central, convenient location and potential respondents are invited or recruited to come in and participate. For more sophisticated buyers who have easy access to their own computer, it would be possible to send a computer diskette with the conjoint routine through the mail to be completed and mailed back.

Conjoint Simulation

Once utilities have been estimated for a market segment, then additional analyses can be performed. The use of "conjoint simulators" is common and arguably at the heart of what conjoint analysis is all about. It is an available feature of most conjoint software packages. The simulator routines allow you to estimate the ideal feature combinations for your customer, or various customer segments, or to simulate changes to your product or service features. You can easily expand or reduce the competitive alternatives in the market and estimate your product's share of preference, or likelihood of being purchased. By simulating anticipated changes in your competitors' product line, you can estimate the impact these changes will have on your product.

11 Multidimensional Scaling and Preference Mapping

Multidimensional scaling (MDS) is another small group quantitative technique. It quantifies the perceptions and images that people have about a market, a brand, or any concept by assessing how similar or dissimilar people perceive them to be from various other related concepts. *Multidimensional scaling* is often called *perceptual mapping* because, in addition to deriving the perceptual "distances" among brands or concepts, the program will plot these concepts as points in a geometric space so that they are visually shown as a picture—a "perceptual map." From this map you can quickly and intuitively see the mental picture people have of a particular market or topic area. By interpreting how near or far different points in the map are from one another, and by interpreting the dimensions by which the points are plotted, you are able to gain insights into how different brands or concepts are positioned in the minds of your audience, what the perceived relationships among these concepts are, and why these perceptions exist.

MDS Uses and Benefits

Designing the most effective messages for an audience in order to strengthen or change their mental image is a side benefit that MDS offers. If maps are created and compared for two different audiences—for instance, loyal customers versus nonloyal customers or noncustomers—it is often possible to find even very subtle differences in their perceptions that explain the differences in their buying behaviors, just by the way the points appear to shift within the space from one group to the other. This then leads to the development of a communication strategy that targets differentiated messages toward different perceptual segments.

Exhibit 11.1: Multidimensional Scaling "Perceptual Map"

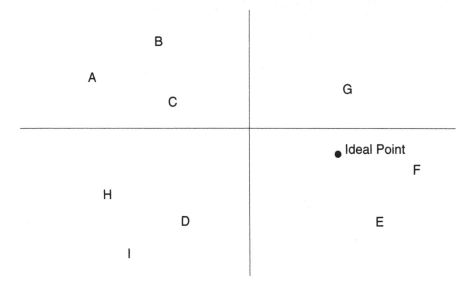

Preference mapping is a related procedure that measures people's preferences for the same concepts used for the MDS; from these preferences it derives the most preferred point and maps this "ideal" point back into the perceptual map, as shown in Exhibit 11.1. In this way, a market researcher would not only know how brands or topical concepts are currently perceived, but also how they fall short of the ideal. Together, MDS and preference mapping can reveal opportunity niches for developing new products or for repositioning existing ones.

Used individually or in conjunction with preference mapping, MDS is powerful in its ability to reveal the structure of a marketplace from the customers' viewpoint. As an example, if your company is a rental car agency, you would probably be very interested in understanding the perceptions people have about the rental market; the images they hold for the various competitors such as Hertz, Avis, and National; how your company is positioned relative to these competitors; how you might improve your standing in the marketplace; and what message strategies would best help you accomplish this. Multidimensional scaling will help you to visualize the perceptual differences among these companies by plotting the concepts you select (or that customers use) to define the market. Key competitors such as Hertz, Avis, and National would be included in the study, in addition to adjectives such as *convenient, affordable, quality, reliable, prestigious, friendly,* and *fast*.

After all is done, the MDS map will show how each of these agencies and your own is positioned with respect to each other and to the selected adjectives. Do the agencies all cluster together, indicating that they are perceived as being very similar? Or, are they scattered across the space showing very different "brand" images for each? Is a "prestigious" agency perceived as an "affordable" agency—in other words, do these two concepts appear together on the map? Or, are these on opposite sides of the map, each aligning with a different mental set? The way the points are positioned within the map will tell you a lot about the image of these companies in your audience's eyes.

By including the concept "Me" in the space to represent the respondent or by plotting an ideal point using preference mapping, you can also learn which agencies your audience most relates to and which attributes are most important to them. This, in turn, will suggest alternative message strategies for repositioning your agency to "move" it closer to "Me," or the rental agency ideal point on the map.

MDS Applications

Multidimensional scaling can be applied to both consumer and business-to-business problems where understanding, developing, and tracking perceptual images are important. Just some of the questions MDS can shed light on are:

- What is my brand/company/service's image or perceived position in the marketplace?
- Who are my key competitors in the customers' eyes?
- What are my perceived strengths and weaknesses?
- What are the underlying perceptual dimensions that are determining the perceptions people have for my product/service?
- How do I best position my new product/service or reposition my existing product/service?
- What are my best message strategies?
- How are alternative creative executions perceived, and which is the "ideal" execution for my brand?
- Are there different "perceptual" segments in the market to which I should communicate/sell differently?
- How has my company's image changed over time relative to the competition's?
- Are there untapped opportunities in the marketplace that are as yet unmet by the competition?

Obviously, by the creation of a "map" that lays out the position of one brand relative to another brand or descriptive concept, you are able to see the perceptual structure of a market and the positionings of brands within that market. Your key competitors from your customers' perspective would be revealed to you as those brands that visually cluster near your own. By scrutinizing and interpreting the dimensions on which the brands or concepts appear to be differentiated, you can learn the strengths and weaknesses of your own brand and your competitors'.

Multidimensional scaling even yields useful information to guide how you communicate with or sell to your market. Much of business-to-business marketing communication is based on the assumption that customers' buying behavior is patterned after their attitudes and beliefs about the product/service category and the available brands. Marketing communications are developed, then, in an attempt to change people's perceptions in the hope that buyer behavior will also change in the desired way. Unfortunately, communication tactics frequently go awry. And when they do, it is often because the marketing strategist did not fully understand how the audience perceived the brand in the first place or how the communication would be perceived by the targeted audience. For this reason, a marketer has an advantage whenever he or she can visualize—or make a mental picture—of what the audience perceptions actually are and develop message strategies based upon what would drive those attitudes and beliefs about the brand in a positive direction.

The concepts within the perceptual map can lead you to those ideal message strategies. In this rental car agency example, the concepts included such descriptors as "affordable," "prestigious," "reliable," and "convenient." Any one of these concepts could become the foundation for a communication strategy if by associating your company with one or a combination of them appears as though it will reposition your name in a desirable way within the perceptual framework. Once you have initiated a communications strategy, you can then reevaluate your audiences' perceptions later and compare the two maps to see if the desired effect has taken place.

If you have several creative pieces, you can show them to your intended audience and ask them to rate how similar these are to one another as well as to individually rate their preference for each, thereby creating a map of the executions with an ideal point plotted as well. Once you have learned how the audience has perceived the various creative pieces, and you know what the ideal execution should be, you can start to speculate on what it is that perceptually differentiates these pieces and how to refine them appropriately.

You might even find that after looking at what the ideal concept is, and where the existing brands are, that there is a gap—an opportunity to develop a new product or a new positioning to take advantage of the "hole" in the perceptual space. The justification for this, of course, is that no brand already holds that viable position so the competition is less.

MDS Procedure

Multidimensional scaling begins with the task of selecting the concepts to be included in the map, or those brands, adjective descriptors, and other key concepts and/or phrases that define the topic or market under study. This is a critical stage because the map will only be as good as the concepts within it. If the wrong brands are selected in that your audience is not familiar with them, or the adjectives are not meaningful, relevant, or clearly understood, then respondents will not only have a difficult time completing the necessary tasks, but the resulting map will be useless. Time taken in the beginning to refine the concept set is well worth the wait.

If any competitive positioning is needed, then obviously you will need to determine which competitive brands, and how many, to include in the study. Often, market share figures, past quantitative research, and insights from the sales force or focus group discussions with your customers will provide you with the appropriate set of brands. It is possible, and sometimes desirable, to *only* plot brands, without any other descriptors or concepts at all. The first column in Exhibit 11.2 shows the brands that might be included in a perceptual study of the copier category.

When there are very few brands within a field, or when the purpose is to better understand your own brand's positioning on key criteria—such as affordability or quality—you may want to include these other descriptors. Again, the specific adjectives or criteria should be selected with care based on input from those close to the market and the research, as well as from actual customers.

In fact, if you want to know what concepts people use to define a topic or a category such as the copier category, doing qualitative research is quite helpful. Simply ask people to talk at some length about copiers and copier brands and record the words they use to describe the product, like "office equipment," "complicated," "expensive," "reliable," "big company," and "aloof." At first, many such descriptors will become apparent from the interviews, but somewhat surprisingly, after a short while, people begin to repeat the same words and ideas. After five or ten interviews, very few new concepts emerge. In fact, while as many as forty or fifty such concepts may sometimes be discovered in a series of twenty-five to fifty interviews, those that are repeatedly mentioned very seldom number more than a dozen.

The second column in Exhibit 11.2 shows the concepts that might be included in an MDS study, again in the copier category, when descriptors are mixed with brand names. In this case, only three brands were included for study, the top three in this particular small business market: Canon, Sharp, and Xerox. The other 12 concepts are descriptors to help determine the positioning of these three copier brands in the customers' minds.

Once the concepts are selected, data on how similar the concepts are to one another need to be gathered in order to construct the map. This is usually referred to as "similarities" or "proximities" data, although "dissimilarities" data could be collected depending on how you flip-flop the similarity scale. Respondents are essentially asked to judge how similar or different each pair of brands and/or concepts are

Exhibit 11.2: Example MDS Concepts for the Copier Category

Brands	Brand and Descriptors
1. Canon	1. Affordable
2. Kodak	2. Aloof
3. Konica	3. American
4. Minolta	4. Approachable
5. Mita	5. Bureaucratic
6. Panasonic	6. Conservative
7. RICOH	7. High quality
8. Sharp	8. Innovative
9. Toshiba	9. Intimidating
10. Xerox	10. Me
	11. Prestigious
	12. Reliable
	13. Canon
	14. Sharp
	15. Xerox

to one another. This translates geometrically to how close together or far apart they are in the map. Such "distance" measures are needed for every concept relative to every other concept in a complete pairwise fashion in order to derive more stable coordinates for each in the map.

Obviously, then, the more concepts that are included in the study, the more pairs there will be to evaluate. To make the point, if there are 8 concepts, then 28 pairs need to be judged; if there are 16 concepts, then 120 pairs need to be judged. The number of pairs increases more rapidly than the number of concepts and respondent fatigue can become a serious issue. Weary respondents will estimate distances poorly and inconsistently. You need, therefore, to keep the concepts you use to a reasonable number.

Going back to the copier concepts in Exhibit 11.2, notice that the two lists are relatively short. In the first scenario, there will be forty-five pairs from the ten brands. The average respondent will need less than ten minutes to estimate distances for the forty-five pairs. In the second example with fifteen concepts, the 105 resulting pairs are just about the maximum number that the average respondent is able to evaluate at one time. Respondents begin losing interest after 100 or so pairs; hence, you would be best advised to limit your study to around fifteen concepts or less.

The similarity judgments can be measured in many ways: using a line scale or other direct estimating rating technique to assess the perceptual distance for each pair; comparing two pairs at a time and having the respondent select which of the two pairs are more similar to each other; or rank ordering all the pairs relative to one another. Examples of some of these methods are shown in Exhibit 11.3.

Notice that respondents are given no criteria on which to make their similarity judgment. This is purposeful. Without predetermined criteria, such as "based on cost" or "based on quality," respondents are left to their own devices, preconceptions, and criteria. This ambiguity, uncharacteristic for most other kinds of survey research, has distinct advantages here. It eliminates any bias the researcher might have of what is important and allows the research method to uncover the actual dimensions on which these judgments are being made. In addition, in many instances, an individual might not really know *why* two concepts seem to be similar in his or her mind, or cannot clearly verbalize his or her sense of what is similar because it is complicated by the fact that it is "multidimensional" in nature. This notion of multidimensionality is at the heart of multidimensional scaling, as its

Exhibit 11.3: Examples of MDS Similarity Measures

A. How similar or different are:

Canon and Xerox

Very Similar _____ Very Different

Canon and American

Very Similar _____ Very Different

B. How similar or different are:

Canon and Xerox

Very Similar 1   2   3   4   5   6   7   8   9   10   Very Different

Canon and American

Very Similar 1   2   3   4   5   6   7   8   9   10   Very Different

C. On a scale from 0 to 100, how would you rate the similarity of the following pairs of concepts? If you think two concepts are very similar, seem to go together, or are often associated with each other, then write a *small* number. On the other hand, if you think the concepts are very different, do not seem to go together, or are seldom associated with one another, then write a *large* number.

   Thus a zero means that you believe the two concepts are identical, while a 100 means that you believe the two concepts are as different from each other as they possibly could be. How similar are:

   Canon and Xerox _____
   Canon and American _____
   Canon and My Business _____

D. Which pair of words seem to be more similar or seem to go together better? Choose one.

   1. Canon and Xerox   Canon and Sharp
   2. Canon and American   Canon and My Business

E. Please rank order the following concept pairs based on how similar the word pairs seem to be. The pair that you think seems the most alike, rank first; the pair you think seems next most similar, rank second; and so on. The pair that is the most different in your opinion should be ranked last.

   Canon and Xerox
   Canon and American
   Canon and Sharp
   Canon and My Business

name implies. The art of MDS is trying to understand what the perceptual dimensions in a customer's mind are—without leading him or her.

By quantifying how similar an individual perceives all the pairs of MDS concepts, the computer can convert these similarity judgments into actual distance measures that can be plotted on a map. Exhibits 11.4 and 11.5 show two maps for the copier example, one with just the brands and the other with mixed brands and descriptors.

Interpreting the Perceptual Map

The payoff in MDS comes from interpreting the perceptual map. The wonderful aspect of MDS is that, while the MDS algorithm is statistically complicated, the output is highly readable for just about anyone, regardless of their statistical prowess. The maps are friendly and most people intuitively understand how to read them. However, interpretations are often subjective. Everyone who looks at the map may have a different idea of why the brands are positioned in a certain way or what the "dimensions" defining the space represent. Before you accept one interpretation, consider sharing the map with others who will be using the results, such as a creative team or members of the sales force, to see if they might have new and different interpretations based on their particular realm of experience.

There is no one right way to interpret a perceptual map, but knowing how the map was created helps you to understand how to begin the process. The concepts are plotted based on a coordinate system in two dimensions at a time. Each dimension is shown as a line, one horizontal and one vertical. The point at which the lines intersect is the origin and it is from this point that the computer begins to measure and plot the concepts based on an estimate of their distance along each dimension. Therefore, you can interpret the map in two ways. First, you should look to see which concepts tend to "cluster" with which other concepts in the space. Second, you should try to identify what each dimension defining the space means.

Interpreting concept clusters can be very revealing. If two concepts are very near one another, you could say they are perceived as being very much the same. Concepts that are isolated must be perceived that way—as alone. In Exhibit 11.4, the ten copier brands are scattered across the four quadrants of the space, but the first thing that is noticeable is that the Xerox brand stands out all by itself, distinctly separate from its competition. No other brand is perceived to

Exhibit 11.4: Copier MDS with Brands Only

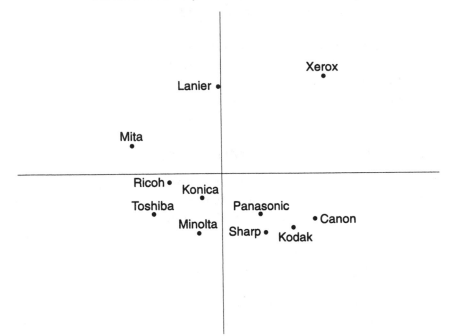

be like Xerox in the minds of these respondents. On the other hand, you can clearly see that Panasonic, Canon, Kodak, and Sharp all appear to cluster together in one quadrant, while Toshiba, RICOH, Konica, and Minolta form another, much looser cluster in a different quadrant. The respondents whose perceptions are captured in this map believe that there are three distinct competitive groups, where brands within each cluster are perceived very similarly. What do the brands in each cluster have in common that is different from other brands?

Exhibit 11.5 shows another perceptual map for copiers. In this map you can see many interesting associations. Notice that, on the one hand, Xerox is clustered with adjectives such as "bureaucratic," "aloof," and "conservative." On the other hand, Xerox is also perceived as "high quality," "reliable," and "relatively prestigious." In fact, you see that "quality," "reliability," and "prestige" all cluster together as attributes that are perceived to be similar in nature, the same way that "bureaucratic," "aloof," and "conservative" all are perceived as associated with one another.

Sharp and Canon are perceived as being very similar brands and much closer to "My Business" than Xerox. The reason may lie in the

Exhibit 11.5: Copier MDS Map with Descriptors

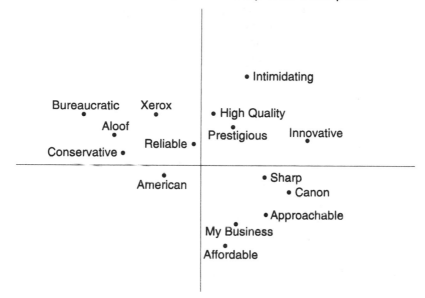

fact that these respondents see their businesses more associated with affordable products and approachable companies and both Sharp and Canon are considered approachable and more affordable than Xerox. It is interesting to note that while Xerox is perceived as more American than its competitors in the map, Sharp and Canon are not that distant from this concept either, indicating that these two Japanese companies are perceived as being almost as American as Xerox.

What is just as interesting is what concepts are *not* associated with one another. Companies that are bureaucratic and conservative in nature are not readily perceived as being innovative or approachable or having affordable products. Higher quality products are not believed to be affordable. And Xerox is not the first choice copier brand for those responding to this study.

Simply scrutinizing the map for these kinds of associations is a natural lead-in to the second interpretive step—identifying what the dimensions in the space mean. This is not always necessary since the concept associations in the previous step should tell most of the story. However, sometimes interpreting the dimensions will impart additional insight.

The best way to understand a dimension is to mentally draw lines from each concept perpendicular to first the horizontal axis, and then the vertical axis, and view the order in which they line up along each line. In Exhibit 11.4, the horizontal dimension is anchored at one end by Mita, Toshiba, RICOH, and Konica (in that order) and, from the other end, Canon, Xerox, Kodak, Panasonic, and Sharp. You might interpret this dimension as representing familiarity, extending from the unfamiliar to the more familiar. Or perhaps it is a continuum representing Japanese/Foreign companies on the left side to American or American-sounding company names on the right side.

The vertical dimension starts at the top with Xerox, followed by Lanier, Mita, and RICOH and continues down to Toshiba/Panasonic/Canon, Kodak, and Minolta/Sharp. One good interpretation for this is that respondents are differentiating based on how much the company specializes in copiers. Xerox and Lanier are best and only known for copiers, while Minolta, Sharp, Kodak, Canon, Panasonic, and Toshiba are all recognized brand names in other electronic industries such as cameras, televisions, VCRs, microwaves, and computers.

In Exhibit 11.5 the same dimensional interpretation can be accomplished. Here the horizontal dimension is anchored on the one end by concepts such as "bureaucratic," "aloof," and "conservative" and on the other end with "innovative" and "approachable." This dimension could be labeled "Conservative/Innovative" or "Traditional/Progressive." From this perspective, Xerox is seen as a traditional, conservative company and not as a progressive or innovative one. Canon and Sharp are both perceived to be more progressive or innovative.

The vertical dimension in this case is anchored by "intimidating" and "high quality" at the top and "affordable" and "approachable" near the bottom. This could be interpreted as a High/Low Quality dimension, a High/Low Cost dimension, or a Less/More Approachable dimension. All of these interpretations go somewhat hand in hand and clearly show Xerox to be a higher quality but higher priced and less approachable/more intimidating company than either Sharp or Canon.

Once again, keep in mind that labeling dimensions is subjective and relatively arbitrary. It often depends on the perspective and/or knowledge of the person doing the interpretation. Dimensions can also come in two varieties. In the copier examples, most of the dimensions were characterized as continuums along which the concepts gradually changed from high to low or more to less of some attribute, such as cost or quality. A dimension may also simply separate category types, however. In the copier brand map, the American vs. Foreign dimension might be merely dichotomous in nature rather than a continuum. To better clarify, in an MDS study of print advertisements for a car manufacturer, a dichotomous dimension was found to exist separating those executions that contained people from those that were void of people and contained only cars and inanimate images.

Mapping Preferences

Preference mapping works best in situations where you are plotting brands only. Though the perceptual map portrays the similarities and differences among the various brands, since no descriptors are included, there is no indication of which brands or brand types are most preferred by the respondent(s). To understand brand differences, preference mapping can be invaluable. To assess preference, an additional set of questions is required in the data collection stage. Respondents are shown each of the brands and asked to either rank them from most to least preferred or to rate each individually on a scale. From this data, then, an "ideal point" can be plotted back into the original perceptual map. This point probably will not coincide with one of the actual brands but instead represent the ideal combination of attributes for a brand as defined by the dimensions.

In the copier example, the ten copier brands were defined by an American/Foreign dimension and a Specialist/General Electronics dimension. Exhibit 11.6 shows this same plot with an ideal point added. Interpreting this added information, you can see that the ideal copier company from the perspective of these respondents is one that is American rather than foreign and more of a copier specialist rather than a general electronics company. Knowing these preferences gives some indication of what to emphasize in your selling or communication effort. You may find that different market segments have similar perceptions of the industry (their perceptual maps are the same), but have very different preferences and views of what they consider "ideal." In this case, you could map more than one ideal point back into the space to show how these market segments differ in this respect.

Preference mapping is not necessary in the other copier example because one of the concepts included in the map was "My Business." This concept substitutes in a way for an ideal point because it reflects the respondents' views of what they would prefer. As shown, the businesses prefer a company that is more affordable and approachable than any of the brands represent in the map.

Exhibit 11.6: Perceptual Map with Preference Mapping

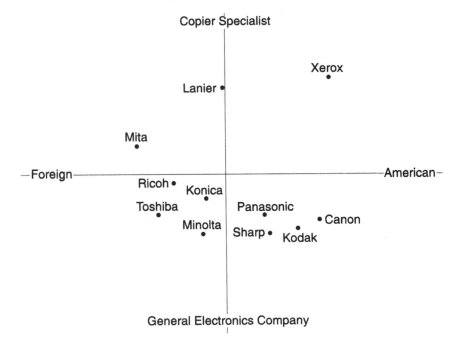

Developing Message Strategies

Earlier, the application of MDS to message development was mentioned. It is possible to use perceptual mapping to identify key concepts that might be used in creating alternative message strategies
with the purpose of changing the market's perceptions in a way that is
desirable to you. Visualize moving your brand closer to the ideal
point, or "My Business," in the two maps already presented. Alternatively, you could strategize to move the ideal point, or "My Business,"
in the direction of your brand and its image, but it is probably easier
in most situations to change the one brand's image than to alter respondents' perceptions of who they are and what they prefer.

One metric MDS routine, Galileo, can identify the best concept or
combination of concepts that, if associated with your brand, should
have the impact of moving it closer to the respondents' position. Exhibit 11.7 illustrates how this might be done. Let's say that the goal is
to move Xerox closer to "My Business" in the space. Examples of alternative message strategies would be to emphasize:

Exhibit 11.7: Message Strategies for Copier Example

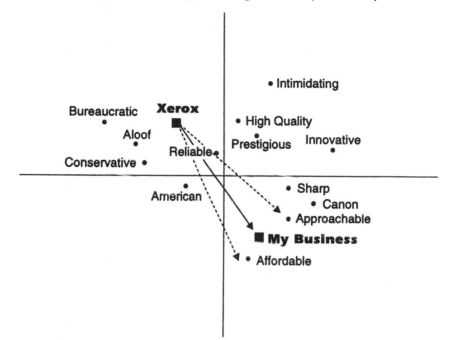

1. Reliability
2. Affordability and approachability
3. American, affordability, and innovativeness

To understand how this works, imagine that by associating the Xerox name with a concept, such as affordable, the Xerox point moves toward that concept. Moving Xerox toward affordable is indeed in the right direction but a bit off the path to "My Business." By associating Xerox with approachable, however, you are moving the brand toward "My Business," but once again it is slightly off the direct path. By emphasizing both *affordable* and *approachable*, the impact would be to move Xerox squarely on top of the ideal point since the sum of these two "vectors" is the solid line shown in Exhibit 11.7. The Galileo computer routine will calculate the best combinations quantitatively.

Metric Versus Nonmetric Measurement

Two models of multidimensional scaling have developed over time based on the way respondents estimate the differences between concepts. Metric measures are those that use higher level measurement, such as ratio scaling techniques that require respondents to (1) estimate actual distances between concepts with a number or (2) mark on a line scale that can be directly related to a number. Examples of metric measuring scales are A, B, and C in Exhibit 11.3.

The precision available to respondents with metric procedures allows the creation of a more exact map. The metric multidimensional scaling algorithm will attempt to plot each point so that it is exactly as many units from every other point as the respondent indicated. If that cannot be done in a simple two-dimensional plot, the computer will plot it in three or more dimensions. Rarely, however, are more than three dimensions ever used and interpreted because a fourth or fifth dimension cannot be plotted or physically modeled and most people cannot visualize beyond the three-dimensional world that we live in.

If you used the actual air distances (rather than perceptual distances) between pairs of key cities across the United States as input data for a metric MDS routine, the computer would print a map that looks exactly like it should with New York in the Northeast, Chicago in the Midwest, and San Francisco in the West. You would find, however, that the fit in two dimensions is not perfect. Some of the distances do not exactly coordinate with one another because you cannot account for the curvature of the earth in only two planes. The first plane is the vertical plane and represents north/south on the map; the second plane is the horizontal plane, or east/west on the map; a third dimension, the curvature of the earth, is needed to explain the distances perfectly.

Nonmetric techniques do not require a direct estimate of perceptual distance. The nonmetric techniques ask the respondent only to make rank-order judgments about the differences between the pairs of concepts; in other words, respondents must only compare the pairs to each other and say which is more or less similar than the others. Parts D and E in Exhibit 11.3 are both examples of nonmetric measurements.

One of the biggest problems with nonmetric methods is that they do not reliably reproduce the space or map. In the example of the U.S. cities, you would see the key cities in the nonmetric version are positioned approximately where they should be but not as precisely as in the metric map. This is because when you say that Chicago and Denver are closer together than Chicago and Seattle, you have not indicated how much closer together. The nonmetric computer algorithm can apply an "elastic ruler" approach to fit all the cities into a spatial configuration that does not violate any of the rank-order specifications.

Ironically, the less precise nonmetric MDS methods were developed *after* metric MDS (MMDS). The reasoning behind nonmetric methods is almost a philosophical one. Some market researchers believed, and still do believe, that people cannot make the kind of distance judgments required by the metric approach. They argue that the task of placing a number on your perceptions, attitudes, and beliefs is unnatural, ambiguous, and difficult. After all, is the difference between Brand A and Brand B 80, 85, or 90? Could there be error in the judgment? If some of the precision is sacrificed and only rank orders are required, you obviously make the measurement task much easier for a respondent and yet maintain the overall integrity of the perceptions (the placement of the cities on the nonmetric map <u>was</u> more correct than incorrect).

Other researchers would argue heartily in favor of the metric approach, even if it can be awkward at times, simply because it is so much better at reproducing perceptual maps. They believe that metric judgments are actually not that difficult for people to make because the concept of a ruler and of measuring things is well developed for most individuals. No doubt some respondents have difficulty with the metric task, but over several respondents, the too-high estimates will average out with those that are perhaps too low and result in a stable pattern that represents a market's true value.

Perceptual Mapping and Qualitative Research

In Chapter 9, focus group discussions and one-on-one interviewing techniques were discussed at some length because of their importance in business-to-business research. However, one disadvantage to using only these kinds of qualitative research methods is that you never have any quantitative information on which to base decisions. The numbers of respondents are typically too small and the mode of questioning is too unstructured to even begin to quantify what is voiced within these interviews. This makes analysis of individual or group discussions somewhat subjective.

Recently, however, software has been developed that will computer-analyze the interview transcripts and, by content analyzing the words and word sequences that are used repeatedly within the interview, quantify the strength of word associations in order to create a map of those conversations. The software is based on the principle of a "neural network" and patterned after the way your brain works. Neural network models have been gaining attention in the scientific community because of their obvious scientific and physiological flavor. The Galileo System™, which was originally developed by Terra Research & Computing for perceptual mapping, today includes routines for analyzing text (CATPAC) and developing sophisticated artificial neural networks (ORESME).

The topic of neural networks needs a chapter of its own, but at this stage in its development, an in-depth discussion is not warranted since its application to business is still so new. However, a brief overview will give you the flavor for the concept and briefly explain how text can be converted into perceptual maps.

Self-Organizing Neural Networks

To briefly explain the idea of a neural network, consider how the brain functions. Your brain is actually a network of "neurons" that are all interconnected. Information is processed through the interactions of large numbers of these neurons that store and retrieve patterns of information. When a neuron is stimulated, it becomes "active" and sends signals to all the other neurons to which it is connected. Neural networks store information as patterns in the same way that a TV screen or electronic scoreboard does: by activating some of the dots or light bulbs and leaving others off, any pattern can be displayed. Because the neurons in a neural network are connected to each other, the neural network can do more than simply display patterns of information: it can store and retrieve those patterns and recognize patterns it has stored even if they are distorted or incomplete.

In an artificial neural network, such as the Galileo System™ uses, products, attributes, and people are represented as neurons. Each of these products, attributes, and people may be more or less tightly connected to each other. Products that are similar may be tightly connected, so that activating "airline" in the network will probably activate "United," "American," or "Delta" as well. Products will also be tightly connected to their attributes, so that activating "on time," "nonstop flights," or "bad food" will probably activate "United" and "American."

People can also be represented as neurons—connected to both attributes and products. People neurons are connected to attributes that are important to them, and they are more tightly connected to products and services that they buy and use than to those that they do not buy or use. All product development, communication, and marketing strategies are essentially efforts to connect a product or service more tightly to people.

In a Galileo system, neurons are not simply connected or not connected to each other, but instead the strength of each neuron connection is stored. Therefore, if the attribute "comfortable" is connected to an airline such as United, *how* comfortable United is perceived to be, is known. A product, service, or object does not just belong to a category, it belongs to that category to a certain degree. In a natural neural network, neurons that are tightly connected are typically located close to one another. Hence, it is possible to diagram the connections among neurons or concepts such as people, objects, or attributes, in the form of a map that can portray a picture of the structure of the network. One of the major reasons Galileo has such utility in advertising and market research is its ability not only to map the perceptual network, but also because it can calculate optimum strategies for strengthening and weakening the connections between the concepts.

Mapping Qualitative Data

A most interesting application of artificial neural networks is in the analysis of focus group transcripts, open-ended survey questions, newspaper and magazine articles, customer comments left on a telephone hot line or written on comment cards, or just about any text. The program works by designating each word in the text as a neuron (automatically eliminating words such as *the, and, but,* etc.) and then scanning systematically through the text, blocks of words at a time, looking for word associations. For any two words that appear together in the same block, the connections between those "neurons" are strengthened. Therefore, words that occur in proximity to one another repeatedly become associated in the program's memory. Any words that appear at least twice are identified as key concepts.

Because this is an artificial neural network, the activation of any neuron travels along the connections to all other neurons, and other neurons whose associated words may not be in the window can be activated. These neurons can, in turn, activate still other neurons, and so on. The program cycles through the text, usually more than once, in order to identify the key associations and calculate the strength of each word association. These weights can then be used in the same manner that similarity data is used to create a perceptual map.

One of the benefits of this kind of text analysis is that the program will pick up on words and word associations that you—as a casual listener—may not always be aware of. Whereas in the typical perceptual mapping procedure, you must derive the concepts for the space yourself, in this procedure, the program identifies the key concepts for you based on what is actually said by respondents. If these are too numerous to plot practically, you can then cull them down to those that are most meaningful.

Exhibit 11.8 shows an excerpt from text taken from an interview with a corporate meeting planner who was asked the differences between two alternative convention sites being considered in the planning of the company's next corporate meeting. Asking people to describe the differences between products is usually a good approach, since they then usually report attributes that make a difference, instead of attributes that all the products might share.

Exhibit 11.9 presents the key words found in the text in descending order of frequency of occurrence. As shown, *ranch* was the most frequently used word, occurring 24 times. Words such as *mountains, away,* and *travel* occurred only three times each. The program did not consider any words that occurred fewer than three times. These, then, are the key words that will be plotted according to the strength of their associations with the other frequently mentioned words.

Exhibit 11.10 shows these concepts arrayed in the form of a perceptual map. As you see immediately, Hilton Head and words associated with it are located toward the top of the map along the vertical axis, while words associated with the dude ranch are shown along the horizontal axis at the bottom of the map.

Hilton Head is most associated with words such as *resort, water,* and *Westin*. This, of course, makes complete sense since the convention site being considered was the Westin Resort on the water at Hilton Head. Also associated with this site are the words "easy," "travel," "golf," and "everything." Referring back to the original transcript, you'll remember that an important consideration to this meeting planner was that travel be easy and the Westin offered more ease of travel than the dude ranch. Golf was a big activity on Hilton Head, and there was some discussion of this convention site having "everything" right there to offer in the way of activities and having "everything" done for you. The reason everything is located at the mid-axis closer to "Westin" and "resort" but also further down near "ranch" is that at one point in the interview, the meeting planner said that the ranch also had "everything"—just on a smaller scale.

Exhibit 11.8: Example Interview Transcript

The choices were a ranch out west—a dude ranch—in the mountains in Montana versus a seaside resort on Hilton Head, the Westin. One of the major considerations was to find something different from where we worked, a whole new environment that would take us away from our typical corporate daily routine.

There emerged very early on a debate of where we should have the convention. Half the people wanted to go near water and that was the only driving point— water. The Westin at Hilton Head offered water. The other faction was more concerned with the karma of the place itself—the dude ranch offered karma.

Hilton Head offered a good, safe alternative. It was closer, you could get direct flights, easy access from the airport. Hilton Head was tried and true, where there was something in detail written up that you could refer to and travel agents who could give you firsthand information on the place. Hilton Head offered a very safe option. You couldn't really go wrong. Hilton Head is also exotic because of the water. It's so easy.

On the other extreme was the dude ranch in Montana. It had very limited capacity. The ranch was smaller, more exclusive, more casual. You know, fresh air, checkered tablecloths, lots of outdoor bonding experiences. You could divide up into different groups and set up different activities. The ranch got everyone away from the corporate setting. The ranch seemed very health- and nature-oriented. A spa was attached so it appealed to the health conscious. This particular ranch specialized in nutritional food. It had early morning runs. It offered a very tailored and healthy environment for a meeting. The concern was that the ranch might actually be too tailored and that some people might dislike it.

With the Westin, you had a more generalized experience. The Westin definitely had something for everyone. At the dude ranch, you were more contained, nowhere to go. You were stuck there on the ranch. But it was thematic, which was appealing. The ranch seemed exotic in its own way—in the mountains. Since not as many people have been to a ranch, there was a certain mystique about it that was appealing. However, a ranch isn't as fancy, so there was a concern from a planner's point of view that these high-powered executives, as much as they say they are in for this kind of back-to-nature kind of experience, that once they settle in they may not actually like it. You certainly wouldn't have the five-star posh amenities that you would have at a golf resort. No 24-hour room service, comfortable rooms, bell hops, and concierges. More like a B&B in a way. You have to conform to their routine. At Hilton Head, you had more or less a standard resort. Hilton Head would cater to you. No matter what you wanted or when, there would be someone to offer it to you.

Hilton Head had an advantage in that travel was easier. The cost of the flight was less; it was more direct, less time. It was much easier to get from the airport to the resort. Travel to the ranch was more unusual. For instance, people are used to taking cabs and shuttle buses, but if they are required to find the one man to drive you one-by-one to the ranch in a station wagon . . . It's not as easily explained.

Food is a big issue. Food at the Westin resort would mean white tablecloths, full wait staff, many menus to choose from. A resort can handle small groups or big groups, one as easily as the other. At the dude ranch, only one basic food option was available. You'd have to find something within the menu that you like. You need to be more creative at the dude ranch in order to find food that will work for everyone.

At the Westin, there is every corporate amenity. Boardroom tables and an executive setup. A hotel certainly makes the meeting planner's job easier. Everything's basically done for you and pleasing and comfortable to the participants because it is so typical. Work would get done very efficiently at Hilton Head because it's just like stepping into the boardroom back at the office. With the more exclusive ranch setting, they offer everything but on a much smaller scale. It's done in a slightly different format that goes along with their setup there, just enough different to be unsettling perhaps. We feared that there would need to be more adapting and adjustments on the part of the participants.

The big thing that comes out of this is how daring you want to be. It's so easy to go with the tried-and-true seaside resort. It's done every day of the week every day of the year. Resorts like the Westin know what they're doing and you can't go wrong. The dude ranch is on a smaller scale and not so commercialized. But you wonder if there is not more room for human error since they're out in the middle of nowhere. Will they cater to you? Will they be in step with the high-tech corporate world? By virtue of their location, will they be more laid-back about things, and not have the same high standards? Will they maintain things the way we are used to having them maintained? We worried about that.

Hilton Head you have the resort with everything right there, the beach, the game rooms, the courts, the golf, a theater; you have everything right there. You never have to leave. Yet if you want to leave, there are a variety of excursions. You can go shopping in Hilton Head, go to other plantations and play golf—there are several award-winning golf courses down there. You can get off the island entirely and go to Charleston, Savannah, and the other islands. There are so many different flavors you can bring into a one-week convention, one of which is bound to appeal to everyone.

Back in a lodge in the mountains you are more limited to what is there on the ranch. It's secluded. It's a longer trip to go anywhere from the ranch; a much more major effort to go. And, besides, why should you leave since the whole point of being there in seclusion was to get away and not go anywhere else? You'd defeat the purpose.

Exhibit 11.9: Key Words in Sample Interview Text

DESCENDING FREQUENCY LIST

WORD	FREQ	PCNT
RANCH	24	22.0
HILTON HEAD	12	11.0
RESORT	8	7.3
WESTIN	7	6.4
DIFFERENT	6	5.5
EASY	6	5.5
EVERYONE	5	4.6
FOOD	5	4.6
CORPORATE	4	3.7
WATER	4	3.7
GOLF	4	3.7
MOUNTAINS	3	2.8
AWAY	3	2.8
TRAVEL	3	2.8
SMALLER	3	2.8
NATURE	3	2.8
WORK	3	2.8
EVERYTHING	3	2.8
LEAVE	3	2.8

The ranch convention site is most associated with key words such as "different," "mountains," "smaller," "nature," and "away"—to name a few. These were all used as descriptors of the ranch in the interview. Food was also discussed extensively as a possible negative, and the map draws attention to the fact that it was a point of some discussion. The word everyone—similar to everything—was used in connection with both the ranch and the resort but was associated more with the ranch. The comments in the transcript ran something like, "The ranch will take everyone away" and "It will be more difficult to find food that pleases everyone."

This technique obviously should not be applied in isolation of consideration of the actual interview(s) that took place, but as you can see, it summarizes some of the key points made surprisingly well. The critical step forward is that the map quantifies the information in the text in a way that was never before possible.

Exhibit 11.10: Map of Qualitative Text on Two Convention Sites

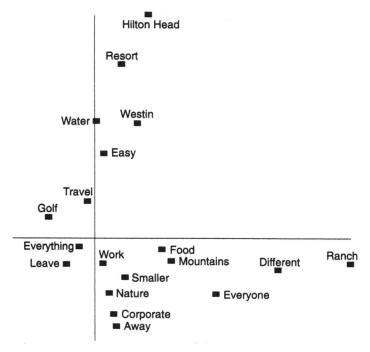

Statistical Software

What makes these techniques, such as conjoint analysis and MDS, so accessible is the availability of low-cost computing. Both conjoint analysis and multidimensional scaling require a considerable amount of repetitive computation to generate solutions or results. Neither technique is practical without specialized software. The computations required are beyond what could reasonably be completed within a spreadsheet program. While an in-depth discussion of the various algorithms is not warranted here, it is probably worthwhile to mention that several options are available to you.

Several software products have been written for conjoint analyses. In fact, these days you'll find many companies that specialize in software only for conjoint analysis due to its popularity and application in business. The two major statistical software competitors—SPSS™ and SAS™—now both include modules, or routines, that will do conjoint analysis. Sawtooth Software (Sawtooth.com) is one of the better known companies that has developed conjoint programs widely in use today.

Again SPSS™ (SPSS.com) and SAS™ (SAS.com) both have a multi-dimensional scaling routine. The Galileo System™ (Terraresearch .com), available through Terra Research & Computing, offers an MDS package, complete with software to develop message strategies.

12 Marketing Mix Models and Financial Returns

The quantification of marketing variables leads naturally to the analysis of financial returns to overall marketing programs. However, marketing programs generally consist of many elements, such as advertising, promotion and sales activities, that are commonly referred to as parts of the marketing mix. In order to assess the impact of changing the allocation of funds among the various promotion, advertising and selling activities, the financial returns from each type of marketing activity must be evaluated.

A marketing mix model relates the various selling and marketing expenses of an organization to the sales revenue. The primary purposes of the marketing mix model is to understand the relative responsiveness of the marketing efforts in order to aid in future planning and budgeting.

For this discussion of marketing mix modeling, a product or service in the mature phase of its life cycle is assumed, where sales and profits are relatively stable. The interest is in determining financial returns as part of the planning and control assessments that determine quarterly or annual budgets for the various types of marketing activity. The purpose is to illustrate the considerations important when quantitatively evaluating the allocation of funds among various marketing activities.

Most marketing mix models are regression based, with the criterion or dependent variable being sales and the predictor or independent variables usually being marketing program spending. The model requires both the predictor variables (typically marketing communications spending) and historical sales data to be available by uniform time periods (typically weeks or months) over an extended period of time (several years). It is also necessary for the building of such a

Exhibit 12.1: Marketing Mix Model

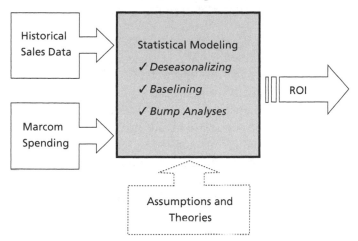

model to clearly understand the assumptions underlying how the particular market is defined and operates. Typical assumptions would involve the definition of the market and competitors, marketing channels, timing, and characteristics of customers.

Variables need to be appropriately created and transformed where necessary for a marketing mix model. The model usually must include a variable that allows deseasonalization or the removal or adjustment of seasonal factors. If, for example, the product normally sells more in the summer, then this needs to be adjusted so that the normal summer increase is not interpreted as an increase due to any marketing effort.

A baseline must also be estimated. The baseline is the estimate of sales if no short-term marketing effort were used. The difference is defined as incremental sales, or the sales attributable to the short-term marketing effort which is usually some form of special price or promotion. This process of identifying of the incremental sales or volume is often referred to as bump analysis. Long-term impacts can be estimated as well if there is sufficient data. The marketing mix model and its associated analysis becomes the basis of a return-on-investment or ROI model.

Determining Financial Values

The general formula for assessing the financial value of marketing activity is:

> Value = Incremental revenue due to the marketing activity −
> Incremental costs due to the marketing activity

Unfortunately, specification of the incremental costs and proper measurement of the incremental revenues is not easy and can present problems initially. There are three types of costs. Direct costs are those that can be directly linked to a particular marketing expenditure. For example, the costs of a print advertisement for specific products can be directly assigned to that product. Traceable common costs are costs for marketing activities that are shared by multiple producers and that can be divided in some logical way among those products. Here an ad that promotes three products together can be divided, with a portion of the expenses being assigned to each. Nontraceable costs, such as top management salaries, taxes, and other overhead expenses, cannot be directly linked to any particular product and must be arbitrarily apportioned across all products.

For many companies, the way in which financial reporting occurs makes even the proper assignment of direct costs difficult. In many companies, the total cost of sales promotion may be distributed across several organizations or departments. For the sales organization, managing sales promotion is only one of several functions performed by the sales force and their salaries and expenses associated with sales promotion can only be assigned as allocated traceable common costs. Costs associated with the production scheduling and inventory management of the promotional product may be reported through the manufacturing organization and may also be difficult to properly allocate.

Recording the discounts and incentive payments made to resellers, brokers, and agents as well as the allocation of such incentives to specific products and promotional programs is often difficult. For example, costs attributable to an Internet-based advertising campaign, particularly when incurred as part of a multibrand theme, may be difficult to accumulate and allocate.

Assessing the incremental revenue due to marketing activities presents similar difficulties. Again, the concept is simple:

> Incremental revenue for marketing activity =
> Incremental volume due to marketing activity ×
> manufacturer gross margin per unit of volume

While a reasonable definition of gross margin may be determined, the measurement of incremental volume often presents problems. Three key problems are (1) assessing short-term cannibalization effects among existing product or service users; (2) assessing the long-run impact on the brand due to attraction of new category buyers, conversion of buyers from competing brands, and stimulation of increased consumption; and (3) assessing the impact of retaining existing buyers who might otherwise be lost to competition.

Because of these difficulties, critics of any particular analysis can generate a variety of reasons why key cost or return elements were improperly evaluated. For this reason, the use of marketing mix modeling and financial value assessment of marketing mix elements has been most successful when it is reviewed and adopted as a corporate method with everyone agreeing with the initial assumptions. As part of this review, standards will be set for determining which costs will be included in the analysis, and consideration will be given to the balancing of financial trade-offs with no financial objectives to be achieved by the marketing program.

Unfortunately, specification of the incremental costs and proper measurement of the incremental revenues is not easy and can present problems initially. There are three types of costs. Direct costs are those that can be directly linked to a particular marketing expenditure. For example, the costs of a print advertisement for specific products can be directly assigned to that product. Traceable common costs are costs for marketing activities that are shared by multiple producers and that can be divided in some logical way among those products. Here an ad that promotes three products together can be divided, with a portion of the expenses being assigned to each. Nontraceable costs, such as top management salaries, taxes, and other overhead expenses, cannot be directly linked to any particular product and must be arbitrarily apportioned across all products.

Models for Analyzing Response to Marketing Activity

A variety of stand-alone models can be used to evaluate various types of marketing activities. Many of these activities are aimed at changing average buyer behavior over time. While even small increases in average buyer purchasing can lead to significant product sales gains, such changes are difficult to measure in aggregated sales data confounded by competitive marketing. The design of choice for such longer-run effects, such as those generated by media advertising and Internet-based advertising, and by promotional activity, such as product sampling and direct mail, has long been controlled experimentation. The typical experiment consists of random assignment of customers or markets to either a test group, or a control group. Data is collected over a base period, and then one group is subjected to some alteration in the marketing mix element under study. Data collection continues, and statistical analysis methods are used to test for significant changes between the test group behavior and the control group behavior.

Among the mix activities that have been extensively studied using controlled panel experiments in both business-to-business and consumer marketing are:

—Advertising copy (copy A vs. copy B).
—Advertising spending levels (standard vs. heavy or standard vs. light).
—Long-run advertising effects.

While such studies provide accurate measurement of individual aspects of the marketing mix, it is difficult to test the entire range of alternatives across all the various mix elements. Marketing mix model systems based on weekly sales data have been developed to address the need for more comprehensive models covering the entire marketing communications program. Such models incorporate the information about the causal relationships among the various marketing mix elements to provide an integrated system of models that relate short-term sales fluctuations to short-term variations in the elements of the marketing mix.

The database for such items is typically built at the week level (Sunday to Saturday). The dependent variable is generally product or brand sales. There are typically eight sets of predictor variables.

1. Seasonality Estimate. This recognizes that markets have different seasonal patterns due to temperature and average weather conditions or local consumption preferences. The seasonality estimation will also adjust for extreme deviations from the average sales.

2. Pricing. Analysis for most categories is typically at the product level. Where there are different prices for different package sizes (e.g., different package sizes of nuts and bolts and other fasteners), price is usually converted based on a standard weight or size unit (e.g., price per pound). This converted price averages all the individual differences in the prices of various sizes and is relatively insensitive to short-run volume fluctuations in package size sales.

3. Promotion. Promotional activities and events are often executed on a subset of sizes rather than all sizes of the product.

For example, discounts are often given for a two-for-one purchases of a particular size of a product, not on all. Promotional activity must be aggregated across various sizes into an average for the product. Hence, there would be a separate variable for each historical promotion in the database.

4. Internet. The impact of the Internet and electronic commerce activity on sales needs to be considered. If there are multiple programs or Internet sites, separate variables are required.

5. Direct Mail. Each catalogue or direct mail piece again requires its own separate variable.

6. Print Advertising. If print advertising is an important element of the marketing mix, then a variable is needed for each placement. However, some models will aggregate all magazine placements into one overall print variable.

7. Competitive Marketing Mix Activity. To account for competitive promotion and advertising, one or more variables are created that reflect activity across all competitors or a particular competitor. This data is often difficult to obtain.

8. Market Normalization. This accounts for nonseasonal fluctuations in sales volume that may be driven by activity outside of the product category. For example, sales of paper and toner might be indirectly driven by the sale of new printers and copiers. In its simplest form, it may be necessary to transform volume sales into volume sales per size of retail or wholesale outlet.

Interaction and Synergy

Within any given cross section of customers or prospects, whether by market, region, or account, a marketing mix model must accommodate the effects of all the possible interactions and synergies among marketing activities. One such consideration may be: How does response to any marketing activity related to seasonality? In other words, does the seasonal characteristic amplify the response to a marketing tactic? For example, a manufacturer's sales of building supplies to contractors may increase in anticipation of the spring and summer construction season, making the manufacturer more promotion responsive. However, for many products with pronounced seasonality, there may be lead or lag effect that the model should account for. The lead-lag effects are caused by the time the product is in a distribution channel on its way to the final consumer.

The modeling system should also consider interactions and synergies among various elements of the marketing mix. For example, are price offers more effective when coupled with high levels of advertising, and less effective at times of low advertising levels?

If multiple advertising copy executions are used during the study period, the question may arise regarding whether there were significant sales differences related to advertising copy differences or not. Ideally, the model should be able to accommodate regional differences in copy, time series differences in copy, and even overlapping utilization of copy.

Almost surely, the model will generate estimates of marketing mix effects that vary across cross sections of the data (i.e., market, region, account, etc). Initial applications of marketing mix evaluations focused on generating reasonable estimates of national response.

If synergy exists, the two working together will generate a greater response than either working alone. Thus, a print ad alone or a price-based promotion alone will each generate a $1,000 increase in sales. Together they may generate a $2,500 increase.

Analytical Problems

Assembling the data for a model into a set of observations and variable values for those observations involves a number of key decisions. There are a number of trade-offs among model complexity, usability, interpretability, and robustness of the results.

Aggregation

Three key aggregation decisions influence the entire design and estimation of the modeling system. These are the level of aggregation in the product or brand dimension (size, package, etc.), the level of aggregation in the geographical dimension (regions, markets, territories), and the level of aggregation in the time dimension (week, month, etc.). Numerous academic studies demonstrate that significantly different estimations of marketing mix effects may be obtained depending upon the level of aggregation used. However, if the accurate estimation of certain effects is more important than the accuracy of estimation of certain other effects, then aggregation levels may be chosen that favor the accurate estimation of highest importance effects.

Brand-size aggregation is a key decision. Different sizes or packages might react differently to promotion, advertising, and selling efforts. Constructing a model that attempts to estimate such differential effects would become very complex, particularly when cross-size and cross-package cannibalization effects are incorporated. The usual assumption is that advertising and promotion are brand-level effects. In this case, the individual brand-size items are aggregated into one total brand specification for sales volumes and promotional effects. Where measurement of advertising and promotion effects is the primary focus, some models will aggregate data to the market level. The primary justification here is that all buyers within a market are exposed to the same schedule of advertising and that promotion is generally applied at the market level.

Typically, aggregating sales by week is most useful and desirable. However, in situations where there is very little variation in sales from week to week, or where promotions are scheduled as month-long events, aggregating sales by month may be sufficient to demonstrate effects.

Data Points

The finer the division of data into observations, the more likely is the occurrence of extreme data values (outliers). The analysis procedure should include screening methods to identify such outliers and mitigate their impact on model estimates by (1) omitting such observations from the analysis, (2) giving them reduced weight, or (3) replacing the extreme values with less extreme, more plausible values based on past history. Similarly, particularly for models with lagged or carry-over effects, observations with missing data may require imputation of reasonable values to complete the data set.

An important problem with data generated from a POS (point-of sale) system is the stability of store management conditions over time. Stores may be sold, extensively remodeled, or subjected to major changes in management procedures, such as a change in pricing policies. In such cases, the store may generate two different data streams—one with an identification prior to the changes and one with a different identification after the changes. Data from the final weeks prior to a store closing, or data from the first few weeks after opening of a new store may need to be deleted from the analysis.

Characterizing Variables

The final model may contain hundreds of different variables with many different characteristics and functions. The dependent variable in the model usually is a (possibly transformed) measure of volume sales for a product specification at some level of geographic summarization for some summary time period. The balance of the variables are collections of nonmetric and metric variables that describe the various marketing tactics and other customer or market characteristics.

When so many variables are included in a marketing mix model, care should be taken to be sure there are a sufficient number of data points to support the number of variables. A general rule of thumb is to have at least ten data points for every variable in the model.

Variables may be characterized by their level of measurement as discussed in Chapter 4.

Nominal variables may be coded as alphabetic or numeric variables. The codes are labels that serve to identify objects or response conditions. Such labels can be interchanged or altered without altering their interpretation. In multiple regression, each different value of a nominal variable typically generates a dummy variable. Examples might include store identification, market identification, time period identification, or promotional condition identification.

Variables whose values indicate an ordered relation, but neither the differences nor ratios of variables are meaningful are ordinal level. Examples might be rank orders, rating-scale scores with unequal intervals, or partitions of some numeric variable (e.g., high, medium, or low market shares).

Finally, a variable may be ratio level where its values represent a constant unit of measurement. For ratio data, the zero point is unique, and ratios of data values are meaningful. Examples are age, weight, and calories.

SIMPLIFIED MARKETING MIX MODEL EXAMPLE. An example of a typical marketing mix model follows below. It begins with product or brand sales over time.

Sales are typically converted to its logarithm to keep data manageable. Therefore, the dependent variable for this model is:

Sales = the log of sales

The model is based on a nominal variable, **COND,** for identifying the promotion condition by week and a variable, **DSCT,** giving the price discount in percent by week. The promotion or advertising condition variable is translated into dummy variables such as that shown below:

Adv is 1 if advertising only, and 0 if not advertising only.

Prom is 1 if promotion only, and 0 if not promotion only.

Exhibit 12.2: Response Function

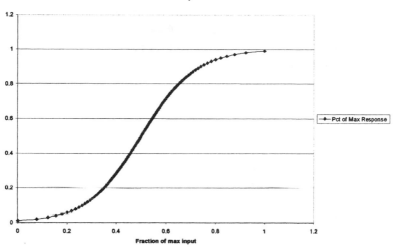

Discount variables for the various conditions are obtained by multiplying the condition dummy variables by the **DSCT** variable. Thus,

Adv*Discount = Adv × DSCT

Prom*Discount = COND × DSCT

These variables are entered into a regression analysis with **Sales** as the dependent variable, and **Price, Adv, DSCT, Adv*Discount** as the independent variables. Observations with no promotional activity may or may not be included.

The response curve for a price discount is obtained by selecting various values of variable $\underline{X}$ representing discount levels and plotting the predicted value of Exp (**DSCT parameter + Adv*Discount parameter**). Curves for other conditions are obtained in a similar manner.

If the relationship between marketing inputs and sales responses has been verified and validated across a broad range of products and across broad ranges of marketing inputs, then a functional relation may be specified in the model that allows forecasts to be made well outside the range of observed data.

Exhibit 12.2 illustrates a case where the global response function has an s-shape. A global response function represents all the marketing mix variables taken together. For such a function, sales predictions work best in the tested range, usually the middle, more linear portion of the S-curve. An S-shaped function implies there is an initial threshold level of marketing activity that is required for even minimal sales response. At the upper end of the curve, an S-curve shows diminishing returns from additional marketing effort, whereby more marketing expenditures will not presumably result in further sales gains.

Return on Investment

Calculation of return on investment depends upon the estimated relation between investment in a marketing activity and is modeled by a global response function. If the model for a marketing activity is a response function that includes a large number of observations, then the calculation is straightforward:

> Estimated Incremental Volume (X) = expected volume for marketing activity at spending level X – expected volume for marketing activity at spending level 0.

> Then **Net $ return (X)** from the activity is Gross margin per unit times Estimated Incremental Volume (X), minus the cost of the activity at spending level X, and the **Return on Investment** is **Net $ return (X)** divided by cost of the activity at spending level X.

> Gross margin ($10) × Incremental Volume (200,000) –
> Cost ($500,000) = Net $ return ($1,500,000)

The return on investment calculation becomes the basis for reallocating funds from one marketing activity to another, or for evaluating proposed increases or decreases in funds for the entire set of marketing activities. In most cases the interest is in making evolutionary changes to the allocation of funds for a marketing activity, and not revolutionary changes that take us far outside the historical range of levels for the activity.

The basic process of determining financial return is shown in Exhibit 12.3. This process is merely an extension of the simple return on investment calculation just discussed. One important difference is that there are separate calculations against different customer segments. Shown in the exhibit are separate columns for best customers,

Exhibit 12.3: Basic Financial Return Process

	Best Customers	Good Customers	Price Customers
1 Present Income Flow in Category	$	$	$
2 Share of Requirements	%	%	%
3 Customer Income Flow to Brand	$	$	$
4 Contribution Margin %	%	%	%
5 Contribution Margin $	$	$	$
6 Income Flow Without a Brand Communications Program	$	$	$
7 Contribution Margin Without a Brand Communications Program	$	$	$
8 Income Flow With a Brand Communications Program	$	$	$
9 Gross Contribution Margin With a Brand Communications Program	$	$	$
10 Brand Communication Investment	$	$	$
11 Net Contribution Margin	$	$	$
12 Difference in Contribution Margins With and Without Brand Communication	$	$	$
13 Incremental Gain or Loss	$	$	$
14 Return on Investment	%	%	%

good customers and price customers. These segments are entirely arbitrary to illustrate the concept. Best customers might be those that have historically purchased large quantities and contribute substantially to company margin, and price customers might be those that seem to respond to special prices.

The top line begins with the income flow in dollars for the entire category including all competition. This is the estimate of the total market size. The next line shows the market share requirements. Line 3 then shows the income flow for the brand or company.

Lines 4 and 5 are the contribution margin percentage and the corresponding contribution margin in dollars. The margin percentage is typically averaged across items. Lines 6 and 7 require establishing the base line from a marketing mix model. The income flow and contribution margin without a brand communications program is that associated with the base volume. Remember: Total volume is equal to the incremental volume (generated by the communications program) plus the base volume (what would have been sold if no program were employed).

Lines 8 and 9 show the total income flow and contribution margin in dollars after a communications program has been employed.

Line 10 shows the total cost or investment in the communications program.

Line 11 shows the net contribution margin, that is the total margin less the cost of the communications program.

Line 12 shows the difference in margin between the total and the estimated base margin (margin with the communications program). This is the incremental margin in dollars that results from the communications program.

Line 13 compares this incremental margin with the total cost of the communications program. Hopefully this number would be positive showing a gain, but could be negative showing a loss on the communications program effort. The communications program in order to be successful needs to generate incremental margin in excess of its cost.

Line 14 shows the return on investment, which is simply the net gain (or loss) in dollars divided by the cost.

The basic financial return process is fundamental to integrated marketing communications (IMC). The process must be based on the analysis of real data that allows for the estimation of base sales and response. Strategic marketing communication activity must be related to short term changes in incremental sales and put in a financial context.

Assembling sufficient disaggregate historical data is still a challenge for most marketing organizations. Determining synergistic effects and the overall value of multiple communications programs is also an analytical challenge beyond simple regression. Sorting out short-term and long-term impacts adds to the analytical challenge.

Market Response and Marketing Mix Models

The measurement and analytical procedure, often called "marketing mix modeling," is offered today by a limited number of external vendors. For the most part, all use some type of black box system and generally serve consumer goods marketers, although a few business-to-business marketers are now getting into the act.

The marketing manager typically provides sales data by product or service by month or preferably by week, over a relatively long period of time. This lengthy data stream enables the consulting company to identify seasonal variations, competitive activities, new product introductions, and the like. Note here, the data used in this analysis is internal data commonly held as sales records by the organization or firm. The external vendor simply takes that data, massages and manipulates it, and returns the results of the analysis to the manager.

These services are based on the common annuity model of consulting, where the research or consulting organization charges the marketing firm for each analysis or the firm agrees to pay an ongoing fee for the services provided. While this is a most profitable approach for the marketing research group, it is an ongoing expense for the organization. Since the solutions provided are proprietary, the marketing manager typically has little or no choice in how the data is analyzed or whether or not the measurement model is relevant to the market or the marketing activities being measured.

There is no reason why the marketing organization, with a limited amount of investment, cannot develop the necessary tools and techniques to perform this analysis internally. Indeed, that is what several marketing organizations are doing today—authorizing the development of transparent analytical models that the marketing communications group can then manage, adapt, tweak, and dynamically adjust to fit their own needs, not the needs of the outside research firm.

The two key elements needed to carry out the analysis in-house are historical sales records in dollars by product or brand to be measured and the marketing communications investment records by type of activity for the same period, again in dollars. By statistically correlating sales and communication investments, it is possible to parse out the financial returns on marketing communications financial investments. Further, with a bit more analysis, the marketing manager can decompose the incremental results generated and identify which type of activity or program generated what return.

Thus, using your own internal data, an approach to internal measurement can be developed that allows research and modeling to be conducted by any organization in any market in any culture in the world.

Index

About TEXERE

Texere, a progressive and authoritative voice in business publishing, brings to the global business community the expertise and insights of leading thinkers. Our books educate, enlighten, and entertain, and provide an intersection where our authors and our readers share cutting edge ideas, practices, and innovative solutions. Texere seeks to cultivate, enhance, and disseminate information that illuminates the global business landscape.

www.thomson.com/learning/texere

About the typeface

This book was set in 10 pt New Aster. New Aster was created in 1958 by Francesco Simoncini of Italy. This typeface is known for a stylish oldstyle face with some similarities to Times Roman.

Library of Congress Cataloging-in-Publication Data

Block, Martin P.
    Business-to-business marketing research : a value-based approach / Martin Block, Tamara Block.—2nd ed.
        p. cm.
    Includes bibliographical references and index.
    ISBN 0-324-22230-0
    1. Industrial marketing—Research. 2. Industrial marketing—Management. 3. Marketing research. I. Block, Tamara Brezen. II. Title.
    HF5415.1263.B565 2005
    658.8′04—dc22

                                                    2005004871